The Three Lives of
HARRIET HUBBARD AYER

By Margaret Hubbard Ayer and Isabella Taves

J. B. LIPPINCOTT COMPANY   PHILADELPHIA   NEW YORK

The present ownership and management of Harriet Hubbard Ayer, Inc. have no connection with any of the persons mentioned in this story.

THE THREE LIVES OF
HARRIET HUBBARD AYER

INTRODUCTION

In the early eighteen hundreds, a typical eulogy of a great man in Chicago read something like this: "He was a crack shot, drove a hard bargain, was loyal to his wife, and got the best of the Indians."

Chicago was then a wilderness of prairies where wolves and bears roamed, with swamps filled with bloodsuckers and virulent mosquitoes; what is now State Street was an insect-infested bog, with a sluggish fern-bordered stream oozing into a river called Chi-cack-o (onion weed) by the Indians, and Checagou by the French traders.

Harriet Hubbard Ayer's cousin, Gurdon Saltonstall Hubbard first saw Chicago in 1818, when he was sixteen years old, and a trading post clerk for John Jacob Astor. He liked to remember that he found there only two and a half buildings: Fort Dearborn; the log cabin of an Indian trader named John Kinzie; and a tumbled-down "half-a-shack" occupied by a French squaw man. But wild little Chi-cack-o was exactly what Gurdon Hubbard was looking for. He had been born in Windsor, Vermont, the eldest child of a lawyer named Elizur Hubbard. His mother, Abigail, wanted Gurdon to be a lawyer, too. But books and school bored him. At thirteen, when the family moved to Montreal, Canada, he left schooling behind and clerked in a store, which bored him equally. So at fifteen, when he heard that the huge fur trading firm of John Jacob Astor was looking for young men with a taste for adventure, he signed up.

A tall man, well over six feet, with big bones and tremendous vitality, he was a crack shot and drove a hard bargain. But, from the first, he was friendly with the Indians and they both loved and admired him; in a period when the white man had only one object, to cheat the Indian, to get the best of him, to get rid of him, Gurdon Hubbard was a rebel and an iconoclast.

Until a short time ago, it was only the rare and enlightened historian who set down any idea of how badly our pioneer fathers cheated and misunderstood the Indian. Books dwelt on the bloody massacre of Fort Dearborn in 1812, and there was an oft-repeated tale of how the Indians forced one young woman to watch while they killed her uncle, a Captain Wells, and ate his heart. Gurdon Hubbard was among the few who knew both sides of the story, and realized how the whites had again and again violated their pacts with the red man, or used him to their advantage.

At twenty-two, he was in charge of all the Astor fur posts in Illinois. A few years later, he struck out on his own, and there is hardly a civic or business enterprise of early Chicago in which Gurdon Hubbard did not have a finger. He wrote the first fire insurance policy in Chicago; built the first packing house—so big it was called Hubbard's Folly; helped organize the Episcopal church there; built the first big hotel; inaugurated the first line of packet boats between Chicago and Buffalo; was a director in Chicago's waterworks and one of the first trustees of incorporated Chicago; and once owned over two hundred buildings.

He had the brains, the ingenuity and the physical endurance to make him a natural leader. (When Gurdon Hubbard was nearly seventy, his son declared that his father was still stronger than he was.) He made portages under all kinds of conditions: floods, blizzards, steaming summer heat. His wagons were equipped with sails and his boats with rollers. In the fall of 1829, he drove four hundred hogs to Chicago. When ice prevented the ship from Buffalo getting through, Hubbard slaughtered the hogs and piled their carcasses in snow on the banks of the Chicago River, near the site of the present Chicago Tribune building. He broke the trail from Danville to Chicago; it was first called Hubbard's Trail; then State Road; and is now one of Chicago's leading industrial streets, State Street. He helped organize the Chicago Board of Trade, became a member of the state legislature, and a director in both state and city savings banks. A street, the one that runs by the Blackstone Hotel today, was named Hubbard Court in his honor; but later it was changed to Seventh Street and is now called Balbo.

In an era when Chicago was a rough, tough frontier town, of booming taverns, and ugly huts set crazily on lots of sand and clay, of wigwams and filth and din, of hard-drinking men who wore leggings and fur hats and fought each other for the handful of women, Gurdon Hubbard was a note of sanity. Most of the settlers had no idea of improving Chicago; they had come for booty alone. But Gurdon Hubbard loved Chicago from the first, and had faith in its future. Never a drinking man, a member of the "respectables" as opposed to the roistering-drinking crowd, he yet managed to keep the respect of the toughest troublemakers.

He died at the age of eighty-four. During the last two years of his life he was blind and, according to the family history "patiently and in darkness awaited heavenly light, which came September 14, 1886." But up until the last few years of his life, his hair and curling beard were still black, and his vitality and love of life, still strong. His home on the north side was always a gathering place for the leading citizens of Chicago and the most distinguished guests, among them Abraham Lincoln, both before and after he became President. Early settlers remember an incident during the Lincoln-Douglas debates when Lincoln was a guest at the Hubbards', and Douglas was staying with his neighbors. When both families congregated on their front porches with their guests on the warm summer evening, there was an awkward moment. Then Hubbard went over and shook Stephen Douglas' hand and the two groups joined in neutral conversation.

A Chicago judge, in an address before the Chicago Historical Society said: "In Ancient Greece or Rome, the memory of Gurdon Hubbard's deeds of heroic endurance and self-sacrifice would have been perpetuated in bronze or marble, and glorified in song." However, although he was considered one of Chicago's first citizens, and by many its first citizen, he never was one of its front-ranking millionaires. A Chicago newspaperman of the time put it this way: "Hubbard all too frequently paid for the seed, while the others waited for the harvest."

And it is also significant that, along with the prominent and important people who stayed in Gurdon Hubbard's house, any Indian who happened to be in the vicinity was always welcome. Neighbors remember that, long after the red man was supposedly gone from Chicago, Indians could still be seen knocking at Gurdon Hubbard's door—which always opened promptly.

An illustrious relative is no guarantee of brilliance. Undistinguished parents have produced multi-talented children, and some of the dullest people have inherited the proudest names. However, in Chicago, another Hubbard was to attain distinction. Her name was Harriet Hubbard (after her marriage, Harriet Hubbard Ayer) and she was a cousin of Gurdon Hubbard.

Her father, Henry George Hubbard, came west from Connecticut in 1837, excited by the rumors he had heard of his cousin Gurdon's success. By that time Chicago had a harbor, a scattering of flimsy frame houses, and a few brick buildings, among them Lake House, built by Gurdon Hubbard, the first big hotel in the city. There was also a drawbridge across the Chicago River, although the area to the east and north—the Sands—was then a red-light district. The population was considered roughly to be forty thousand, but much of it was transient, and covered wagons and prairie schooners camped in the fields across from Fort Dearborn. Wolf packs still roamed the outskirts and the children whose families lived as far south as Twelfth Street spent many a night with the covers pulled over their heads to shut out the eerie howling of the animals. Chicago had been incorporated as a city in 1837, but it was still considered a speculative risk. Men shook their heads over the swamp that is now the business district; one early settler wrote that when he was looking for land on South Water Street he found a stalled wagon mired in the property and decided against buying a lot, for the expense of hauling out the wagon would come to five or six dollars, an amount the value of the land did not warrant.

Hank Hubbard was a keen sportsman, who took great pleasure in hunting, and a crack shot. But his education had gone on longer than had his cousin Gurdon's, and he was qualified for a clerkship in the courthouse, which was located on La Salle Street, between Washington and Madison—behind it a huge prairie, which remained vacant until 1864, and was often used as a site by traveling circuses. Hank married Juliet Elvira Smith, daughter of a judge in the circuit court, and sister of Mrs. Stephen Gale and Mrs. Levi Boone, both prominent early Chicagoans—Dr. Boone later became mayor.

Harriet was the sixth child born to Henry and Juliet Hubbard in their big frame house on Michigan Avenue and Hubbard Court, now the site of the Blackstone Hotel. She was not an interesting baby, or a pretty child. Her schooling, as was customary with girls in that period, was extremely sketchy. She did not go to school at all until she was twelve years old, because she was supposedly sickly, and even after she attended the Sacred Heart Academy, she remained painfully shy and ill at ease in any situation calling for social grace.

Yet she was to achieve great beauty, great fame—and great notoriety and heartbreak. Her story is even more exceptional than her cousin's; not only because she was a woman, and a beautiful one, but because she was such a controversial character. Like her cousin, she was a rebel. She fought against rules which she considered silly, and traditions which to her had no meaning. She shocked less daring critics and made enemies of both stupid and jealous people. A book called *Chicago Yesterdays*, reminiscences of pioneers, published in 1919, and "garnered" by Caroline Kirkland who knew Harriet all her life, makes this appraisal:

"In a strait-laced, conventional community, Mrs. Ayer ventured to be and do what she wanted. As I look back on her, she seems like some rare, tropical bird of gorgeous plumage strayed into a simple country hen-yard. . . . She was the first to fill her house with bric-a-brac, to read French novels and, worst of all, to act French plays. . . . She distressed the high principles of the community by giving Sunday breakfasts at which she served *omelettes aux fines herbes,* chicken livers *en brochette, café noir,* and alas! *vins Graves, Sauternes* or *Chablis*; and to which she invited well-known stage celebrities such as Edwin Booth, Lawrence Barrett, and John McCulloch, all of which was not done at that time in Chicago. . . .

"So it was really but a just fate which overtook the Ayers when Mr. Ayer's firm suffered in a panic; he failed and had to go out of business. Mrs. Ayer gave up her luxuries and undertook to support her two daughters and herself by the manufacture and sale of a cream known as the Récamier. Later, she retired from the undertaking and became head of a department in the *New York World* where she made much newspaper fame for herself.

"Whether she was rich or in restricted circumstances, she was always generous in sympathy and money to those with whom she came in contact. . . . She loved life and especially its beautiful, luxurious, amusing side, yet when reverses came to her she faced and conquered them with a gay courage which, in time, I think, disarmed some of the critics who had watched her earlier career with disapprobation."

This book tells the extraordinary story of Harriet Hubbard Ayer from the summer of 1864, when she was fifteen, until her death in 1903, when she was fifty-four. Although she outlived many of the scandals which surrounded her, she never would write the truth about herself, because it involved too many people she loved. Of her three girls, the only one who survives today is the youngest, Margaret Hubbard Ayer Cobb, widow of Frank Cobb, famous editor of the *New York World.* She is now in her seventies but she felt she must wait to tell her mother's story until the rest of the principals in the story were dead. However, her determination to print the whole truth dates back to the 'thirties, when she was teaching at the Dalton School in New York. She was summoned to court to testify concerning her mother's cosmetic business, sold by Harriet's heirs after her death. When Margaret was on the stand, one of the women litigants stood up and screamed at her: "Whatever Harriet Hubbard Ayer thought or said has no value. Everybody knows she was a lunatic!"

At that moment Margaret vowed that sooner or later she would make it plain to everyone that her mother was not only sane, but a remarkable and brilliant woman. This book, of which she is co-author, was a labor of dedicated devotion to a mother who would never allow anyone to say a person was crazy—even in fun.

Everything in the following pages is based on actual happenings as recorded in family stories, newspaper accounts and letters; even the occasional, apparently broad use of the writer's imagination has been founded at least on probability. Fortunately, her daughters saved much of their mother's correspondence, even from the time they were small. Harriet also wrote drafts of important letters, which were found among her effects, including letters she wrote to the man she loved but never married. The files of the *Chicago Tribune,* the *New York Herald,* the *New York Times* and the *New York Sun* furnished valuable source material.

The description of the months Mrs. Ayer was kept prisoner in a private asylum in Bronxville, New York, where she suffered the ignorant and brutal restraint which was then routine treatment for those suspected of mental disorders, are taken directly from her own manuscript of the lecture given in 1894 from the stage of the Central Music Hall in Chicago where other controversial figures of the day, like Oscar Wilde and Henry Ward Beecher, had also entertained audiences. During the last seven years of her life, Mrs. Ayer was a feature writer for the *New York World* who specialized in interviews of women involved in notorious crimes, and also edited the woman's page. These interviews and pages were used as source material, as were her pamphlets on beauty, written at the time that she was making her Récamier face cream, and her 543-page book, published in 1902 by King-Richardson, called *Harriet Hubbard Ayer's Book of Health and Beauty.*

The Chicago Historical Society, the Newberry Library of Chicago and the Mercantile Library of New York have also been extremely helpful.

The rights to the beauty products created by her, and to the use of her name on these products, were sold by her heirs after her death. These heirs have no connection today with any preparations for beauty sold under the name of Harriet Hubbard Ayer, and have not had for fifty years.

ISABELLA TAVES

PART ONE

CHAPTER ONE

IN THE summer of 1864, because of the war and the demands President Lincoln was making on Chicago for more and more recruits, there were no Independence Day celebrations. The Fourth of July was like any other summer day, hot and dry, with clouds of interminable dust in the air, even over on fashionable Michigan Avenue and Hubbard Court.

The fruit trees, the almond trees, the flowers, the bushes and even the grass were coated with dust. No matter how often Madame Hubbard ordered the streets around the house sprinkled, the winds from the west and south brought new baked soil to sift over everything. Harriet, just turned fifteen, in a high-necked, long-sleeved organdie dress—worn, of course, over many petticoats—was hot and restless. She jumped up on the lower rung of the white wood fence—disregarding the fact that her hoops bulged indecorously out behind her—and peered at the crowds on the lake front.

What is now Grant Park and Outer Drive was then only a strip of parched grass, in some places less than a hundred yards wide, with the Illinois Central Railway trains running on tracks which had been built on a breakwater across the lake, and a basin for small boats between the railway and the grass. The railway, with its soot and noise, added no charm to the most exclusive residential district in the city; the rows of tall elms and even the new marble "palaces" languished under a constant bath of smoke and grime. But it had only been thirty-one years since a whooping band of eight hundred Indian warriors staged a war dance down Lake Street to Michigan, the present site of the public library. Only fifteen years before, Chicago had been such a welter of mud and bogs that the city had gladly given the railroad the right to build the breakwater and run tracks across it in the hope that it would be some additional protection against flooding from the lake. And by 1864, the tracks and trains were such familiar sights that Chicagoans no longer noticed. On hot days like this, the lake front did provide a popular breathing—and courting— place for young people who didn't have the advantage of living on the lake shore.

Harriet watched the crowds enviously: the star male boarder, with the landlady's daughter on his arm; the pert little waitress, in hoop skirts every bit as wide as those of the young ladies of fashion, and a bonnet just as heavy, laughing up into the face of a Union soldier. The United States was split apart by war; even in Chicago there was bitter feeling between the Southern sympathizers, the Copperheads, and the Unionists. Every day funerals passed through the streets bearing their burden of military dead. Yet the young people continued to laugh and flirt; the soldiers particularly, those with empty uniform sleeves pinned to their sides, or the even sadder ones who limped painfully along with canes and wooden stubs for legs.

It didn't occur to her that she might also be an object of envy to the paraders—the slim young girl who was perched on the inside of the rail fence, looking out from the grounds of one of the handsomest houses in the city. The Hubbard house was a big square frame building with a hall through the middle and a white-pillared veranda, where Harriet and her sisters and brother sat on warm summer evenings. It was set far back on a vast lawn planted with shrubbery and flowers and trees, and dotted with outbuildings: a carriage house, greenhouses, fruit houses, even a barn for their cow. A fifteen-year old girl named Harriet Hubbard was worth staring at—even if she wasn't pretty.

But Harriet was far too shy to imagine herself interesting. She had had the misfortune to be born into a family which prided itself on the beauty of its women. Her mother had been a dashing belle, much sought after as a cotillion partner even after her marriage; Jule, Harriet's older sister, had inherited her mother's height and chestnut hair and pale skin—at nineteen, she boasted that she had already had twenty-nine proposals of marriage; even May, who was just twelve, was already a beauty, with red-gold curls and tiny features. But Harriet had a straight, uncompromising nose, the Hubbard nose, which was far too large for her small face. Her eyebrows and eyelashes were as pale as her fair hair, no complement for her heavy-lidded dark blue eyes. Her fair skin was covered with freckles. And her mouth had a tendency to pull down at the corners, for she was unhappy and ill at ease much of the time. Even when alone, she was pursued by feelings of inadequacy. There is no question that the basic unhappiness that always lay deep in Harriet, even when she was most sought after and admired, went back to her childhood.

She had been born on June 27, 1849, upstairs in the Hubbard house, in the big walnut bed where her mother now lay reading and nibbling candy. She was the sixth child; the three oldest were dead before Harriet was old enough to remember them. Chicago was still a pioneer town in 1849. In wet seasons, the roads were bogs. Chickens and pigs roamed at will. The winters were bitter and central heating was rare; most of the houses were kept sealed tight, stifling and airless with deadly airtight stoves. Water came from the lake or river; no one had yet thought to boil it. Cholera, the "whiteman's plague," galloping consumption and so-called "brain fever" were common. Parents bore the loss of children stoically, and went on having them.

Juliet Hubbard was always more of a wife than a mother. She accepted the loss of three children. But in 1853, when the youngest and seventh child, May, was just a baby and Harriet was only four years old, Henry Hubbard died suddenly in Sandusky, Ohio, from pneumonia contracted on a cold, wet, all-day ride on horseback, and that was a blow from which she never recovered. Before her husband's death, she had been one of the liveliest of the married crowd, who never tired of dancing the night away. When her husband hunted wolves on the west side, she would bundle the children up and they would all ride in the sleigh with him, crouching in delicious terror under the buffalo robes while the horses flew after the baying hounds. When word reached her that her husband was dead, at the age of forty-three, she was ready to die, too.

Urged by her sisters, she tried travel. The four remaining children, ranging in age from Jule at eight years to May at eleven months, were divided between her two sisters. She went to Paris; the property her husband had bought in the land panic of 1839 had increased tremendously in value and she was a rich widow. But external sights had ceased to interest her. The only souvenir she brought home was the French *Madame* in front of her name; she insisted on it though the Anglo-Saxon "Madam" was currently used to designate older women with married children. She went back to her house on Michigan Avenue and Hubbard Court and tried to interest herself in what went on. For a short time, she was married to a poet who came to Chicago to give cultural lectures in the churches. But the liaison was so brief and so shadowy that the daughters couldn't remember his name afterwards, or what he looked like. And even during the marriage, Juliet Hubbard had continued to answer to the name Madame Hubbard. After the poet left, she had taken to her bed —the same big walnut bed where she and her husband had slept and she had borne her children—and lay there, propped up by innumerable pillows, surrounded by books, dipping occasionally into the dish of candy or nuts that was always at her left hand.

It was not unusual for Victorian ladies to take to their beds when the world became too much to face. Often, with the aid of doctors and relatives, they coddled themselves into permanent declines. But Juliet Hubbard was not a usual Victorian lady.

Her father had been a traveling judge in the Eighth Circuit of Illinois, a territory of some twelve thousand square miles, ex-

tending from Springfield to the eastern border of the state. Juliet
went with him on horseback, as he visited each county in rota-
tion, with court terms lasting from three days to a week. A large
part of the country was so sparsely settled that they would ride
for hours, or sometimes a whole day, without seeing a house. In
the early spring or late fall, when roads were muddy, they could
average only about twenty miles in a long day's ride, bundled up
against blustery winds and drizzling rain, swimming their horses
through swollen streams. Traveling the long, slow miles on
horseback gave Judge Smith plenty of time to teach his daughter
what he considered the essentials of an education: history, philosophy and literature—with emphasis on poetry. As they rode
along, they weren't alone, for they had as companions the characters of fiction, and the great poets.

When Juliet's husband died, she discovered the value of the
education her father had given her and turned to the world of
books. But in the process, her children were left largely to their
own devices. Juliet "took to her bed" at the age of forty-three,
and spent a good deal of her time there until she died, at seventy-
three. Her chestnut, and later graying, hair was always carefully
brushed and piled on top of her head; her fine cambric night-
dresses were always fresh, and topped by exquisite lace jackets.
Cleanliness was an obsession. It was the one thing besides manners that she taught her children. Otherwise, their actual care
was left to servants, and Juliet lived on the principle that household troubles, if ignored, usually solved themselves.

Jule (named Juliet after her mother) was the eldest and
seemed as a young girl to have suffered least from the loss of one
parent and the indifference of the other. She had inherited her
mother's imperious disposition and enjoyed being mistress of the
house, bossing her sisters and brother. Eventually, Jule was to
have her own problems. But as a nineteen-year-old in 1864, she
was pleased with herself, and her situation. Henry, who was just
a year older than Harriet, had the advantage of being a boy. He
had the freedom and indulgence that all Victorian males, even
young males, enjoyed; and his mother sometimes favored him
because he had his father's name. But Henry never quite got
over missing the opportunity to be a soldier in the Civil War,

because of his youth. Although he had his Cousin Gurdon's impatience with school and taste for adventure and excitement, he lacked his sanity and balance. In Henry, high courage became recklessness and eventually he deserted a wife and family to run away to Montana and become a forest ranger. Red-headed May was the lucky one of the four. May, although she was twelve in 1864, was still the baby, the charmer; Henry spoiled her, Harriet took care of her, and even Jule sometimes weakened when May coaxed.

Harriet was the odd one who took everything hard. She was the most fun to tease, because her reactions were so violent and so prompt. She was younger than her actual years—both physically and emotionally. She took no interest in clothes; when the dressmaker Miss Mahoney came to spend several weeks with them each season, she took without interest whatever styles the other girls discarded. When she ran away one day with Henry to explore the lake shore of the river north as far as the cemetery (now Lincoln Park), both of Madame Hubbard's sisters made special visits to warn the widow about the dangerous little tomboy she was rearing.

Madame Hubbard, in an odd way, had moments of liking Harriet as a person, but not as a child. As they both grew older, and Harriet was able to see her mother with a sense of humor and detachment, this friendship grew deeper. But a normal mother-and-daughter relationship was impossible, for Juliet Hubbard had dedicated herself to the passive role of observer. The world outside, although it was going through one of the most dramatic eras in our history, failed to move her. In 1858, Abraham Lincoln came to Chicago and stayed with Henry Hubbard's cousin, Gurdon Hubbard. Although Juliet had met Abe Lincoln many times when he was a young lawyer traveling the Eighth Circuit, she did not even ask him to call on her, though his star was rising. Two years later, when the political convention which nominated Lincoln was held in a new building only a few blocks north of Hubbard Court, on Michigan Avenue, Juliet stayed home and read about it in the *Chicago Tribune*. Even the war did not stir her to real anguish, though she deplored it philosophically. She had lost the one person around whom her life revolved. She sympathized with the sorrow of wives and mothers who had lost men in battle, but their predicaments seemed less real than those of the fascinating characters created by the popular English author, Charles Dickens.

Later, Harriet was to share the bond of reading with her mother. But as a child, she was too intellectually impatient to enjoy the sessions when Madame Hubbard read aloud, in the fashionable Victorian manner. Consequently, although she was able to read before she was five years old, she was supposed to hate books. This was not considered too important; higher education, or even education, for young women in those days was scrappy, at best. What nobody realized was that Harriet had such a quick mind that she often was far ahead of the tutors who were hired to teach her; consequently, they complained that she was naughty and indifferent. And, because she was supposed to be "sickly," in the vague Victorian term, she did not go to the Sacred Heart academy until she was twelve. Unused to school ritual, she felt too shy to answer the nuns' questions, even when she knew the answers. As a result, she was often unfairly punished for inattention and lack of preparation. The nuns gave her poor grades. Madame Hubbard privately thought poor Harriet was dull in brains as well as in looks. The other children, taking their cue from the leader Jule, took delight in teasing Harriet, especially about her phobia, fear of the dark.

Modern psychologists might have helped her, and certainly wouldn't have laughed at her. But no one, not even a doctor, in 1864, thought it was anything but ridiculous for a great girl of fifteen to cry in a dark room with the door bolted. The result was that the fear continued until the end of her life. When she had a choice, she always chose rooms flooded with sunshine, with big windows, with light draperies and walls painted pink. It is particularly poignant that a woman with an ingrained terror of the dark should have been shut up by her enemies in an asylum for over a year.

Just before Harriet's fifteenth birthday on June 27, 1864, her fear of the dark had been pushed to the point of hysteria. Jule had planned a dancing party for a new beau, a senator from whom she hoped to extract her thirtieth proposal. He was a pompous little man with a fine stand of chin whiskers, who looked remarkably like a goat. Knowing Jule had no sense of humor, Harriet took revenge for the merciless teasing she suffered in mischievously asking her sister if she didn't think the senator looked like some animal. A pig? No. A cow? No, not really. But maybe a goat, an old goat . . .

Jule grabbed the younger girl and shoved her down the dark cellar steps and bolted the door. To do Jule justice, she didn't realize that there was a basket of live lobsters in the cellar, ready to be dropped into boiling water and made into lobster salad, which was one of the senator's favorite supper dishes. Harriet, trying to control her fright, tiptoed carefully down the cellar stairs, telling herself it would not be long before she would hear one of the hired girls, or cook, upstairs, and she would scream to be rescued. But, as she reached the bottom, she put her foot into the basket, and the weaving claws touched her leg.

She screamed. She lifted her foot, one lobster clinging to it. Panic-stricken, she crawled frantically back up the stairs, kicking her leg to get rid of the horrible thing, believing it still there long after she had lost it. She tore her hands and her dress. She beat on the cellar door with her feet, her hands, even her head. Blood was streaming from her forehead before Nora, a new Irish girl who had been hired to help cook, heard the screams in the kitchen and ran down to investigate.

Even after Harriet was standing outdoors on the clean grass, she could not believe the crawling things weren't still running up and down her legs. Nora, who was hardly older than Harriet herself, held the girl tight and tried to explain that the crawling things were nothing but poor old lobsters who didn't have long to wait for their bath in boiling water. But Harriet was incoherent with fear. Nora's anger at Jule grew. The older girl was not a favorite with any of the servants, for they resented her imperious ways and her rudeness. But they all loved Harriet. At last, Nora could keep silent no longer. She blurted out: "I wish that Miss Jule would get married and good riddance. Only I pity her husband."

Harriet was startled enough to stop crying.

"But Nora—Jule can get any man she wants. She's had twenty-nine proposals."

Nora frowned. "She'll be a bad wife, mark my words. What good is her beauty, with that temper? Not like you, my darling. The man that gets you will be lucky as a prince."

"No one will ever marry me."

Nora put her arms around Harriet and gave her a hug. "Listen to the child! I'll bet you're married before her. Now, what do you say?"

Harriet couldn't say anything. She was too shocked. But many times in the days following, she took out Nora's words and examined them. Even when she couldn't quite believe, they made her feel better. In her mind, marriage became not only an escape from the loneliness and tedium of the life she led, but a goal in itself. How she was to arrive at it—or how to deal with her mother who, in spite of many unconventional notions, still clung to the old tradition that the eldest daughter of any household must also be the first-married—Harriet could not guess. But it was the stuff that daydreams are made of. Like many lonely people, Harriet indulged in daydreams. Her lively imagination, which was to make her famous in later life, evolved extravagant plots and fantasies which were only of temporary comfort, and made real life even grimmer by comparison.

And on a dusty July 4, a dull day made already duller by the sight of the lively group on the lake front, daydreams were weak solace. But even they were snatched away from her abruptly. For Madame Hubbard, rising from her bed to open another box of candy—a new variety called Turkish Paste which the storekeeper had recommended—saw her next-to-youngest daughter perched stupidly on the fence, staring at what seemed to be nothing. Impatience overwhelmed her. It was characteristic of Madame Hubbard's inconsistency that she hoarded her own daydreams but hated any like tendency in others. Without attempting to analyze why—she was never guilty of the weakness of doubting herself—she swept on a black silk peignoir from Paris and rang for one of the maids to tell Harriet to come up to her mother's suite.

Hastily smoothing her always rebellious hair, straightening her sash and crinoline, Harriet appeared before her mother, eyes downcast, and mouth turned down. She listened meekly enough to Madame Hubbard's lecture on slothfulness, then opened her dark blue eyes—in later life, one infatuated man referred to them as "navy"—on her mother.

"But what do you want me to do?"

Madame Hubbard hesitated. Finally, in the rich voice that she used to recite Chaucer, she boomed: "Exercise! Exercise is excellent for the young."

"How, mamma?"

"You can roll your hoop."

"Where, mamma?"

"Any place you please." Madame Hubbard picked up her book and ended the interview.

Harriet found her hoop in the carriage house. Listlessly, she gave it a push. The chances were that her mother was back in bed, deep in the problems of one of Mr. Dickens' new books. But Harriet could not be sure. Then an inspiration seized her.

The gates had swung open to admit the Hubbard cow that was being driven home from pasture on Twelfth Street. Harriet ran through the gate and fled toward the lake front. The footing was perilous. The city fathers had hit upon the idea of "jacking up" that part of Chicago which was south of the river, to lift it out of the swamp. Whole blocks of buildings were being "screwed up," much of it by a young man named George Pullman who also had the crazy idea of a "Palace" car for train travel. Michigan Avenue had been raised, and you had to go up six steps from Hubbard Court to reach it and down four steps on the other side. Clutching her hoopskirt, Harriet managed the plank steps up. But on the other side, the last hoop of her skirt caught on a projecting nail. She was saved from a bad fall by a sandy-haired young man, who appeared out of nowhere, like the hero in a Victorian novel.

But he was far from being the hero of her dreams. He was short and smelled of whisky. His clothes seemed almost flashy, used as she was to the somber, baggy trousers and loose jacket of Civil War fashion. Long-held prejudices of the era that stamped

a well-dressed man as a ne'er-do-well or a fool, made her doubt
the elegant suit, the broad-brimmed panama hat. His bristling
moustache and his robust laugh frightened her, too. But she was
held there, caught on a nail. Gasping, Harriet reached down and
gave her skirt a vigorous yank. Suddenly released, she tumbled
on her knees in the dusty street, her skirts billowing up around
her, making her more ridiculous than ever, and now so helpless
that she had to be picked up by the young man, abetted by his
tall companion who, too, smelled of whisky.

Harriet's flush made her freckles stand out in hideous relief.
Her skirts and hands were thick with dust. Suddenly, it was all
too much. Tears sprang to her eyes.

Herbert Ayer offered to take the child home. It was a story-
book beginning to a romance and the tale of this meeting was a
story Harriet told her daughters many times. When Herbert
Ayer and John Lockwood presented themselves at the Hubbard
door with a dusty, bedraggled Harriet in tow, the household was
upset to such a degree that Madame Hubbard came downstairs
dressed in one of the dark formal house dresses that she affected.
She was a strong and impressive woman, even to young men as
skittish as Herbert and John, and Herbert was undoubtedly
frightened into giving his credentials—which were acceptable
enough for he was the son of John Vanessa Ayer, who had made
a fortune in iron.

Madame Hubbard was not a grasping or scheming mother, but
she was not completely unworldly, either. Jule was growing no
younger and her strong will and temper made her something less
than a comfort to a lackadaisical mother. Madame Hubbard in-
spected Herbert sharply and decided that he would make a good
match for Jule—despite the fact that the top of his head came no
higher than the girl's ear.

Herbert was never a strong character. He had been spoiled by
a selfish, willful Southern mother who thought education and
brains were nonsense, and by a father who refused to see his
son's faults. At the saloons along Wells Street, particularly the
notorious Under the Willow, Herbert was known as a sport—a
gambler, a heavy drinker, and a good-natured fellow always
ready to help out a friend who was down on his luck. But, like

many weak men, he could be stubborn. Madame Hubbard's determination to have him as a husband for Jule made him look at Harriet with added interest. And the more Madame Hubbard refused to see him as anything but a suitor for Jule, the more interested he became in the younger girl. As for Harriet, she was so starved for attention that she was hopelessly grateful to anyone who was kind to her. This emotion she mistook for love. But her marriage to Herbert was the first step in her inevitable progress toward freedom and self-sufficiency, for it took her close to John Vanessa Ayer, who was to have an important influence on her character.

CHAPTER TWO

J OHN Vanessa Ayer was one of the hundred original members of the Chicago Club, which included all the important citizens of Chicago who had any use for a club: Potter Palmer, George M. Pullman, Robert Lincoln, and Marshall Field. In 1864, he and his family lived at 1 Park Row, on the south side of the river.

Like most of Chicago's builders, he had humble beginnings. When a newspaper reporter once asked him to talk about them, he said impatiently: "Of course I was born poor," and went on to talk about his iron mills. Other early Chicagoans, including the merchant Marshall Field, were bored with their humble origins, and mentioned them seldom, usually when making a point with an employee. But John V. had more important reasons to be reticent. He had a past which was as wildly romantic and improbable as any novel.

He had been born in 1814, in Kenosha, Wisconsin. His father was a farmer, but John V. was given an education, for his parents hoped, with the growing population in the United States, that there would be opportunities for teaching. But John V.'s ambitions outstripped theirs; education only fed his impatience with the profession of teaching.

He decided that the money which would make him rich lay in the earth—not in farming, but in the minerals in the great unexplored areas of land which could then be obtained for a few dollars an acre. He confided in a young man he knew in town, named Samuel Hale. Sam had a little money. John V. showed him maps and persuaded him that Ohio, where land was cheap and iron mills were already springing up, was the land of opportunity.

Sam went to Ohio. John V. had to make enough money to go into partnership with him, so he took a position teaching in New Orleans. New Orleans was gay and hospitable—and an inexpensive place for a personable young schoolteacher to live. He boarded for a few dollars a week, and was asked out socially by the friendly mothers of the children he taught. He was tall, with a physique developed from farm work, and with charming manners which he quickly picked up from his Southern hosts. He also copied their ruffled shirts and conservative but elegant waistcoats. But, although he had a good head for the "wet stuff" and was a shrewd man at "draw" in the taverns, he was very thrifty, saving his money to join Sam Hale in Ohio.

John V. was popular, after the fashion many a young man without prospects may be. The mothers and fathers liked him, but they did not like him as a possible husband for their daughters. The line was firmly drawn and the young women understood. But one strong-willed young woman defied her father.

She was Sara Lynch, a tiny belle from Charleston, South Carolina, whose father was "in rice." She had been raised like a princess, surrounded by slaves who catered to her whims. The schoolmaster interested her; it amused her to reduce him to a state of hopeless infatuation. She had no idea of anything more than that until her father ordered her never to see him again.

Sara listened, her big brown eyes bright with deviltry. At the ball that night, she suggested to John V. that they elope. He was so befuddled with love that his natural good judgment completely deserted him. They ran away and were married secretly. John V. went back to his teaching and she returned to the big house her father had rented for the winter. They saw each other alone only rarely, when Sara was supposedly visiting friends and John V.'s landlady could be persuaded to look the other way. It was tantalizing and terrible for the young man; the clandestine romance only whetted his appetite for more of Sara. Sara, on the other hand, soon lost her taste for John V.'s modest surroundings. She still wanted her husband, but she wanted him on her own terms. She told her father that she was married, and begged for his blessing. For once, he denied her. She was packed off to John V. with only her trunk of clothes, not one gown among them suitable for a boardinghouse.

John V. took every cent he had saved and rented larger rooms, and begged a slave girl from rich friends, to take care of the housework. But the larger rooms were still miserable and mean to a girl raised on a plantation in South Carolina. And the slave girl was impossibly ignorant. Sara, who was too ignorant of housekeeping to train her, took out her frustrations in screaming at the two people who had to listen: the servant and her husband.

The slave didn't have to stay. She ran home to her owners. John V. apologized to his lovely wife and promised to find her someone more efficient. But it was difficult, and the young people passed from lovers' quarrels to bitter arguments. She went to her father and begged him to help. He told her that so long as she lived with John V., he would not give her a cent.

John V. tried desperately to save enough so that he and Sara could join Sam Hale in Youngstown. His wife accused him of being cruel and mean. He knew in his heart that he could not hold her. An epidemic of yellow fever hastened the end. John V. came down with the sickness and Sara fled to her father who took her back to South Carolina.

John V. was very ill, but he was strong, and survived. He was angered by Sara's desertion, but he loved her still and was determined to make enough money to claim her. Then a mutual friend brought him news which had been kept from John V. until he was stronger. Sara was dead of yellow fever.

John V. never spoke of Sara, or of her disappearance. But he took every opportunity to make money, and he spent little on himself. His clothes grew shabby; he didn't care. He took

night jobs; he grew gaunt and his face became lined. Although
he was still under thirty, he looked middle-aged.

But he soon saved enough money to have a stake, and he
joined Sam Hale.

Sam had prospered. The time was ripe; the railroads were
multiplying; McCormick had invented the reaper. Iron was in
demand. But John V. made the difference between modest success and big business. He had a quick mind, and he knew how
to make a sharp deal. Nothing interested him but money. He
got up early in the morning and was at work in his office "before
the boys with the polished nails" showed up.

It was in 1849 that he decided to move to Chicago, where opportunities were greater. Sam Hale was reluctant; he was satisfied in Ohio and felt it was the place for his sons. But Ayer had
his way.

In 1849, he and Sam Hale established their offices in Chicago—
Hale, Ayer & Co., Iron Merchants. It was the year that Harriet
Hubbard was born.

Dirty little Chicago was then a wild melodrama of growth.
The merchants who stood behind the counters of the brick stores
on Lake Street were the tycoons and aristocrats of tomorrow—
men like Potter Palmer and Marshall Field. Land had already
increased phenomenally in value. Gurdon Hubbard had paid
$66.66 for two lots on Lake Street in the 'thirties; now he sold
them for $80,000, though when the storms were bad on Lake
Michigan, the easterly wind dug up the coffins from the old
Madison Street burial ground, spotting the shores with ghastly
remains. There was no water system; the drinking water was
dipped from the lake or Chicago River. There was no lighting
system. The stockade of Fort Dearborn was still standing, but
deserted and filled with honey-locust trees. The only means of
communication was a weekly steamer from Buffalo. Indians
were still seen on the streets, but they carried no tomahawks and
accepted gratefully whatever hospitality was offered to them in
the way of food or drink. A ferryboat hauled by a rope joined
the north and south sides at Rush Street. A town crier, a Negro
with a bell, announced lost children. There was only one form
of public transportation, a State Street coach (which went down

the trail broken by Gurdon Hubbard in 1818) which made two journeys a day from the Chicago River to Eighteenth Street, with a long, much-needed rest for horses on either end.

But it also was an exciting, vigorous city. Underneath the muck of the old lake bed, there was a shallow bowl of rock on which someday tall buildings were to rise. The Chicago millionaires of the next few decades owed most of their fortunes to this rock base. Because of it, they were able eventually to fill in and "jack up" the level of Chicago some ten feet in all; because of it the tall buildings now stand in the Loop. But the first raisings were not done in a day. For years, the wooden sidewalks were a series of steps, for not every property owner agreed on the same level when he jacked up his building. At every corner there were steps, and some of them were more like rotten ladders, which gave many a pedestrian a bad tumble. In places the sidewalks were four to six feet above the roadway, and in the wet season, a tumble frequently sent the victim waist deep in mud, for drainage was an ever-present problem. The first public loan made by Chicago's trustees was for $60 to drain a mudhole in Clark Street.

Young George Pullman made his first fortune as a house wrecker; then engineered raising buildings; he got $45,000 for jacking up the Tremont Hotel four feet. Most of the buildings weren't worth the money spent on them. Long before the great Chicago Fire, in 1871, the *Chicago Tribune* predicted that Chicago's hasty and flimsy construction would someday result in a major disaster. In 1849, all the fire engines were, of course, pumped by hand and manned by volunteers, among them the sons and husbands of all the best families. Fires were frequent— and great social events, for the wives went along to pour coffee and otherwise make themselves useful. In fact, the social life in those days was so limited that one of the diversions offered visitors was the fires. A housewife of early Chicago wrote a friend in the East: "Our house burned last month. We were very much distressed when our neighbors turned out, not so much to sympathize, but to be entertained. I must admit, however, that last week when a barn belonging to our new neighbor burned to the ground, we got the children up and let them enjoy the excitement."

In a city so rugged, there was naturally a dearth of young women. For a long time, the percentage was about seven to one. Even in 1849, the young ladies who came from the East to "winter" in Chicago were quickly snapped up. But John Vanessa Ayer, although he was already wealthy, and in his middle thirties, showed no desire to find a wife. It was a strange reversal of circumstances. When John V. had been deeply in love, he had not been considered a good match; now that he was indifferent, the mothers and young women worked their wiles on him. And his strong views against slavery identified him with the growing and powerful abolitionist movement.

Eventually, he married a shy young farmer's daughter from his home state; for her, it was a great match. But there was never any romance in their marriage. John V. had had his romance. Now his business and his city were his main interests. The Civil War brought him more and more profits; railroads were booming, ground had already been broken for the Union Pacific in Omaha. The iron horse was making John V. a very rich man—and so was the war. But, unlike some other war profiteers, he subscribed heavily to the government loans.

As John V. grew richer, he grew more restless. Money and success were not enough to satisfy him. He was ripe for adventure. It might have come to him in the form of a woman, but instead he found a son he didn't know existed.

Near the end of the war, during one of his many trips, he stayed overnight at the resort hotel in White Sulphur Springs. It was an elaborate establishment, noted as much for its social life as for its baths, whose health-giving properties had been known to the Indians. Both Northerners and Southerners could be found there even during the war, though by 1863 few Southerners were seen, for money was too scarce.

In the dining room, a couple caught John V.'s eyes—a still-beautiful gray-haired woman and a young man in Confederate uniform. At first, he could not understand why the woman attracted him so, but gradually he realized it was her resemblance to his first wife. He was ready to leave when a waiter brought

him a message from the lady, asking him to take coffee with her
and her son in the parlor afterwards. However, it was not until
she addressed him by name that he knew she was Sara; Sara
Copeland now, for she had married again.

When she returned to her family after her brief message to
John V., her father had sent word to New Orleans that Sara was
dead of the fever, just as he told Sara that John V. had died. She
had no particular desire to return to her miserable married life,
but her family feared that the birth of the baby might change
her viewpoint.

John V.'s head jerked up at that point. What baby? Then
Sara, smiling, put her hand on the gray-uniformed arm of the boy
with her.

"I named him Herbert," she said. "Herbert Copeland, for he
took my second husband's name after we were married. But it
really should be Herbert Ayer—he is your son."

It was a shock, but a wonderful one. Avidly, John V. pressed
for more details. The divorce had been obtained before the child
was born, before they even lied to her about her husband's death;
Sara's mother had come from a family of lawyers and it had been
managed with such felicity she now hardly remembered anything about it. But, some time after she had married Mr. Copeland and had his children, she had heard rumors that her first
husband was alive; and before the war visitors to Chicago had
brought back news of him. In fact, Herbert had known all about
his father for some time and, if the war had not intervened, he
might have made a trip to Chicago to see him, for he was of an
age when he should have some kind of a profession. . . .

Dazed and dizzy with emotion, John let her talk on. Sara's
husband was now very ill, his money gone, his plantation ruined,
but it was characteristic of Sara that she had taken some ready
cash she had hidden to spend on a holiday for herself and her
son. Her three daughters, Mr. Copeland's children, had been left
at home. Listening to her complain about her situation and her
hard life, John V. found his heart pounding with excitement. He
no longer craved Sara. What he wanted was their son. Until
now, children had meant nothing to him. The children by his
second marriage had been his wife's concern. But this boy was

different. He had Sara's eyes, and like her, was small and delicately boned, and John V. thought he saw something of himself
in Herbert, too. . . .

Before the evening was over, he had made a deal with Sara.
In exchange for a large sum of money for herself and her family,
she gave him permission to buy Herbert out of the Confederate
Army and take him back to Chicago with him, as the heir to his
name and business.

It was a selfish move, John V. knew, and it was not fair to his
second wife, or her children. But John V. could not help himself.
He was as dazzled by the newly discovered son as he had once
been by Sara. Herbert became his whole life, his reason for ex-
isting. After the war and the death of her husband, Sara moved
to Youngstown, Ohio, where John V. had his mills. He always
took care of her and her daughters, until they married, and she
became something of a local legend. The story of her strange
meeting with her ex-husband and his discovery of his son was
reprinted in the Chicago papers whenever Herbert broke into
the news.

Harriet, who knew Sara as a spoiled, difficult old lady, found
it hard to understand why she and her son had such a hold over
John V. It was not until her father-in-law's death that she realized Sara had represented high romance and youth to him—so
Herbert automatically stood for the same things. John V. laid all
his hopes and ambitions on the boy's shoulders, a heavy burden
for any young man to carry, especially one who had been
brought up by a woman like Sara.

For several months after Herbert had met Harriet, he did
not tell his father about her. He was employed as a clerk in the
National Bank, where John V. was a stockholder, waiting the
day when Sam Hale would retire. The work bored him, and he
had no special supervision. So he found time nearly every day to
ride over to Hubbard Court.

He still dutifully attended social gatherings, dancing well, but
was painfully silent at supper, and even more silent at theatre
parties, where the stifling air grew so bad, with its overpowering
smell of gas lamps, that he often fell asleep through endless dull
Shakespearean tragedies at McVicker's. He still also frequented

the notorious Under the Willow on Wells Street and drank with his cronies in Billy Bolshaw's. But the little girl whom he had literally picked up on the lake front stayed in his memory. She wasn't a child; Jule Hubbard had told him her sister was fifteen, which was considered a marriageable age in South Carolina. And she had a delicacy and sweetness that pleased him. She was not beautiful; but Herbert, who had a beauty for a mother, knew the pitfalls of marrying a belle. He fell into the habit of riding around to Hubbard Court often on summer evenings, and sitting with the group on the veranda, most of them Jule's friends. Harriet said very little, and whatever she said was pounced on by Jule, and criticized. The only way Harriet had of retaliating was by irony, quietly dropped, which went over Jule's lovely humorless head. But Herbert always laughed. It was one of the things that endeared him to Harriet. Once, when she made a face behind Jule's back, he turned and responded immediately with a hideous grimace. While they rocked with laughter, and Jule looked bewildered, Herbert made up his mind that he was going to marry Harriet.

He did not talk to her about it until after Christmas, in 1864. The war news was good. On December 26, Savannah fell. Even President Lincoln said that the South had no chance, any more.

Harriet was surprised when Herbert mentioned marriage. She was not so stupid that she hadn't realized that he liked her, but when he told her that he had spoken to his father about her, Harriet was genuinely startled.

So, as a matter of fact, was John V. He had made plans for Herbert to take over the iron business; and he had great dreams of building it into an empire for Herbert's sons. Somewhere along the line, he wanted Herbert to marry a sound Northern young woman who would be a good mother for the sons. But he was not eager to hurry the marriage; he enjoyed having Herbert under his own roof.

On the other hand, the Hubbards were a fine family. Harriet, when she came of age, would undoubtedly inherit a small fortune of her own. John V. had not known her father but, like everyone else in Chicago, he knew and respected her cousin

Gurdon. After a few minutes of completely selfish annoyance, John V. told his son that he was sure he was making a wise choice. Herbert's stepmother was sent for, and instructed to call on Madame Hubbard immediately, and prepare her for Herbert's formal demand for Harriet's hand.

It was a trying visit for Mrs. John V. Ayer. Madame Hubbard took a long time getting dressed to come downstairs to the parlor and receive her. Then, when she appeared, she kept insisting—at first, in a normal voice, and then, as Mrs. Ayer grew bewildered, talking louder and louder—that she was sure Mrs. Ayer was mistaken. It was Juliet, of course, whom Herbert wanted to marry. Poor Harriet was only a child. Herbert never noticed her. Harriet was still too young for beaux. She had not yet gone to her first ball. Mrs. Ayer had better return home and straighten out the whole thing with her son. Or was Herbert her stepson? Well, all the more reason why Mrs. Ayer could be mistaken.

Harriet, crouched on her bed upstairs, suffered tortures of anguish. But later that evening, when she walked to the gate with Herbert, she acted out her own version of the meeting and Herbert roared with delight. Then he promised to send his father to pay a call on the Hubbards, and make the whole situation plain.

John V.'s first reaction to Harriet was shock. Jule was a dazzler, and he would have been delighted with her as a daughter-in-law, even though she was taller than Herbert. But poor little Harriet was dull—as uninteresting in manner as his own poor wife, Mrs. Ayer, and even more mouse-like in appearance. He had somehow imagined Herbert would capture a girl as dazzling and enchanting as his mother had been. But Herbert, if he lacked his mother's ruthlessness, was as stubborn as she when he wanted something. John V. realized the fact when Herbert told him bluntly that he never was, and never would be, interested in Jule; that she was a bore. Madame Hubbard realized it when she told him that it was impossible for Harriet to be married until her older sister was engaged and married; that Harriet was too young, too inexperienced; that—

Herbert interrupted firmly: "I'll wait until Harriet is sixteen. But then we are going to be married. My father and mother eloped. But I'm sure Harriet would rather be married at home."

John V. had a talk with Sam Hale. Sam wanted to leave the business and start another mill with his two sons. If the boy married, this might be a good time for him to come into the business.

It was an eventful spring. On April 10, a Sunday, Richmond fell. War was over; all the churches held special night prayer meetings; shouting, singing crowds gathered in front of Tremont House far into the night, while the courthouse bell pealed and rockets illumined the sky. The next day the parade took four hours to pass along Michigan Avenue and even Madame Hubbard was among the crowds that watched. It was announced almost immediately that President and Mrs. Lincoln would come to the Northwestern Fair, which was to open in Chicago on May 30.

But on April 15, Abraham Lincoln was assassinated. The train bearing his body traveled all over the North. On May 1, the coffin was borne up Michigan Avenue to State Street, while the courthouse bells tolled solemnly and nearly every house displayed black crepe. Harriet, wearing a black silk dress, and a heavy shawl, stood on the veranda and watched the cavalcade move past. The body was to lie in state in the courthouse from five o'clock until midnight. John V. had decided to go at midnight and Harriet surprised him by asking if she could accompany him.

Harriet never forgot that night. There was a strange silence over the city. It was cold and wet—the *Tribune* said next day: "The falling of rain seemed like the weeping of nature over the loss of her favorite son." Yet the waiting line, even at that late hour, was nearly a block long. People seemed to tiptoe as they climbed the long flight of steps to where the President lay, General Sheridan on guard at his head, and General Logan at his feet. As Harriet walked past the body, a male chorus, with torches and music books, stood out in the street in the rain to sing a requiem for the dead.

The preparations for the wedding were already under way, although it would not take place until the last of June. Madame

Hubbard had sent to New York for a white satin wedding dress, which was to be trimmed with some of Madame's own precious Venetian lace. Nora had been given permission to help make the wedding cake, which would be large, even though only relatives and close friends of both families were to be invited. And Harriet was busy in the garden and greenhouse, holding some plants back and forcing others, for Madame Hubbard had told her that she could decorate the house herself, and Harriet had dreams of making the parlor into a bower of bloom. She wasn't doing it for herself, really. It was a way of saying goodbye to the garden at Hubbard Court, the garden which she had loved. It was also a way of saying goodbye to the father she could hardly remember who had also loved the garden.

May was thrilled with the prospect of a wedding, and even volunteered to stand in for Harriet when she got tired of fittings for her trousseau—which, unfortunately, was being made entirely by the unimaginative Miss Mahoney, who was sewing the same high-necked, long-sleeved dresses for the bride that she had made for the schoolgirl. Harriet did not know the difference and Madame Hubbard quite frankly did not care. She had taken to her bed, shutting the door against the loud and bitter arguments Jule had with everyone.

There was no question that Jule was being even more difficult than usual. She gave the busy servants added chores. She made fun of Harriet's looks, and shook her head when she saw the wedding gown—"Imagine, lace and satin on *you*." She even was snappy with poor little May. Once she locked her in a cupboard and, although it did not frighten the younger girl, she was bitterly resentful.

"What am I going to do when you're gone?" she begged Harriet.

Harriet used to hold her sister close, promising her that she wouldn't permit Jule to abuse May, that she would let May live with her if Jule didn't behave well. Secretly, she was bewildered. It was impossible that Jule had been interested in Herbert Ayer, even though she had always accepted him as one of her beaux. It was impossible that a girl of such beauty and spirit could be jealous of a plain younger sister. It was also impossible that Jule could be upset that her mother had disregarded convention and allowed Harriet to marry so young simply because, as Madame Hubbard explained to her sisters: "The poor child might never get another chance." Yet Jule had been strange, secretive, recently. . . .

The answer came when Jule eloped with John Lockwood a week before Harriet's wedding. They went east to New Jersey to live. Harriet's first shocked thought had been: "Then I needn't marry Herbert after all!"

But she had gone too far now to draw back. Her trousseau was finished. The wedding dress was ready and Madame Hubbard had personally supervised its final fitting. Nora was counting on beating the eggs for the wedding cake. And Herbert—she couldn't disappoint him. He told her constantly how much he loved her.

The house looked beautiful for the wedding, the big parlor transformed into a rose garden. The guests politely told Harriet that she made a sweet-looking bride; privately, they commented that she was an uninteresting little thing, but at least she seemed eager to please.

When John V., having asked who had arranged the flowers, was told it was the bride herself, his pleasure was obvious. During the few weeks he had known his son's bride-to-be, he had been surprised to find himself enjoying her company. She had curiosity; she asked questions because she was interested in learning the answers, not to show how smart she was, a fault of some young women. She was not beautiful, poor child, but she had a shining cleanliness that in itself was appealing. Her hair was a beautiful color and always sparkling with life and light— although badly dressed. Her clothes, dowdy as they were, always shone with freshness. And now she seemed to have a talent with flowers. Perhaps poor Herbert hadn't done so badly after all.

CHAPTER THREE

HERBERT had no reservations; he was delighted with his bride. He was also delighted with the white frame house on tree-shaded Wabash Avenue, which John V. had rented for them. It wasn't large; Harriet could manage it with one hired girl. And, although she had much to learn about housekeeping, she was interested and eager to improve. Unlike Sara Lynch, she was neither spoiled nor lazy.

She made the usual mistakes; mistakes which Herbert loved to talk about at the Chicago Club. Once she had attempted to roast a chicken on Lizzie's day off. She had taken the bird whole, as it arrived from the butcher, cut off the head and plumped the rest of it in the oven, uncleaned. When it exploded and filled the house with the smell of burning entrails, Harriet burst into tears. Herbert came home from the mill that day in time to discover the disaster, before Harriet could run over to Nora at Hubbard Court for help. He laughed until he cried.

Harriet found marriage a great deal better than she expected. For one thing, Herbert was both kind and generous; he laughed at her mistakes, but he was proud of her developing competence and skills. The nuns had already taught her to sew; now she went to Hubbard Court to take cooking lessons from cook and Nora.

Clothes also became important—and interesting to her. On her honeymoon at White's Hotel, she had been shocked to realize how ill-dressed she was, more like a child than a young matron. In White Sulphur Springs, while Herbert played cards in the saloon, Harriet visited the dressmakers, who brought out the latest fashions from Paris for her when they discovered she had money to pay for them. For the first time in her life, she had a bank account; John V. had deposited a sum of money in the bank in her name that she could spend as she wished, without accounting to anyone. Harriet was at first ashamed to admit that she had never shopped for a dress in her life, but had accepted what came from the dressmaker's hands without comment or interest. Now she was learning that clothes could be amusing— and shockingly expensive. However, since it was her own money. . . .

Soon after they came home, while she and Herbert were still living with his father at 1 Park Row, she showed her mother the Paris dress she had bought for dinner at White's. It was rose gauze, with an overskirt of deeper rose velvet, and a cascade of ruffles down the back. Harriet was still not pretty, in the conventional sense, but the tone of the dress gave her face color and made her eyes more interesting. Even Harriet's figure had matured amazingly, her mother thought.

"I'm wearing a corset," Harriet told her proudly.

And she continued to wear a corset, much as she hated the discomfort it caused her. She was growing up fast. She and Herbert became part of the young married group on Wabash Avenue; they sometimes went up to parties on the north side. Harriet loved the dancing; particularly the square dancing, although she caught on quickly to the newly fashionable "round" styles, in which Herbert was adept. She was still shy, and younger than most of the wives; but, bit by bit, they began to accept her, to invite her to call and bring her embroidery. She was bewildered and bored a great deal of the time among these other young women; she would much rather have been working in her own garden. But she was still too uncertain of herself to dare express her feelings. Consequently, if she was not very popular, she was not unpopular, either.

She saw a great deal of John V. Nearly every day he stopped by the small house, sometimes with Herbert, sometimes alone.

Her freshness, and her sense of fun, the qualities which had first attracted Herbert, gradually began to interest John V. The schoolmaster in him also delighted in her eager mind; she was hungry for knowledge and it amused him, after all these years, to teach again. Her first quarrel with Herbert came after she had proudly given him a display of the twelve lines of Latin which John V. had taught her. Herbert stormed out of the house and over to his bachelor haunts on Wells Street, the first time he had been there since their marriage. He came home very late and very deep in his cups, so befuddled that Harriet gave up trying to put him to bed and let him sleep downstairs on the hard horsehair sofa, with a knitted shawl over him. The next morning, he was miserably repentant, and Harriet was glad to forgive him. Only she wasn't quite sure what she had done, and she didn't want to expose her family troubles to John V.

The steel mills interested Herbert. John V. had started him at the bottom in the office, but Herbert's easy manners and cheerfulness won him friends. John V. was pleased. The boy would do, and the mill was booming. In fact, industry was booming better than ever since the war, especially in the West. Chicago had grown phenomenally; in 1866, nearly nine thousand new buildings were erected and land on Michigan and Wabash was selling for $400 a front foot. Chicago was the "Hog-Butcher for the World" and, if the city trees and gardens were suffering under increasing clouds of industrial smoke, and the Chicago River was dark and malodorous with soot and grease, few people minded. For the river was choked with boats, and crossed by no fewer than ten swinging bridges; everybody was getting rich, at least everybody Harriet and Herbert knew socially. They all had carriages or broughams and victorias. They traveled on the luxurious Pullman Palace car which George Pullman had been laughed at for building. (It had come into prominence when Mrs. Lincoln collapsed on reaching Chicago with the funeral train, and Pullman had offered his coach to take her to Springfield.)

The two-mile tunnel under the lake was finished and the new

municipal water crib was opened. The Atlantic cable had been laid under the ocean. Women were reading a new poem called *Snow-Bound* by John Greenleaf Whittier, and whispering about suffrage. The gambling palaces and saloons and theatres were jammed; there was a frantic search for excitement, diversion. Over twenty-five hundred people crowded into the circus-like grandeur of Crosby's gold and white opera house to see *The Black Crook*, in which blondes in black stockings and tights were seen "capering lasciviously."

One era of Chicago's history was coming to a close, and another one about to begin. The industrialists and business tycoons had their troubles cut out for them with the so-called "Communists" who were to demand eight-hour days, and unions to strike and dicker for salary increases. The city directory listed 1,481 saloons and only 1,056 groceries, but only a few prohibitionists and reformers worried. While the women of fashion took their "airings" every day from five to six in their carriages, along the lake front, the men gathered in the saloons, drinking and playing cards. Everything was pitched at a high key. Uranus Crosby, the spirited society bachelor who had built the opera house, declared himself in need of funds, and raffled off the house at a lottery, selling some 210,000 tickets at $5 each. In the end, fraud was strongly suspected because an unknown out-of-towner had supposedly held the winning number, whereupon Crosby promptly bought the ticket for $200,000. (The building was soon to be destroyed in the Chicago Fire and never rebuilt.)

The few millionaires who had continued to plow their earnings back into property never regretted it; they were the ones who had real survival insurance. Madame Hubbard had been left with valuable holdings in what is now the Loop; but she was improvident enough to sell them off, piece by piece; it was said that whenever Juliet wanted to buy a box of candy, she sold a piece of real estate. John Vanessa Ayer, on the other hand, had most of his holdings in the Youngstown mills. True, they were vast, but it never occurred to him that his empire would ever be threatened by the employees he hired and fired as casually as he replaced machinery. Like many self-made men before and since, John V. had little sympathy or compassion for the indigent and inefficient. He still worked long hours and had small patience with anyone who seemed to him to lack ambition.

Without a twinge of conscience, he and his friends demanded the best: the "palace" hotels and riverboats and Pullman cars. Potter Palmer, who in 1868 built a marble "palace" on State and Washington which housed "the grandest and most fashionable dry goods store in the city," was rumored to have settled a million dollars on his bride, the former Bertha Honoré. But their cook, like all the cooks for the best families of Chicago, earned $4 a week and had one day off a month.

Harriet's background did not provide her with any yardstick by which to measure the injustice of the pattern. But she had a life-long tendency to identify with the underdog. She hated to see suffering. Her generosity to those in need came not only from a lack of reverence for money, but from a genuine desire to eliminate suffering.

She was, of course, naïve. When she became pregnant, and was ill with such blinding headaches that she could not move or sleep, the doctor suggested that she be sent to a hospital, where she could have the benefit of some nursing, which was a newly popular occupation for young women. She went (taking, of course, all her own bedclothes and having her food brought from home) and there she discovered two things: the novels of Charles Dickens and the poverty of some of the people who lived only a few blocks from Hubbard Court.

Madame Hubbard brought Harriet Dickens' novels. They were supposed to be proper for a gentleman to read aloud to ladies, and shock-proof for young women whose sensibilities were so delicate that they clothed the nudity of piano legs in panties and ruffles. But he had a feeling for the poor that moved Harriet immediately.

One day the doctor found her weeping. When he protested that this was no way to get well she cried: "How can I be happy about my baby if I know that somewhere, other women haven't enough to eat?"

"You can't help everybody," he warned her.

"But I can help a few people. Tell me about some of your patients that are in trouble. Let me do what I can."

Actually, she was playing the lady bountiful; real philanthropists scorned such feeble efforts. But she was sincere, and too young to realize how small her efforts were. She bought a layette for a young mother who could afford nothing for her baby; the doctor was surprised at how sensible Harriet's selections were. She paid the hospital bill for a woman who had broken her hip, and sent food to her three children and unemployed husband. Later, after discussion with Madame Hubbard's coachman, she found the man work in a livery stable. She was sensitive enough to demand that her gifts remain anonymous; but, of course, they didn't. It was too much to expect that gifts from the daughter-in-law of John V. would remain unidentified. John V. and Herbert soon discovered all about Harriet's "lame ducks"; they had little sympathy with the unfortunates, but it pleased them that Harriet was so womanly.

She came home to have her baby, of course; it was unthinkable that John V.'s grandson should be born in a public hospital. But the baby, born in the middle of an insufferably hot spell in August, was a little girl. Harriet was meekly apologetic. Herbert, however, was delighted. His sense of dynasty was then far less compelling than his father's; he loved all babies; and this one was his own. He pleased Harriet by insisting that the baby be named after her.

Little Hattie was pretty from the first. She had her father's brown hair and her grandmother Lynch's huge brown eyes. She was compact, like her father and paternal grandmother. Soon John V. was just as fatuous over her as Herbert. He had broken his long hours at his roll-top desk to come and see Harriet while she was pregnant; now he also stopped by on his way to work in the morning to visit the baby. Even while Hattie was too little to recognize anyone, he showered her with presents; no baby in Chicago had finer embroideries and laces. The laundry and housework were soon too much for Lizzie to handle, alone. So Madame Hubbard sent Nora to her daughter; and Nora was delighted. She was far better at taking care of Hattie than was Hattie's own mother, as Harriet acknowledged with a laugh. She allowed Herbert to send away the baby nurse, and let Nora take charge of Hattie.

Before she could begin the entertaining which both John V. and Herbert were urging on her, Harriet discovered she was pregnant again. John V. was delighted. This time he was certain he would have a grandson. Harriet tried to share his enthusiasm, but she felt too ill most of the time. She refused to go to the hospital, because it meant leaving Hattie who was growing more charming every day. But she was not capable of much more than lying on the sofa reading—she reminded herself of her mother—or walking in the garden, supervising the care of the small grounds.

Herbert, delighted as he was with Hattie, grew bored and petulant. A household with a baby and an ailing wife was trying to a young man. A new saloon had opened on Clark and Lake, which was much the rage because of a new feature—the delicious free lunch. Herbert met his cronies there after work and sometimes did not come home until very late. Harriet felt sorry for her husband; he meant so well that she did not dream of reporting his defections to his father.

"I'll be better company," she promised, "after our son is born."

But the son was another daughter, and sickly at that. Herbert was not impressed and John V. was openly disappointed. Even Nora, sighing, remarked that Baby looked like a poor little plucked chicken. Harriet felt more fiercely maternal than ever; she named the baby Gertrude after a beautiful aunt of her mother's and insisted on doing many things for Gertie herself, despite Nora's protests.

Madame Hubbard spoke to her sharply: "A man hates sickly children. Besides, Nora knows much more about taking care of babies than you do."

"But I'm the only one who loves her! She's so—"

Madame Hubbard studied her daughter, almost as though she were seeing her for the first time. Harriet was wearing a white peignoir; her red-gold hair, which she hadn't dressed yet, fell loosely around her face. Her cheeks were pink and her skin was clear; the freckles of childhood had vanished. And her lashes and brows had darkened, accenting the large blue eyes that were set deep in enormous sockets.

"Harriet, are you using paint?"

Harriet's face became even pinker. "Mamma, of course not; what are you talking about?"

"You've turned into a beauty."

Harriet looked at her mother in astonishment. But Madame · Hubbard was not one to flatter, or tease. Still holding Gertie, Harriet picked up a looking glass on the bureau and studied her face. It looked back at her much the same as always, the strong nose, the corners of the mouth pulled down. And yet . . . She turned around. "Oh, mamma, if it could be true—"

"You must buy some new clothes. Hoops are definitely out; you'll want some dress improvers. And you must start entertaining. Herbert has an eye for pretty women; let him meet them in his own home instead of at the burlesque."

"Mamma, don't say things like that!"

Madame Hubbard stood up. "Don't be a child, Harriet. Your body is grown-up now. It's time you began to understand men. It's simple enough if—" Her voice trailed off.

"If what?" Harriet asked.

"If you care enough. Only—let Nora take care of Baby. Now that your looks have improved, you won't find parties quite so dull, I promise you."

Harriet selected a modest wardrobe in the new fashion, with the "dress improvers"—bustles made of horsehair or steel casings. She felt ridiculous until John V. looked at her with sharp surprise.

"What's happened to you?"

"It's the new style."

"I'm talking about you, my dear. I always thought Jule was the beauty of the family. You knock the spots off Jule any day. Look at her, Herbert, hasn't she changed?"

To her surprise, however, Herbert was less pleased than either John V. or her mother. He was sulky and, for the first time, criticized her clothes. But John V. laughed at him.

"Forget about entertaining here, my dear. I'm going to build you a house that will be the kind of a background a beauty like you should have. We want a palace, Herbert, fit for your queen. What do you say?"

Herbert said little. He realized that now his father was making him take over more and more responsibility at the mill, he should have a show-place worthy of his position. If nothing else, it would impress the men with whom he did business. At the same time, he felt sands shifting uneasily under him. The girl he had married had grown into a beauty; he had seen enough of Southern beauties to suspect how it might change her. She also had developed a taste for study; and there was nothing he deplored more than a bluestocking. On the other hand, there were the children—at least, Hattie. And maybe the next one would be a boy. Children would be the answer, even though it was a pity that Harriet didn't feel better during the process of having them. But perhaps she would get used to that, too; and enough babies would keep her nose out of books.

CHAPTER FOUR

ALTHOUGH it was the eighth of October, the weather was so hot that the women at church all wore summer dresses. And a relentless breeze from the stifling south brought sand and dust and more discomfort. Chicago needed rain badly. Old settlers like Gurdon Hubbard said they'd never seen Chicago baked so dry, so badly in need of rain. In the country, the crops were ruined. The city's fifty-six miles of wooden block pavement and almost 560 miles of brittle pine sidewalks were dry as tinder; grass and flowers were parched and stiff; the leaves had long since dropped off the exhausted trees and lay in rustling drifts along the roads and gardens.

The whole city was like an enormous pile of kindling, waiting for the match. Block after block consisted of hastily erected frame buildings. The newspapers scolded constant warnings; the city was paying more for fire insurance than was collected for state, county and municipal taxes. Yet there were only fourteen fire engines and one pumping house, with a wooden roof that was just as dry as the sidewalks. Although the spectacular new waterworks' building on the north side, which had been finished in 1867, gave citizens a sense of security, actually it was more decorative than adequate. The day before, Saturday, there had been a bad fire on the west side. The papers said it had been dealt with, but there was a current uneasiness throughout the city.

Herbert refused to go to church, claiming that he had a headache. Hattie had broken a French music box her grandfather had given her, and was in bed as a punishment. The baby had been sick and fretful all day; it was the unseasonable heat, Harriet assured herself, and yet Gertie's slightest whimper worried her. The big Sunday dinner had hardly been touched; afterwards Harriet sent the maids home to the west side, for they wanted to be sure their families had not been burned out in Saturday's fire. After washing up the dishes from the evening high tea, almost as unappreciated as the dinner, Nora went up to put the children to bed. She had a hard time. Hattie, after having slept most of the day, was cross and rebellious, and poor little Gertie was crying again.

Herbert flung down the newspaper and announced he was going out for a breath of air. Harriet did not blame him, she was restless herself. But she hoped he wouldn't drop into one of the many saloons that defied the Sunday closing law. It was her only complaint against Herbert, really; but perhaps she was naïve, as he told her, for all his cronies seemed to drink whisky by the tumblerful and their wives didn't seem to notice.

She tried to read. But after an hour or so, her eyes grew heavy. She dozed in her chair, not wanting to go to bed until Herbert returned. Finally, she was awakened by the book falling from her lap. She picked it up and walked to the door. The air was heavy with haze—and something else. Her mind flew to poor little Gertie who, among her other trials, suffered from asthma. She hurried to close the windows, and called upstairs: "Nora, you had better be sure none of the windows are open. Smoke seems to be coming from somewhere; I'm afraid there must be a fire."

Nora did not answer. Harriet waited for a minute, and then ran upstairs. To her surprise, Nora was standing in her nightdress at the head of the stairway, her face gray in the harsh light of the gas jet. She was shivering, in spite of the warmth of the night.

"Are you ill, Nora?"

"No, ma'am, it's—I don't want to talk about it."

Harriet's glance sought the children's bedroom. It looked toward the west. The windows were closed, but there was a strange light in the sky. She said sharply, half to reassure herself:

"You aren't afraid of a fire, after all these years in Chicago? It's only on the west side again and the wind is from the south, I noticed particularly a little while ago. Besides, the flames can't jump the river." Harriet touched the girl's wrist; it was cold and bathed with sweat. "Nora, you're ill; go to bed and I'll send for a doctor as soon as Mr. Ayer comes home."

Nora shook her head, leaning against the wall, her eyes closed. "No, ma'am, it's something the doctor couldn't help, I—"

"Then what is the matter?"

Nora opened her eyes. "I've seen it, ma'am. I was closing the children's windows because of the smoke and I turned around and it came out of the corner—the corner by Baby's bed—and looked me in the face."

"You saw what?"

"The ghost, ma'am. It means someone is going to die."

Harriet shuddered involuntarily. Then she straightened up. She was no longer a foolish girl; she was a grown woman, married, with two children. She said briskly, "When Mr. Ayer comes back, I believe we should drive out to his father's house on Park Row. Mother Ayer has been wanting to see the children. The air is better there; and I don't like to think of Baby having another attack of asthma."

Nora stared at her stupidly. Harriet gave her a push. "Run along and get dressed. Pack a box with some warm things for the children. We had better take that, and some blankets. It might turn cold."

She went downstairs, trying to keep calm, to smile at Nora's foolish Irish ideas. But the incident had upset her. She checked to be sure all the windows were tightly closed and went out on the porch again. Now the air was thick with smoke and the sky in the west had a violent color unlike anything she had ever seen before. For the first time, she was genuinely frightened. She ran down to the gate; as she reached it the fire bells began to toll. A neighbor, a pretty young woman from Cleveland, hurried by with her husband and another young woman, a guest from the country. The girls looked gay and excited in their light clothes and flowered bonnets.

"My friend has never seen a fire, Mrs. Ayer, so we're trying to find it. Where do you suppose it can be?"

Harriet shook her head. Fire had never frightened her abnormally, and as a child she had occasionally even enjoyed an exciting one. But Herbert was not home; her mother and May were in New York; and John V. was on the south side, too far away to be much comfort. Their frame house was charming; but it was a firetrap.

A sudden blaze made her turn. The garden was lighted with a scarlet flash, it seemed bright as day. The air grew hotter, and a burning shingle flew through the air and landed in the grass. Harriet ran to stamp it out, calling to Nora that the wind had changed and was bringing burning brands from across the river. But almost as soon as she called, Harriet realized that there was no time to waste. Although their livery stables were several blocks south, she must get the horses and carriage; she could not wait for Herbert.

She ran in to give Nora instructions to have the children ready, wrapped in blankets, when she came back with the carriage. Now that there was something to do, Nora was calm. She even remembered to insist that Harriet put a shawl over her head, to protect her hair from the flying cinders.

In the few minutes spent talking to Nora and getting the shawl, the street had already begun to fill with carts and people. There was a red glow over everything, and the ominous roar of the fire grew louder. People were loaded down with fantastic burdens, from empty bird cages to broken mirrors, and Harriet saw her pretty neighbor from Cleveland, now white-faced and minus her bonnet, trying to drag a heavy trunk behind her. If it had not been so horrible, it might have been ridiculous. Choking back an hysterical laugh, Harriet tried to push her way through the crowd. She heard rumors: the lumber yards were aflame; the opera house was gone. She tried not to listen, but

people, like maniacs, paused and shouted at her, and then she
was carried away on the wave of the crowd.

She had almost reached their stables when she saw Herbert.
His hands and face were black with soot and his coat was torn.

"Go back!" he shouted at her. "Our block will be in flames any
minute."

"But the carriage and horses—"

"Gone. God knows where. I've been trying to bribe somebody
to drive us. If worse comes to worst, we'll have to spend the
night on the lake front. They're blowing up houses trying to
stop it, but this wind is like a blow-pipe."

Together, they pushed their way back through the screaming
crowds. Harriet clung to him, sure she never could have made
it alone; but she pushed, too, with all her strength, for she had
to reach her babies. The air was suffocatingly hot; she pulled
the shawl off her head and then replaced it when a hot cinder
fell on her head. Herbert tried to stop wagons and carriages,
begging them to take his wife and wait until he could get his
children, but nobody bothered to listen. Hot ashes and dust
choked Harriet's throat and blinded her, but she pushed on,
sometimes bumping into frightened cows and horses, and once
into the jaws of a huge maddened dog. How she escaped, she
never knew. How long it took for them to get back to the house,
she didn't know, either. Time didn't exist. She stopped thinking; she neither anticipated rescue nor disaster. She just kept
on pushing against the crowds that blocked her path. By the
time they were within calling distance of the house the roar of
the fire had increased and in the distance they could hear the
crackle of explosions. Brighter than the scarlet light, a huge
torch of flame rose into the sky. And the courthouse bell began
to toll, the bell that had told of Northern victories during the
war, the bell that had mourned for Abraham Lincoln. Harriet
clutched the arm of a running man and asked him what had
happened.

"The water tower is gone," he screamed. "There's no more
water anywhere. We can't survive. We're all as good as burned
to death now."

Harriet put her hands over her ears. The tolling of the bell

seemed to heighten the terror unbearably. People dropped boxes
and bundles and rushed off more wildly than before. Harriet
felt panic touch her, too, for there was no sign of Nora or the
children in the yard or on the porch. The door of the house
was shut; the closed windows reflected the light in the sky and
glowed like evil red eyes. "Something's happened to them," she
told Herbert, and would have fallen if he hadn't held her up.

An empty hack without passengers stood in front of their gate.
Herbert left Harriet and ran to scream at the driver: "Take my
wife and children to the south side. I'll give you anything you
ask—anything."

The man didn't answer. Frantic, Herbert grabbed his sleeve.

"Name your price. In another minute, it will be too late for
all of us."

The driver pulled his arm away. "I'm waiting for Mrs. Ayer.
The girl and the children are in the house. She said Mrs. Ayer
wouldn't go away and leave them. She'll be back. And I've got
to save her. My wife saw their boy take her carriage and horses
and run away, and she made me swear before God I'd save Mrs.
Ayer. So I swore before God and—"

"I'm Mrs. Ayer," Harriet gasped. She knew her hair was wild,
and her face and hands covered with soot, but the man gave her
a look of piercing scrutiny and seemed satisfied. He told her to
get in, and she hurried, for fear he would change his mind.
Herbert ran to hunt for Nora and the children, without caring
who the mysterious benefactor was, or why he insisted on saving
Mrs. Ayer.

Nora had closed and locked the door to keep out the pillagers
who were already running wild. She had built a tepee of blankets in the parlor, and she was huddling under that with the
children. Herbert picked up Hattie and ran, and Nora followed
him with the baby and one of the heavy blankets. There was no
time to go back for the box of warm clothing, or anything else.
By this time, the streets were emptying. Holding her children,
keeping the blanket well around them both, Harriet's tears of
thankfulness rolled down her soot-streaked face. But when she
tried to thank the driver, he told her: "Ma'am, you helped my
wife and me when she broke her hip. There was nothing we

could do for you before, but you saved our lives. God willing, we'll all escape."

The drive was a nightmare, and there were times when Harriet was certain they would never see her father-in-law's house. She held the children while Nora and Herbert took turns beating out the blizzards of sparks that fell on the hack. Both of them were badly burned on their hands and wrists. Soon Harriet's early terror gave way to exhaustion. Little Hattie slept with her head on her mother's lap and Harriet once or twice found herself close to falling asleep. Nora tried to take the baby, but Harriet shook her head.

Michigan Avenue was jammed. She caught glimpses of the mass of humanity on the lake front, animals and people pushing each other aside to get into the water, and she thanked God that they hadn't been forced to spend the night there. Although the streets were still crowded, the worst of the mob was gone, and they were able to move toward the south, which seemed to have escaped the fire. The shock of the disaster made Harriet numb. Although she saw sights that night which she never forgot, they didn't horrify her at the time.

Once a horse collapsed in the street and the other carriages rolled right over it, without stopping. She saw a man jump out of a hack, and drop dead on the street corner, from a bullet fired from the same hack. Sometimes a loaded vehicle would burst into flame before the people could get in. Rumors flew from wagon to wagon; once their driver, Garth, reported that the fire was following the river, firing all the vessels; that the bridges were gone; that the mayor had sent as far away as New York for help, but that the city would be rubble before it could arrive.

Daybreak was streaking the crimson sky when they reached Park Row. Everybody there had been up all night, too. John V. had frantically tried to reach Herbert's house, but had given them up as dead. His big house was filled with refugees, including one badly burned woman who had died without anyone knowing who she was. John V. had spread mattresses in rows on the floor of his big basement. Mother Ayer and the servants were making sandwiches and coffee for all who passed by the house. When she saw Harriet and the children, she burst into tears.

She insisted that Harriet and the children take her own bedroom, but, although Mother Ayer tried to get Harriet to go to bed, promising to watch over the children herself, Harriet could not sleep. The baby's breathing was harsh and she lay gasping on Harriet's lap. While they had been in the worst of the fire, the flames had been too hot for much smoke; but now that they were safe, the air was heavy.

Harriet said, "I'm frightened. Do you suppose anybody could find a doctor?"

Mother Ayer went downstairs to find out. Tired as he was, Herbert saddled one of John V.'s horses and started back to the inferno. Most of the streets were deserted except for the litter of discarded possessions and occasional dead horses or cows. He got as far as the Chicago Club on Monroe Street. It was still standing and a scattered group of men who had been burned out in the night had gathered there and were having what amounted to a breakfast of champagne and cigars. Even as they lifted their glasses, word came that the house had caught fire. Tipsily, they filled their pockets with cigars and, carting a red satin sofa and a demijohn of whisky, made their way through the burning streets to the lake, where they finished their "meal" on the sofa in the water.

Herbert learned that the waterworks on the north side had burst into flames at three-thirty that morning. The magnificent marble building built by Potter Palmer for Field, Leiter & Co. had gone shortly afterwards, the iron columns had melted, the marble front powdered to lime. Field, however, had worked all night, getting out goods. His employees, hastily summoned, piled up an estimated $582,000 worth of valuable merchandise, including laces, silks and satins, which he had moved in wagons; storing what he could in Leiter's home at Twenty-third and Calumet, thrusting the rest under a tarpaulin in a nearby schoolyard. Fire engines were buried in the debris. The lighthouse at the mouth of the Chicago River—the same one that had lighted Harriet's dreams as a child—was providing coffee and what food it could find for the refugees trapped on the river front. All kinds of craft, from tiny boats to tugs, were busy transporting the homeless to the south side, which had been partially saved.

The pastor of the Wabash Avenue Methodist-Episcopal Church had persuaded some young men that they could save the building if they would bury it in sand taken from a huge pile on an excavation in the next lot. When General Philip Sheridan saw that they were having success, he ordered that every building in the block around the church be blown up. Everybody believed that his daring decision had kept the fire from going farther south.

The morgue was on Hubbard Court in a barn. Herbert, noting that Madame Hubbard's house hadn't been touched by the fire, went to the morgue and finally persuaded a red-eyed doctor to come and see the baby when he had finished taking care of a severely wounded woman. Eventually, he kept his promise. But he was too late to help the baby. She had died shortly after Herbert went for help, her tired heart exhausted from the effort of breathing. But Harriet would not believe it. The doctor found her still sitting in the low rocker, clutching her baby frantically when anyone tried to take it away from her. She had even tried to feed it, forcing milk into the stiff blue little mouth.

The doctor had a small amount of morphine left. When Harriet fell into a drugged sleep, they took the baby's body away. Then both Herbert and the doctor went down to the basement and threw themselves on mattresses.

The fire lasted until Tuesday morning, when rain fell on the ashes. But downtown Chicago and the north side had been leveled. More than 13,500 buildings had been destroyed, out of an estimated 60,000 in the entire city; out of a city with approximately 340,000 inhabitants, over 92,000 were homeless. The west side, except for the fire area around the river, was intact; the south side was partially saved, thanks to General Sheridan and the pastor of the ME church. The church was taken for a post office on Tuesday and never saw another service.

But the heart of the city was destroyed. Bank notes were baked to a brown crisp in bank vaults. The courthouse was gone, and the city records. The great hotels were in ashes, including the thirteen-day-old Palmer House, which came down like "a castle of cards." Mc Vicker's Theatre was gone. So was Crosby's opera house, which was to have held its gala fall opening on Monday night. The Tribune building, supposedly fire-proof, was given up at ten A.M. Monday when the great rollers on the press melted and the workers had to drop everything and flee for their lives.

The night police reporter for the *Chicago Tribune,* named G. P. English, had been in the middle of writing the story of the fire's origin when he was summoned to the roof to help Joseph Medill and other editors stamp out flying brands. He was never able to finish the story, but he did not believe then, and never did, the oft-repeated tale that Mrs. O'Leary's cow was to blame. He had gone to 137 De Koven Street and talked with the O'Learys and their neighbors. The story of the cow kicking over the lantern when his mistress went into the house to fetch some salt for the ailing animal, had been sent out originally by the correspondent of the *New York Herald.* But Mrs. O'Leary insisted then and later that she and her husband and five children were in bed that Sunday night and never woke up until a neighbor named Sullivan told them their barn was on fire. It caught rapidly, due to the proximity of three barns, a well-stocked paint shop, lumber mills, and a Parmalee stable loaded with hay.

But neighbors told a story about another family named McLaughlin who were supposed to have been giving a special oyster supper that evening, with much singing and gaiety. One of the guests was supposed to have decided, after a few nips, that he was going into the O'Leary barn to milk the cow. . . . Whatever the truth, it was buried in the ashes.

The loss in money was over two hundred million dollars; in human lives over fifteen-hundred people. Buildings covering more than two thousand acres were destroyed. After the fire was under control, clouds of stinging smoke continued to roll over the city, carrying with it sand and dust. There was no water system; for ten weeks people obtained their water in barrels from the water carts. There was no light. The use of kerosene was forbidden and in the few shops left unburned there were so few candles that sometimes only one or two would be sold to a purchaser.

As always, in a period of disaster, some twisted people took advantage of human misery. Looters walked into deserted houses and moved out with whatever they wanted; even pianos, newly fashionable now that young women were learning to play them instead of the harp, were carted away. Some of the criminals didn't even bother with theft; they smashed mirrors and marble-top tables and tore great rents in valuable carpets. And there were also the irresponsible, who fired piles of bedding or heaps of charred wood as a kind of hideous practical joke. A young girl running through the streets with blond hair flaming had a glass of whisky tossed over her by one of these wicked idiots; her scalp burned blue and she fell to the ground in a merciful faint.

Men carried guns for protection; and many a survivor told fearfully of seeing human beings shot to death, or pushed out of fourth floor windows, or crucified for suspected theft or arson. There was no time for trial by jury, and as panic grew, many an innocent was punished with the guilty.

On Tuesday night, although the worst was over, coals still glowed all over the city, giving a weird effect in the blackness. About fifteen-hundred volunteers, all armed, patrolled the city, while women and children huddled terror-stricken in temporary shelters or in what remained of their homes. By Wednesday, the troops from nearby cities arrived to help General Sheridan, and the city was placed under military law, with a nine o'clock curfew.

Thousands of people fled from the city to take refuge with friends or relatives. No one had much money and it was a week before any could be obtained from the banks. On October 12, the *Tribune* appeared again, a crude, poorly printed four-page paper carrying the big news story of "the ruins," with advertising cards telling the new locations of burned-out businesses . . . and the first lists of the missing. Some of the older people left Chicago for good, heartsick at seeing everything destroyed they had worked for. But others set out immediately to build on the ashes. Field & Leiter set up business in a car barn on State and Twentieth Street, and the customers began pushing in to the temporary counters while smoke still hung over the city. Fire engines

were dug up, and fire-fighting equipment was lent to the stricken
city from as far away as New York. Wooden cabins were hastily
erected; the refugees lived in them, or even in tents. Sightseers
poured in, ghoulishly, but so did money from the rest of the
country. England sent $300,000; and gifts for the sufferers came
from as far away as South America. George M. Pullman was appointed treasurer of the Relief Aid Society; the churches were
open every day all winter, feeding the homeless and distributing
clothing. Those whose homes were still standing opened their
own parlors for distribution centers. Those who could, donated
money. Others shared what passed for houses with the less
fortunate. Along with the ugly side, there was much generosity
and heroism. Robert Collyer, the Unitarian preacher, held services in the still-smoking ruins of his church on the Sunday following the disaster, and asked for donations for rebuilding.
Smallpox became epidemic and some of the crude wooden shacks
had to be burned, making their inhabitants once more homeless.
But as Chicago sat up and counted its losses, the pioneer spirit
rose again. There were calico balls for the benefit of the relief
society. A group of young men on the north side started a dancing class called The Cinders. Entertainments were held in halls
where the stage alone was lighted, and that only by candles.

Harriet sewed for the destitute, using the small, beautiful
stitches which the nuns had taught her. Her mother-in-law was
in charge of a center that provided clothes for the penniless;
each day she handed out not only warm clothing but soup and
milk from the cows that had taken refuge on the grounds during
the fire. Harriet tried to help; but the sight of the babies
was more than she could bear. She never wept, but she spent
long hours behind locked doors sewing away fiercely, until her
eyes were red and strained. One day she came into her mother-
in-law's parlor with a bundle of baby things in her arms. With
a sinking heart, Mother Ayer recognized them as garments she
had been sewing on for Gertie.

Mother Ayer accepted the bundle, but after Harriet had left
the room, she picked out a fine embroidered dress and took it to
her daughter-in-law. "Save it for your next baby," she told her.

"You are young. Wounds heal. Think how lucky you are to be alive, you and Herbert. And you have little Hattie."

Harriet took the dress and put it away. After her death it was discovered in a box she had used for the few treasures from which she was seldom parted.

CHAPTER FIVE

MADAME Hubbard had been in New York with May at the time of the fire. Sending May to her old friends, the Wetherills, in Philadelphia, Madame Hubbard returned to Chicago. Harriet and Herbert met her at the station; a station filled mostly with people running away from the ruins. Madame Hubbard came out of the train shed wearing her most imperious expression. The city was a shock; only scorched, blackened trees seemed still to be standing. The burned, hollow blocks of Nicholson pavement gave an added eeriness to their jolting ride through the virtually empty streets to her house. The fire had not touched the big frame building, but the vandals had. The gates were smashed, the yard was filled with broken china and glass, and the house itself was a shambles.

Madame Hubbard did not even go upstairs. Her cook and coachman had fled; strangers must have camped out in the building, and they had taken what they wanted before they left.

"I'm selling the land," she told Harriet. "Sometime, perhaps, I may come back to Chicago. But I'm too old to start rebuilding now. I'm going to Paris for a while; and I think you and Hattie should come with me."

64

Harriet Hubbard Ayer with three-year-old Margaret
surrounded by photographic studio props

The young and beautiful Mrs. Herbert Ayer

Harriet Hubbard Ayer in the dress she wore
for the portrait by William Chase

Blanche Willis Howard

Blanche Willis Howard in 1886, when Margaret first knew her

Dr. Julius von Teuffel;
physician to
the King of Württemberg

Herbert Copeland Ayer
in the 1880's

Hattie Ayer Seymour in her wedding gown and hat

...Central Music Hall...

Chicago,
APRIL 15TH, AT 8.

"FOURTEEN MONTHS

..IN A..

MAD-HOUSE."

AN ADDRESS
BY

HARRIET HUBBARD AYER,

In the Cause of

THE LIVING DEAD.

The poster used to advertise Mrs. Ayer's lecture

Mrs. Ayer in 1897 in the costume—skirt a daring four inches from the ground—she made popular for business women

Harriet and Margaret not long before Harriet's death

Herbert protested; he did not want to be deprived of his wife and little daughter. Hattie was at an age when every day brought new delights and changes. The loss of the baby had been sad; but when he thought that it might instead have been little Hattie, he breathed a secret prayer of thanks. He did not dare admit this to anyone, even his father, but he wondered sometimes if Harriet suspected. She was a changed woman; all the life and spark had gone out of her. Even Reverend Clinton Locke of the Grace Episcopal Church whose wit, he often said, kept him from becoming a bishop, could not make her smile. The doctor told Herbert glumly that a sea voyage might be healthful; Madame Hubbard told her son-in-law bluntly that if he didn't agree to the trip, she wouldn't promise that Harriet would live through the winter. And when Mother Ayer spoke up, in one of her rare spurts of temper, to tell Herbert not to act like a spoiled child, he agreed. But even at the last, he begged Harriet to leave little Hattie with him.

Years later, when Harriet was able to evaluate this period of her life with some objectivity, she realized how much Herbert had been hurt by his separation from Hattie at an age when the little girl was growing so fast. For Hattie was the one thing in Herbert's life that mattered deeply; he would have done anything and given up anything for her. Otherwise, although he was over thirty, he was still immature, more of a gay young sport than a grown man. He was quick at business, and well-liked, but he lacked John V.'s driving force and vision. If he had had his little daughter at home instead of abroad, it might have given him something solid as a basis for his life. Without her, he drifted back into bachelor habits. Chicago was rising from the ashes; so were her saloons and gambling places. He and John V. were at the mill much of the time, trying to replace the records that had been lost in the fire. Herbert's now-widowed mother lived in Youngstown and she was delighted to see her son and indulged him in all his whims—from drink, which she considered quite in order, to young ladies of flexible virtue, against whom she closed her eyes. She even conspired with Herbert to keep John V. in the dark; for, while she enjoyed the fact that her first husband was a rich man, she found him too strait-laced and dull for a steady diet. It amused her to help her son escape from his father occasionally; and she was glad of the opportunity to pamper and flirt with him without the dampening influence of a young wife to hamper her.

Harriet might have sensed some of this, even in the freshness of her grief. But leaving little Hattie was unthinkable; she had lost one child and was haunted by the fear that something might take away the other. She could not bear to be separated from Hattie even for a day.

The loss of her baby was a turning point in her life; abruptly, she became a different person, with depths that might never otherwise have been plumbed. If Gertie had lived, she might have gone on having children and become another rich Chicago matron with no ambitions beyond Chicago society, such as it was, and her family. Harriet had changed physically from a plain, almost an ugly, child into a beautiful young woman. Now the tragedy of her baby transformed her entire emotional outlook on life.

The ocean trip, on the *George Washington*, was either rough and sunny, or fog-bound and smooth. Harriet discovered she was a good sailor; she liked the turmoil of the sea on rough days, and the mystery of it when the fog settled. This was the first of many ocean trips she was to make in her life. From the beginning, the Atlantic, which Oscar Wilde was to find "disappointing" a decade afterwards, fascinated her. Madame Hubbard, who found sea voyages no more interesting than most other phases of her life, spent most of the time in her berth with her books. And small Hattie, when she grew bored with twisting Nora or her mamma around her pink fingers, would go to Gammy's state-room, crawl in bed with her and gravely accept a candy or a litchi nut. Hattie was a revelation to Madame Hubbard; she discovered that it was possible to enjoy a child when you did not have a feeling of responsibility—or perhaps, guilt—toward it. She had never before liked a little girl; May had come as close to her as any of her own children, but even so there was a wall between May and her mother that did not exist with Hattie. Madame Hubbard spoiled her grandchild; she teased her; and she was inordinately proud of her. When Nora disembarked in

Ireland, Madame Hubbard was secretly delighted because that removed one more candidate for Hattie's attentions. And Hattie, young as she was, delighted in her new conquest and the full-time attentions of her mamma. Watching her, Harriet was able sometimes to forget her grief. But she also sometimes made the mistake of looking at her little daughter and thinking "mine" instead of "ours." Herbert was growing dimmer and dimmer in her thoughts; there were days when she did not think of him at all.

The steamer trip had been good for her. The detachment from reality had been soothing. When it was over, she almost dreaded her first look at the beautiful Paris that Madame Hubbard remembered. But Paris, in November of 1871, was by no means at its most gala. Between the Germans and the revolution, Paris was suffering and scarred. Until June, it had been under martial law; visitors were not allowed in or out without permits; curfew had been at eleven; and mounted patrols with their revolvers ready rode up and down the deserted streets. Day and night, the acrid smell of gun powder and fire had hung over the city; all too often the empty streets had reverberated with gunfire. When the frightened and confused Parisians went out, they hurried like ghosts among the destruction; and when they met old friends, they either did not dare to speak or did not recognize them, so changed was everyone from starvation and fear.

After the soldiers left, the populace recovered slowly. The destruction of Paris was painful to contemplate. Whole streets had disappeared. The beautiful, broad boulevards which M. Haussmann had laid out for Napoleon III were punctuated with rubble. There were long lines of gaping roofs, battered walls, and charred façades. The magnificent Hotel de Ville, dating from the sixteenth century and rich with history, had been smashed to a shapeless heap of stones by the Communards. Of all the acts of their madness, this was the one most resented by the Parisians. Monuments had been destroyed; only the base of the Vendôme column remained. In the Champs Élysées stood the roofless Palais de l'Industrie. The Palais de Justice had been fired and between the Arcs de Triomphe of the Place Carrousel and l'Etoile there were desolate vistas through the gutted Tuileries.

When the military rule ended, great crowds of tourists had come to sightsee—first the French provincials, then the English "on pleasure tours" and last of all, the Americans. Jules Bertaut in his book, *Paris 1870-1935*, reported: "It was the Yankees' turn next. The New York steamers brought hordes of them and their wives and their blonde daughters 'doing' the devastated town at a moderate inclusive rate. . . . Although the Germans still remained in the outer fortifications, the carriages came out again, the streets were crowded all the time, and we find the newspapers complaining that the press of carriages was holding up the traffic. . . . The cab drivers resumed normal activities, and the plaint of the mulcted fare was heard on every hand. And the beggars reappeared. 'Most of them,' says *Figaro*, 'are armed with violins or accordions, pursuing the passers-by with an interminable and intolerable *Marseillaise*. At least they might play the *Chant du Départ!'* "

Harriet had read a little about France in the newspapers, but she had no conception of the extent of its sufferings. Paris did not lie in ruins like Chicago, but its destruction had been malicious and deliberate and the beautiful old buildings and monuments could never be replaced. Unlike the sightseers, who were often disappointed because the damage was not as severe as they had hoped, Harriet could identify herself with the Parisians. Many of the women were, like her, in mourning. But their deep mourning was invariably made chic by a touch of bright jet, a hat drowned in waves of black lace. Their faces might be ravaged by privation and suffering, but when not in black their impertinent little hats were loaded with crushed roses, their wide-skirted frocks were bedecked with flounces and ruchings and sleeves of green or heliotrope; under their arms they carried little spaniel dogs, which had suddenly sprung into fashion. Harriet was at first astonished, then admiring. She had lost her home and her baby; but she still had a husband and another child, and money was no problem. The French had lost relatives and their city had been despoiled. Worse, they still had the heavy burden of indemnity to pay off to the Germans. But the women put flowers in their hats; they flirted and argued; they swished their skirts to let passers-by catch a glimpse of frivolous boots.

Harriet and her mother rented a furnished apartment on the Champs Élysées; with it came two servants who spoke nothing but French. Harriet's French was meager; the nuns at Sacred Heart had never been out of America themselves, and their pronunciation was far from flawless. Harriet was embarrassed by her inadequate vocabulary and even when she did dare ask a question, the reply was so rapid that her ear was baffled. Sometimes small Hattie, who was already chattering in a combination of French and English, went so fast that her own mother could not understand her. Harriet felt baffled; not so, of course, Madame Hubbard.

Madame Hubbard had developed her own technique during her first visit to Paris; it had worked then and she saw no reason why it should fail her now. Whenever she wanted anything in a shop, she kept raising her voice until it appeared. She had a strong contralto, well-trained in a Chicago church choir, capable of immense volume. Without anger, without even showing faint annoyance, she boomed out her demands in calm, implacable crescendo. By some miracle, an interpreter or a brain storm, the Parisian shopkeepers always managed finally to understand. If they overcharged her, Madame did not protest. Money meant little to her at any time. Now, after the poor Parisians had suffered such hardships, she was willing to let them make their small extra profits. As a result, she was a welcome customer wherever she went. If they laughed at her behind her back, Madame Hubbard did not care; they were charming to her face. She often told friends that it was a pity the poor Parisians were all so deaf; but she attributed it to the bombardments during the terrible siege.

Harriet, however, determined to learn the language of her hosts. This was considered a rather foolish, even daring, step among the American colony in Paris, many of whom were Madame Hubbard's old friends from Chicago, wintering abroad until their houses were rebuilt. But this was the first sign Harriet had given of being interested in anything outside of her sorrow, and there were few young Americans to give her companionship. So Madame Hubbard and her friends watched with indulgence while Harriet studied French. Her first step was to engage a French nursemaid for Hattie, who soon spoke more often in French than in English—except, of course, to her grandmother, who did not stand for such nonsense. Then Harriet found a French teacher, a young woman who had gone to school in England, Mlle. Frochard. She took a two-hour lesson each morning from Mlle. Frochard at the apartment, and spent long afternoons doing the written work and the practice of verbs upon which Mademoiselle insisted.

The business arrangement grew into a friendship. Mademoiselle had lost her family in the Revolution. She had, of course, never expected to have to support herself. But she did not talk about her troubles. She wore pert little pancake hats which she concocted and she dressed in the same flamboyant silks she had worn before the war. Alarmed by her thinness, Harriet managed after a while to persuade her to extend the daily lesson through luncheon, but she was always amazed at how little Mademoiselle ate. One day, the French girl apologetically explained that her stomach had been poisoned by the straw-like black bread she had lived on during the war. She told of the first evidence the Parisians had been given that the war was over. A little girl walked down the Rue de Richelieu carrying a fresh white roll in her hand, and followed by a dozen or more people gaping at the "unbelievable miracle."

Mlle. Frochard was a true Frenchwoman. She was not easy to know, but as Harriet persisted, she grew to love her, and everything that she stood for. The crowded streets and cafés, the frivolous dresses, she learned to see as symbols of courage. When France launched its Liberty Loans, it was announced that three milliards were needed. Over forty-two milliards were subscribed; in Paris alone, over twelve. Everyone, even the bankrupt shopkeeper, added his sou. Mlle. Frochard explained that it was more than a matter of pride; it was love and sacrifice for the beloved country. And Harriet learned to sing, and love, the song that was heard everywhere, in the streets and theatres and cafés:

V'la l'travail qui r'prend
Espérance, confiance,
V'la l'travail qui r'prend
Paris sera toujours grand!

"Cheer for the work which is returning. . . . Paris will always be great"—it was a magnificent philosophy. Harriet herself began to smile. She had assimilated enough of the French philosophy to realize that the first step in renovating her emotional state was to repair the way she looked. She put away the ugly mourning she had hidden behind. And she went to see M. Worth.

The great dressmaking art of Paris was then in its infancy. The *haute couture* had sprung up around Eugénie, wife of Napoleon III, less than fifteen years before, and now the couturiers were coming to life again. Of them all, M. Worth was the leader. He preferred to dress French women, and only France's bankruptcy made him agree to see Madame Ayer. Mlle. Frochard had told him she was very rich; he expected the worst. But the young woman, scarcely more than a girl, who entered the salon enchanted him, and he was even more delighted at her shy, careful French. He designed several original creations for her—one a black lace dress in which she was later painted by William Chase, another a violet grosgrain trimmed with deeper violet ribbon. For a ball gown, he had his mills in Lyon weave a special material—a very heavy white satin, with an all-over tracery of a rose design in white silk. The most talked about hostesses in France made it a rule always to wear white, with jewels. When he asked her about her diamonds and Harriet said she had none, M. Worth's eyes widened in surprise; surely the rich Americans could afford jewels, and they were such a source of security to a beauty, for when all else failed her, she could feast her soul on their costliness or, at worst, sell them. Harriet was delighted at such a French point of view, both romantic and practical. She determined to remedy the situation. Herbert had sent her a more than generous letter of credit, and she had a feeling that jewels were among the few French purchases he would appreciate and understand.

Her attitude toward her husband worried her. Herbert was

kind and generous. He was looking forward to her return; this he wrote over and over in his letters. But Harriet was sometimes sick at heart when she studied the bad spelling and ill-formed writing. She told herself that when she saw him in person, she would forget these minor faults, and that perhaps he would come to Paris with her next time and begin to share her new enthusiasms. But in her secret thoughts, she knew these were foolish fancies. She was going to have to chart her own intellectual life.

Her French was now so good that she had no need of an interpreter, but she enjoyed Mlle. Frochard's company, and often they would spend their lesson period wandering around the shops of Paris, looking at furniture and glass and bric-a-brac. But Harriet made few purchases except at the bookstalls along the quays, where she carried away volumes on a great variety of subjects. Madame Hubbard looked on amused; she was delighted that her daughter was discovering books, though she considered such academic subjects rather heavy and pedantic for a young woman with so many attractions more obvious than her mind. But she said nothing, because, to her surprise, her daughter had become rather formidable in her own right.

It was partly, of course, her clothes. M. Worth had decided from the first that Harriet's style of beauty demanded purity of line and Grecian simplicity—at least compared with the current fashions. His clothes were designed to display the woman, and before he would let her wear them, he went with her to a hair-dresser who created coiffures for some of the great beauties of the time. After a long afternoon of experiment and argument, the two artists released the exhausted Harriet in a coiffure which hardly seemed worth more than a few minutes trouble—hair drawn back from her face to emphasize her chiseled profile, ending in a small knot of curls at the back of her head, and softened by a "bang" of loose, natural-looking curls over the fore-head, to conceal its height. These were the days of the chignon and the elaborate curl; Harriet's style at first made the American colony laugh. But the French eyed it with interest. Some of Mlle. Frochard's young friends paid Harriet the compliment of trying to copy it, and gave up as a bad job because the only person it seemed to suit was the lovely Mrs. Ayer. During the rest of her life she wore that style, with slight variations.

She was now an object of curiosity; she could have had many invitations to dinner and balls in fashionable French circles. But she unwittingly added to her appeal by refusing everyone except Madame Hubbard's old friends, who still thought of Harriet as the "plain little Hubbard girl." She knew her way around Paris, for she and Mlle. Frochard had covered most sections of it during their daily walks, and she was often asked to make purchases for her mother's friends.

On one such trip, she found a tiny chemist's shop on the Boulevard Malesherbes, where the proprietor, with the assistance of his wife, made his own perfumes and unguents. Harriet talked to him for a long time and he, like John V., was impressed by the fact that this beautiful young woman asked questions because she was really interested and listened to the answers. He took her back of the shop and showed her his laboratory, which doubled at mealtime as the dining room, and his stock of essential oils. Together, they worked out a Parma violet perfume for her, which became another of Harriet's lovely trademarks. He related stories of the old days, when his father and grandfather had mixed creams and rouges and powders for the most famous ladies of the land, many of them by secret formulas.

M. Mirault told her: "Somewhere, there is a cream that was made for the beautiful Julie Récamier; it is said to have been the secret of how she kept her skin looking like that of a *jeune fille* for over forty years. I will look for it, and perhaps the next time you come, you might like to see it. As a curiosity only, of course; madame does not need any artificial aids for her complexion."

Harriet accepted the compliment gracefully; she was learning gradually to have confidence in her beauty. But she had for too long thought of herself as an ugly duckling, to have any false pride about her skin or the color of her eyes. Right now, she needed no artificial aids and she was thankful. But if someday she should . . .

"I'll remember," she told M. Mirault; and remember she did, at a very important time.

Meanwhile, as her house in Chicago was nearing completion, and Herbert was growing increasingly impatient to see Hattie, she intended to perfect her French while she could. Mlle. Frochard suggested the theatre, which was blooming with new vitality. The old opera house on the Rue le Peletier was still open while the new one was being finished. The Gymnase put on Dumas fils' *La Visite de Noces;* the Palais Royal, *Tricoche et Cacolet;* the Gaieté, *La Chatte Blanche.* Night after night she attended the theatre, sometimes seeing the same play several times, if she could persuade one of her mother's elderly American friends to escort her. But at last, she settled on the Odéon. It was a theatre which was sometimes called the second Comédie-Francaise, famed for its excellent plays, and the perfect diction of its actors. The play running was a French triangle and was admirable for her purposes. The actor who played the hero, Armand, had an enunciation so precise that Mlle. Frochard declared he had the best diction in all Paris; and the heroine, Eloise, was playing a lady who was the essence of a true *Parisienne de style.* Every night for a month, Harriet engaged the same loge right beside the stage, from which she could see the actors' faces perfectly. She made a transcription for Mlle. Frochard and each morning, she would recite various sections, copying Armand's precise rhythm and pronunciation. After lunch, she would practice before the mirror. And in the evening, she would study his lips through her opera glasses.

Madame Hubbard's American friends accepted her invitations to see the play for the first week; but more than one evening at the Odéon was too much for their patience. Madame Hubbard refused bluntly to attend at all. And Mlle. Frochard, although she attended more often than the others, was not free every night. There were evenings when Harriet flouted tradition and went alone. After the first week, the theatre was so familiar that she no longer felt ill at ease. During intermission, while the French promenaded and drank sweet syrupy drinks and smoked, she eavesdropped, listening for different accents, memorizing them. Then, back in her loge she would study Armand's diction and Eloise's gestures.

It is quite probable that an older woman, or one who was

less conspicuously beautiful or well-dressed, might have done the same thing without creating comment. But before long, the actors began to notice *la belle Américaine*, and *la belle* herself, mischievously, took to carrying always a bouquet of Maréchal Neil Roses, which she placed on the railing. One night, the actor who played Armand appeared with a small yellow Maréchal Neil in his buttonhole.

The cast looked with interest on what they regarded as the beginnings of an affair; Armand was handsome, of an "interesting" age, and undoubtedly *la belle* was rich—wasn't she dressed by Worth? The American colony took a less easygoing attitude; Mrs. Ayer was going to make a fool of herself, like so many American wives whose husbands were interested only in making money. Madame Hubbard's old friends took Harriet aside to warn her that no one would ever believe that her only object was to learn French. Harriet thanked the visitors for their advice, but she went on attending the theatre each night and carrying her roses.

The night before they were to sail, she attended for the last time. At the conclusion of the play, she leaned forward and tossed her bouquet over the footlights. The French in the audience buzzed with delight and murmured to each other that *la belle* had given the signal; she would soon summon Armand to a meeting at her hotel. The matrons of the American colony who were present took a less indulgent attitude. They drew lots to decide who would visit Madame Hubbard and warn her in blunt terms of the folly her daughter was about to commit. But before they could call at the apartment on the Champs Élysées, Madame Hubbard and her family had left for America.

They went home on a French liner; the trip took only fourteen days and the weather was beautiful. Mrs. Ayer was much admired. The captain, thinking she was one of his countrywomen who had married an American, asked her to sit at his table. Not until the end of the voyage did she convince him that she was not a Parisian. As they drew near the New York harbor, Harriet felt a mixture of emotions. She was coming home, but it almost seemed as though she were entering a strange land, that Paris was her emotional home. Dressed in one of her loveliest Worth frocks she met her husband, who had come from Chicago to welcome her. It was of violet merino, her hat was a soft mass of crushed violets, trimmed with black lace. As she came down the gangplank, people strained to look at her, wondering who she was. It was not Harriet that Herbert yearned for, however. He kissed her, but it was Hattie whom he snatched up greedily. The little girl pulled away and hid behind Harriet's scented skirts.

Herbert pretended not to care. But that evening he scarcely touched the lavish dinner he had ordered at Delmonico's and he finished most of the wine. Usually, he grew more cheerful and boisterous when he drank; tonight, he grew curt and ugly.

Harriet's heart ached. She had been fond of Herbert, and she had been happy in their small house with the two babies. But she wasn't the same person she had been before the fire. Then she had regarded Herbert with respect; even sometimes with a tinge of fear. He was older than she was, and she had been brought up according to Victorian standards. But now all she could feel for Herbert was sympathy. He was not to blame for anything, even this spell of bad temper. She would have to watch the whole situation more carefully in the future.

CHAPTER SIX

To HARRIET Chicago rebuilt seemed depressingly like Chicago before the fire. The Chicago station was still bordered by festering slums, the train shed still roared with escaping steam, and the same confusion reigned outside: whining beggars, barkers for hotels, hacks seeking passengers.

Herbert hired a hack; John V. had not expected them back so soon—he had, in fact, urged Herbert to take a holiday. But New York made Herbert impatient, and Harriet urged him to get reservations for the train trip home under the pretext of her eagerness to see the new city.

"You'll be surprised," Herbert assured her, for what seemed the hundredth time. Harriet tried to be enthusiastic. But the railroad still ran across the lake front, an ugly and smoking spectacle. The buildings that were springing up looked like those that had been destroyed; later she heard the quip that the bad architects had all dug deep holes before the fire and carefully buried their original plans, so the precious blueprints could again be used. Worst of all, as many Chicagoans were to discover in this decade, a glimpse of other places and older civilizations made Chicago look raw and unlovely.

"Wait until you see our house. Everyone's moving to the

north side now. They're starting to call the lake front up our way the Gold Coast, because all the millionaires are putting up palaces there. And wait until you see the Palmer House! Old Potter has paved the barbershop floor with silver dollars. Did you see anything like that in Paris?"

For a few minutes, Harriet wished that she had never seen New York or Paris, that she had never read the books from quays on architecture and painting and design. Then she stepped out of the carriage into John V.'s waiting arms. For the first time, she felt glad to be home.

Mrs. Ayer was waiting in her bedroom for Harriet. She had been feeling unwell for some time. Hardly anyone in the family, even John V.'s children, paid much attention to Mother Ayer, for she seldom voiced an opinion and she never asked for any attention. Harriet had accepted her and disregarded her like the others. But when she took the older woman in her arms and kissed her, suddenly Harriet found herself weeping uncontrollably. Mother Ayer held her hard; it reminded Harriet of the way Nora had held her the day she had been frightened in the cellar. And then she realized that Mother Ayer understood a great deal of what she had been feeling—disappointment, fear of the future and a reopening of her grief when she found herself in the room where the baby had died, looking at the same chair where she had last held her.

"I'll put it away if you like, Harriet, but you musn't be frightened or sad about death. It comes to all of us—to me, one of these days very soon. But I'm not frightened. It makes me happy to look at the chair where you held Gertie and know I will be taking care of her for you."

"Mother Ayer, don't talk like that. You aren't sick."

Mother Ayer shrugged. "Yes, I am, but don't tell my husband. He would worry because—well, because he felt guilty for not having noticed. The doctor told me I did too much after the fire."

"You did, Mother Ayer, and I was too blind to see. Why didn't you make me help you? You were too unselfish."

Mother Ayer turned from the window. In the relentless glare of the summer sun, Harriet could see how pale and transparent she looked. But she was smiling. "I never enjoyed anything so much in my life. It seems terrible to say it, when so many people were suffering, but I felt important and useful. It's been so long since I mattered to anyone."

"We shouldn't be here bothering you when you are ill. We could move to a hotel or a boardinghouse."

"No." Mother Ayer's dark eyes filled with tears. "It—it would disappoint me a great deal, Harriet. I'm not much for talking, I leave that to my husband. But I want to say that one of the nicest things that ever happened to me is knowing you."

Harriet felt a shock of shame and surprise. She had been so concerned with herself and her own trouble that she had accepted Mother Ayer without ever thinking of her as a person. She said quickly: "You must come to Paris with me, next year. I could show you so many things. Paris will make you well again."

During the next weeks, Harriet spent hours with Mother Ayer, talking about Paris. She had little to do. Madame Hubbard had stayed in New York, for May had become engaged to the son of her Philadelphia friends, Alexander Macoom Wetherill. Responsibility for Hattie's care was again in Nora's hands. The little girl's French had gone entirely, except when she was alone with her mother, but that happened seldom for Herbert and John V. were much at the house, and she was soon flirting outrageously with them both and using their influence to win her anything she wanted.

Harriet told herself that the trip to Paris had been worth while to Herbert, whether he knew it or not, for she had learned the French trick of wearing a frivolous mask over a troubled heart. She threw herself brightly into the plans for the house. The Chicago stores were increasing their stocks daily, but for some furniture Harriet went to the exclusive, expensive importing house of Sypher & Co. in New York. Her trips were brief, however, and she never took Hattie with her.

Late in October, they moved into their new home. A year ago, the city had been reduced to ashes, yet now the taxable property was almost equal to what it had been before the fire, and trade and commerce were even greater. Chicago was now one of the great commercial centers of the United States and Harriet began

to understand John V.'s and Herbert's pride in having John V.
Ayer & Sons acknowledged among the houses of importance.
The prospect of entertaining on a large scale suddenly became al-
luring.

The social season, however, was delayed. In November, the
town was disrupted by an epidemic of "Horse Flu" which attacked over a thousand horses and started many young women of
fashion walking again. But by Christmas, Chicago was living in
high key. The Potter Palmers gave a dinner party at which they
served five different varieties of wine—which set Chicago hostesses, who recognized nothing but champagne, atwitter. The
theatres were filled every night. Even Herbert kept awake when
they went to *The Black Crook* or saw the Spanish dancers; when
it came to Shakespeare or the ballet, he deputized John V. or one
of his father's friends as Harriet's escort. The hotels vied with
each other in lavishness. The Sherman House was rebuilt by
W. W. Boyington, who had created the fantastic Gothic extravaganza of the north side waterworks; the Palmer House, along
with its barbershop paved with silver dollars, had a grand dining room copied after the salon of the Crown Prince's palace in
Potsdam, and an Egyptian parlor and a gigantic Egyptian chan-
delier over the reception desk. Field, Leiter & Co. was reinstated
in a magnificent new building at State and Washington streets;
and never before in any western city had there been such an ar-
ray of jewelry, toys and fancy goods displayed for the Christmas
trade.

Both Herbert and John V. gave Harriet jewelry for Christmas.
She put away the rather modest pieces she had bought for herself in Paris, and wore her new ruby and diamond necklace and
bracelet with her white-on-white Worth evening dress for her
first dinner party. The table was decorated with ruby-red roses
swimming in crystal bowls and her red and. gold plates were
French. Although the Ayer house was simple, and the dining
room did not seat more than fourteen people, John V. was
pleased; the food had been delicious, the rather strange French
red wine which Harriet had served had been excellent, and the
hostess had been elegant.

Harriet was not so pleased, however. The conversation, after a few minutes, had limped, and then had finally died. It wasn't until she had taken the ladies into the parlor, leaving the men to their drinks and cigars, that she had heard laughter from the dining room.

"What were you talking about?" she asked Herbert afterwards. He looked at her teasingly. "It's none of your business."

"But I'd like to make my whole party that lively."

Herbert winked at her. "They wouldn't repeat such stuff in front of their wives. Forget it, Harriet."

But Harriet couldn't forget. It was bad enough to be entertained in other houses where conversation languished until the men and women were separated; much, much worse to have stiff, dull dinners in her own home.

She worked hard to make her parties different. Some of the things she did were decades ahead of her time. She loved flowers, but she used them with restraint, and she shunned the traditional bunched flowers on her dinner tables. Instead, she planned her table settings like paintings, seldom using the conventional white tablecloth (except when she wanted white as a background), but choosing lengths of silk in various colors. These she employed as a basis for arrangements of flowers and fruit and even vegetables, such things as shiny dark plum-colored eggplants or even field corn.

Once, when Herbert was giving a stag dinner for some customers in the railroad business, she decorated a tablecloth with fresh flowers—real heads of black-eyed susans pinned thick on a white tablecloth. The day before, when she had been wondering about what effect she might produce, she had taken Hattie and some of her friends for a picnic on the west side. There, Harriet had found the fields covered with the black and yellow flowers and, while the children played, she had filled a basket with what most women then thought of as ugly weeds. Herbert's friends were not men who were usually perceptive about table decorations; but they went home and told their wives about the black-eyed susans.

In Paris, Harriet had studied French cookbooks and learned about French cuisine. She occasionally introduced a special French dish or a sauce at a dinner party if she felt the beef-and-whisky appetites of Herbert's cronies would not be too affronted. She served wines other than champagne; not as many as the wealthy Palmers, but one or two wines of good vintage, carefully chosen to complement the food. She was aware that few of her guests appreciated the trouble she took; that didn't matter, for her time was not at a premium and she enjoyed the preparations —if she did nothing more than talk them over with Mother Ayer afterwards.

She entertained often when a young woman from Charleston who had known Herbert's mother visited them—one of those long visits which were customary in those days. Margaret Mitchell was a lively girl, with huge black eyes, and a gift for flattery. Both Harriet and Herbert enjoyed having her in the house, and small Hattie worshiped her. She had had little formal education and she didn't pretend to compete with Harriet's brains or taste, but she had the knack of making her hostess and her hostess' husband feel brighter than they were. It was this Southern talent which Herbert had missed in Northern girls, and which he was beginning to feel lacking in his wife since more and more she had taken to burying herself in books. He was not intelligent enough to be able to explain what he wanted; she, on the other hand, was too straightforward to understand how much more easily she might have handled him if she had employed a few feminine wiles.

In spite of their differences, they were happier in their new house than they had been for a long time—especially during Miss Mitchell's visit. She admired Herbert's knowledge of business, and her high spirits made him look with more indulgence on some of Harriet's experiments—such as amateur theatricals. In fact, it was Margaret Mitchell who really persuaded him to join the Anonymous Club, which specialized in dramatic productions, some of them given in private houses, others in the parlors of the Unity Church. There was one performance in the basement of Unity Church which Caroline Kirkland reported in *Chicago Yesterdays*: ". . . a series of disasters, which began when the curtain, rising, caught the fringe of a tablecloth on a table at the front edge of the stage, and dragged it up, showering the floor as it rose with fragile and precious *objets d'art*. Everyone in the course of the play forgot his or her part. The final catastrophe occurred when Mrs. Ayer, the heroine, was supposed to conclude the piece by either fainting or dying on the stage and, in so doing, dropped too near the front of the platform and had to draw in her feet and knees to avoid the descending curtain. It is reported that Mr. Ayer was found upstairs in the dark, empty church, lying on the cushions of a pew, his handkerchief stuffed in his mouth to keep in the peals of unholy laughter which threatened the peace of the evening."

When Harriet planned another of the heavy dinner parties which she dreaded, Margaret Mitchell had an inspiration: she suggested that they make the rounds of the bookstores and buy joke books to serve as conversational ice-breakers. They visited all the stores in Chicago and finally sent to May Hubbard in New York for more. The jokes for the most part were either too stupid or too rough for mixed company, but they did find a few which they decided were suitable. Even Herbert forgot his captain-of-industry dignity—which sometimes amounted almost to pomposity these days—and became a party to the scheme. For a little while, Harriet felt close to him again, sharing in the silly jokes that they made over the dinner table, and watching the guests unthaw and attempt some feeble witticisms of their own. The Ayer dinner parties, even after Miss Mitchell had gone home, became noted for their liveliness, as well as the excellence of the food and wines. It became the fashion to save your best anecdotes for Mrs. Ayer's dinner table and, because of his wife, Herbert was treated with new deference in the small crowd of Chicago intellectuals. Instead of pleasing him, this was an added source of annoyance. Herbert Ayer was an important businessman, respected by other heads of corporations; even a brown bear in the new Lincoln Park zoo had been named after him. He didn't think this was anything to laugh at, nor did he laugh at the quips and sallies of the useless young men who hung around Harriet, flattering her outrageously. Unable to escape to more congenial companions, he would take refuge in wine. Sometimes he was forced to retire before the party was over and it added to his annoyance the next morning that Harriet never complained or accused him.

Although he found less and less pleasure in her company, his jealousy seemed to increase in direct ratio. He was surly with the young men who played opposite her in plays, and often rude to them when they accompanied her home from rehearsals. This, far from discouraging them, made Harriet an even more romantic figure, and she found many a melting poem thrust into her hand by callow youths—and some not so callow. She was human enough to be flattered; she had had no experience with flirtations, except vicariously those of Jule's, and she could not help feeling moved and pleased that men found her attractive. If she had been more like Herbert's mother, who had been so adept that she could carry on three and four flirtations at a time and conceal them all, Herbert would have been more tolerant. But Harriet, despite her appearance and wit, was at heart an innocent. She found it impossible to be anything but honest. It was a failing all her life in her dealings with men.

John V. commissioned William Chase to paint Harriet's portrait. Herbert could not, and really did not want to refuse, for Chase was just coming into fashion and it was considered a sign of importance to have your wife "done" by him. But Chase was far too enthusiastic about Mrs. Ayer's beauty. Herbert petulantly criticized every sketch he was shown. Finally, when Herbert complained that the only good likeness that Chase had caught were her slippered feet crossed on a small cushion, Chase was so enraged that he cut the feet out of the drawing and threw them at Herbert—with his "compliments." But he did eventually finish two portraits, both of them of Harriet in the black gown made for her by Worth on her first trip to Paris. One of them now belongs to a grandchild of Harriet's and the other is in the Pittsburgh Museum of Art.

Herbert did not object to Harriet's traveling, so long as she did not take Hattie. It was becoming popular for Chicagoans to go to Europe and many busy heads of industries who felt they could not take off even a few hours from their desks, also felt they gained prestige by sending their wives on jaunts, and filling their houses with their wives' purchases, good, bad and indifferent—but mostly, as Harriet had noted earlier, bad. The wives regarded Europe as a gigantic version of Field, Leiter & Co., and came home loaded down with the results of their shopping tours. Some of them, willy-nilly, eventually acquired some taste and discretion, but at great cost and effort.

Her mother, who lived now in a "French flat" on lower Fifth Avenue in New York, was always willing to accompany Harriet on her European trips. May had been married in 1872 to Alex Wetherill; with no further responsibility to her children, Madame felt less need to retreat to bed, and enjoyed travel. Besides, Harriet was an amusing companion; she could discuss books by the hour and she attracted attention. In Rome, for example, driving out in her smart rented brougham in a lovely new Worth dress, she was mistaken for royalty; soldiers standing guard, saluted her, sure that someone so lovely and so proud was important.

Wherever she went, artists wanted to paint her. She allowed a young Italian sculptor, who had fallen madly in love with her, to sketch her head and shoulders. Before the clay model was finished, she was back in America; but she knew enough about Herbert's artistic tastes by this time not to mention it. However, the young Italian did a statue of Andromeda chained to a rock which was reproduced in a popular art book—and Andromeda had Mrs. Ayer's head and shoulders. Harriet quickly hid the volume, hoping that Herbert's distaste for such subjects would keep him from ever discovering it. But some matrons of Chicago, who were finding Mrs. Ayer altogether too attractive to be tolerated, made sure that Herbert did not remain in ignorance. Herbert stayed away for several nights. Harriet felt she had no one to turn to; Mother Ayer was very ill and she did not want to bother John V. Nora and the rest of the servants suspected something was wrong, but as Mr. Ayer was frequently gone overnight on his mill trips, Harriet held her head high and said nothing. Eventually, he came home, because of Hattie; from that time on, Harriet slept in a separate bedroom, which the doctor had long ago suggested.

Her failure to produce a son had become an issue between them. She had gone through a series of miscarriages, which had left her weak and morose, subject to bouts of insomnia. Herbert, who did not understand the meaning of illness—except perhaps the vapors, to which his mother was subject—was annoyed when she got up and read half the night. Nevertheless he regarded the suggestion of a separate bedroom as an affront, and when Harriet finally took the step, he bristled with indignation.

Mother Ayer died in the spring of 1876. That fall, when the period of mourning was over, Harriet went to Philadelphia. There was a depression going on; men were walking the streets of Chicago with banners screaming "Bread or Blood!" Harriet, as much as she dared, continued her charities, but since Herbert and John V. felt that the avarice of the working man and the greed of the farmer were responsible for bad times, she dared not do too much. She knew nothing of business and, as John V. had been shrewd enough to foresee the panic of 1873 and take steps to guard the firm against failure, she presumed his judgment was right.

Herbert was now glad to get her out of the house, she realized. Twice, she had tried to talk to John V. about the possibility of a separation and he had refused to understand what she was trying to say. So she pretended that the object of her visit was to inspect the Centennial Exposition, which was creating great excitement.

The Centennial brought about a revolution in American taste. Suddenly, the word "artistic" came into vogue. It was to stand for ornamental tiles, peacock feathers, Japanese fans and Oriental domes and silver minarets added to frame houses of good, simple lines. Many things, from ornamental cast-iron walruses to brass chandeliers ornamented with griffins, were exploited in the name of "taste." It was all showy technique, with no real taste or artistry, and critics of today look back on the Centennial (which celebrated the one hundredth anniversary of the signing of the Declaration of Independence) as "an architectural and artistic calamity, the epitome of the accumulated bad taste of the times." As it turned out, the really important exhibits were concerned with the scientific advances: the telephone, the typewriter, industrial machinery. But the new ideas advanced at the exposition were so much discussed that Harriet had a legitimate excuse for attending.

She also wanted to see her sisters. She had seen neither May nor Jule for years: Jule since her runaway marriage to John

Lockwood and May since her marriage in New York to Sandy Wetherill. Jule was living in a small town on the New Jersey coast, but she had made no attempt to come in to New York to see her mother or sisters and she had excused herself from May's wedding because of her husband's poor health. May had recently returned with her husband, now Captain Wetherill, U.S.A., from his post in Indian Territory for a short leave in Philadelphia. Harriet was eager to see her and the new baby, little May. Jule had also had a child, a son, and May was determined to pay her a visit. Harriet, although her old insecurity and feeling of inadequacy returned when she thought of Jule, had agreed to accompany her. She would have liked nothing better than to have taken seven-year-old Hattie to see her aunts, but John V. had begged her to leave the child at home. And certainly she was in good hands, with Nora now graduated to the top position of housekeeper, and with a devoted German governess who was encouraging Hattie's natural talent for music.

Harriet stayed with the hospitable Wetherills. Their friends, some of them more provincial than the cultured Quaker Wetherills, were astonished to find a Chicago matron with such a cultivated voice and charming manners. But Harriet was far less vivacious than May remembered her, although she looked even lovelier than she had in 1872 in New York. When Harriet began to talk of going home, May reminded her of the trip to see Jule. They started out with mixed anticipation and reluctance, traveling by a dirty and dawdling train. When they reached Elberon, both young women were so nervous and ill at ease that they were tempted not to get off the train at all, but to ride on to some nameless destination. Giggling and nervous, feeling more like schoolgirls than married women with children, May and Harriet tumbled out of the train. But the sight of Jule sobered them. She was waiting in a surrey, but she was dressed in such unbecoming, middle-aged clothes that they hardly knew her. And such pleasure lighted up her faded face when she saw her sisters that they were both touched and horrified. Her talk was all of her husband whom she referred to always as "Mr. Lockwood." Her house was furnished in light oak that Harriet found hideous—"Mr. Lockwood says it wears well"—and had no curtains or draperies—"Mr. Lockwood says they catch dust and are not sanitary." The garden, however, was splendid, because "Mr. Lockwood is very fond of flowers and vegetables."

It turned out that Mr. Lockwood was also very fond of whisky, as of old; but Jule, unlike Harriet, pretended that she knew nothing about that—"Mr. Lockwood is subject to unwellness." Harriet also discovered that John, like Herbert these recent days, tended to grow surly after too much to drink. She was relieved when it was time for May and herself to board the slow train to Philadelphia.

On the way back to the Wetherills' they passed the First City Troop, which was acting as guard of honor for visiting celebrities to the Centennial. At their head rode Major General E. Burd Grubb, a magnificently built sportsman with bristling black hair and curling sideburns. Captain Wetherill saluted him and General Grubb returned the courtesy pleasantly; watching them, Harriet had no notion that this was the man whom she was going to love, happily or unhappily, the rest of her life.

He was everything that Herbert was not: an aristocrat, a high-minded gentleman of the old school, and a leader. He had wit, and charm; he was also a scholar and a soldier. His family was an old one. Dating back to the eleventh century in Germany, they had migrated to England, and then in 1661, to America, disembarking at what was known for many years as Grubb's Landing, Delaware. In 1734, Peter Grubb bought land in what is now Lebanon County, Pennsylvania, and acquired a natural wonder, a mountain of iron ore. A few years later, he became an ironmaster, building the Cornwall Furnaces, named after his father's county in Great Britain. In use from 1742 to 1883, the furnaces made iron for the railroads, and farm implements for the people who went west to cultivate the lands. Old Peter died in 1754, but his two sons kept the furnace going; and on October 26, 1776, made their first of forty-two cannons for the Revolutionary War, in which both Grubb brothers were colonels and the eldest was on George Washington's staff.

The furnace today is the property of the state of Pennsylvania, and one of the tourist attractions of Lebanon County. In 1800, General Grubb's great-grandfather sold the control of the Cornwall and invested in three other furnaces, one at Edgewater Park, New Jersey. The latter was inherited by General E. Burd Grubb when his grandfather died; when his father died, the General also inherited his membership in the Society of the Cincinnati.

In the case of some old American families, the fire died out before the middle of the nineteenth century. But General Grubb built up a remarkable career. A brilliant student, he had graduated with highest honors from the Burlington (New Jersey) Seminary, and from West Point in 1858. In the Civil War, he commanded the New Jersey Volunteers and was made a general in 1863. He was a crack shot, an enthusiastic big-game hunter who made frequent safaris to Africa. On October 25, 1873, his schooner *Eva*, sailing from the New York Yacht Club had taken the trophy from England in the race from Sandy Hook to Land's End, England. For many years, he was commander of the fashionable Philadelphia First City Troop.

Coming back from the station, Harriet had felt tired and depressed. She was glad to let her sister and husband carry on the conversation. Her attention had been only mildly diverted by the appearance of the City Troop—and then General Grubb's vigorous eyes met hers. She felt as though she had been dropped into a cold bath. She was shivering, but as awake as she had ever been in her life. She slept very little that night.

"General Grubb is very attractive," she told May the next evening, while they were dressing for the Assembly.

May made a face. "He's married, darling. Be careful; half the women in Philadelphia are in love with him."

"What has that to do with me?"

Harriet was wearing a black lace Empire gown, made by Redfern, with a tight overskirt of the same lace lined with dark red satin. For jewelry, she had left her diamonds in the case and chosen an antique uncut garnet necklace she had bought in Paris. She had never looked more beautiful, her skin more dazzling, her hair more lustrous.

In a small voice, May told her sister: "He has asked to meet you. He's an old friend of the Wetherills."

That night, many men asked Harriet to dance, but she refused

all invitations. When General Grubb came to pay his respects
to Mrs. Wetherill, Harriet was introduced. General Grubb
bowed deeply and asked if she would care to dance. Harriet had
planned to refuse. But she found herself standing up, drawn to
him, walking into his arms.

He danced as well as he did everything else. Harriet felt small
and light in his powerful arms. When the music stopped, he led
her back to Mrs. Wetherill. Not until they were almost within
earshot of her hostess' group did he ask, "May I call on you tomorrow afternoon? I have some violets in my greenhouse at
home that can never be worn now by anyone but you."

He called that afternoon, and every afternoon until she left
Philadelphia. Each morning a fresh bunch of violets arrived for
her. Mrs. Wetherill was kind and charming, but she was very
proper. Perhaps she had no suspicion that any attachment was
developing between Harriet and General Grubb but, with a sort
of sweet obtuseness, she blocked every effort he made to see her
alone.

May, much as she loved her sister, was glad when the time
came for the visit to end. General Grubb had to make his formal goodbyes before the assembled Wetherills. He took his
courage in hand, however, to tell Harriet: "If you ever want me,
for anything, I am waiting."

Returning to Chicago now was much more difficult than she
had expected. Her life there would seem more pointless than
ever. But she had no choice; at least, she told herself grimly,
she was not in a situation as bad as poor Jule's. And she had
Hattie.

She also had John V. Since his wife had died, he had become
more and more dependent on Harriet. He came to her with
every question about his children; and it was she who had persuaded him to allow his son, John, who was also in the ironworks
now, to marry a French girl from New Jersey whose mother kept
a boardinghouse. ("Father Ayer, your parents were farmers;
aren't you always telling me this is a land of opportunity?")

Herbert was hardly aware that his wife was home; he was
drinking more and more heavily. His mother had visited him
during Harriet's absence and under her influence Herbert had

become cockier than ever. To Harriet's indignation, neither of them remembered how opportune their rescue had been during the war; now, as the years vanished, Sara relived the Civil War and became increasingly militant against the Yankees. She boasted proudly that never in her life had she stooped down to pick up as much as a handkerchief; and Harriet found herself asking Herbert violently what her mother would have done if John V. hadn't paid her expenses and those of her family all these years? Herbert's answer was to take another drink—or leave the house.

John V. saw Harriet's problems. One afternoon, he came to the house and bluntly offered her a million dollars if she would renew her marital relations with Herbert and have another baby. Harriet was furious at what she considered an insulting offer, but she could not stay angry with John V. very long. She was too fond of him, and she understood his anguish over Herbert. She also realized that some of the blame for Herbert's action lay in herself. So she closed her mind firmly on memories of General Grubb. She tried to be more patient with Herbert, more considerate. One night when he came home, he found she had moved back into their bedroom.

For several months, Herbert was chastened and sometimes quite sober. Each tried to recapture the spirit of comradeship and affection. But it was not easy.

Harriet, as always, was desperately ill during her pregnancy and weak long afterwards. And the baby was a girl. Herbert and John V. were disappointed at first. But she was a happy, healthy child, named Margaret, after Margaret Mitchell who remained a symbol of one of the Herbert Ayers' happiest periods together. Neither her father or grandfather could long resist her. Soon John V. told Harriet that, if she wouldn't take money from him, he was going to build her a new house as a token of his gratitude.

CHAPTER SEVEN

THE new house at 362 Dearborn, near Maple Street, was the last gift John V. gave Harriet. Perhaps he knew it was to be, for he personally supervised its magnificence: four stories of limestone, with a courtyard paved in black and white stone "for Hattie to skate on," and a huge stable, with accommodations for the men servants on its second floor. The house was in English Renaissance style, with the first floor taken up by a First Empire drawing room, a library, the kitchen suite and a dining room which was lined with walnut paneling taken from an English house, and seated forty people. It was a house designed for entertaining and for show, and required fifteen servants, inside and out, including Nora. The Ayers did not have a butler, although butlers were becoming fashionable, but Harriet did bring back from Paris with her a French nursemaid named Félicie, for little Margaret.

Michigan Avenue was the Gold Coast, where the multi-millionaires built lavish homes on a palace scale; some so pretentious, in fact, that when they were completed the rather simple families who lived in them felt uncomfortable. One former merchant, when he saw the turrets he had ordered, clapped his hands over his eyes and begged the architect to "take them away!" But the area just west of Michigan was elegant enough. Today, Dearborn Street on the near north side is a mixture of shops and movie houses and night clubs. A few old buildings stand, relics of the elegant 'eighties, but they have been converted into night clubs or rooming houses. Cocktail bars run the length of what used to be tapestry-hung living rooms, and young businesswomen cook on gas rings hidden in the old carved marble fireplaces.

Probably never again will Americans live on such a scale. Servants were still comparatively cheap, even though the bosses complained bitterly about labor's inflated ideas, and taxes were still unimportant. Lavishness was the fashion, even for those who couldn't afford it. But many could.

Perry Smith of the Chicago and Northwestern Railroad, for example, had three stories of Joliet marble at the corner of Michigan and Huron. The stairway was of ebony and gold, and the dining room walls were covered with carved panels of ducks, squirrels, rabbits, prairie chickens and other local game.

Cyrus McCormick, of reaper fame, had a house at 675 Rush Street, in Second Empire style, made of Lake Superior limestone. It had two libraries; the master's was in walnut and ebony, the grand library in ebony and silver. There was also a private theatre seating two hundred, where in May, 1880, his parents held a *soirée musicale* in honor of Cyrus II's twenty-first birthday.

After the panic of 1873, and the depression which had sent many big businesses to the wall, the country was again edging into a boom period, and the canny tycoons of Chicago who had seen the panic coming and who had husbanded their resources, were in better shape than ever. In Chicago, twenty million dollars' worth of architecture, much of it gaudily French, was put up by W. W. Boyington, of Chicago water tower fame. And people were splurging in similar fashion at their entertainments. When Marshall Field gave a party for his two children, Marshall, seventeen, and Ethel, twelve, he brought the original sets from the *Mikado* in New York and transformed the entire first and second floors of his house into a Japanese fairyland. Over four hundred boys and girls were invited, some house guests coming from as far away as Boston and Baltimore, and the favors were designed in London by James McNeill Whistler.

If Harriet was not quite able to put on musical soirées in her own private theatre, or send to Whistler for children's favors, she still was able to buy whatever she wanted without asking the price. Herbert and John V. pretended to be horrified at her extravagance, but they were secretly delighted, and encouraged her. It was considered a mark of distinction for a man to be able to afford a wife who had no conception of the value of money.

Several months before the house was finished, Harriet had gone to Europe and come back with magnificent Oriental rugs, carved Dutch highboys, antique mirrors, French Empire chairs and settles, and Venetian glass. Her linens were ordered fifty dozen at a time.

Some of her pieces were heavy and richly carved, but she lightened the effect with Venetian glass and bric-a-brac. She loved mirrors and used them to widen rooms and reflect the out-of-doors. She studied Japanese flower arrangements, and enjoyed creating arrangements simply of reeds and grass and one or two blossoms.

While most other matrons in Chicago were watching the revolt against Victorian stuffiness warily, Harriet espoused it. In England, one of the prime leaders was Oscar Wilde, who made a great show of his aestheticism, flaunting his mannerisms and affectations. In the operetta, *Patience,* Gilbert and Sullivan had deliberately burlesqued Wilde, and he cared so little that he packed his eccentric knee breeches when he went off on a lecture tour of America. One of his early stops was Chicago. It was waiting, chip on shoulder, to receive him and he did not disappoint those who wanted sensation. He criticized the water tower, pride of their prize architect, as a "castellated monstrosity with pepper boxes stuck all over it," a remark quoted by modern critics who view the still-standing tower with the same lack of enthusiasm.

When he returned to Chicago from the West, on his way back to New York, Wilde gave a lecture on decorating at the Central Music Hall (an auditorium where Henry Ward Beecher had

recently lectured, and where Harriet was to take the platform in
the next decade) in which he bitterly criticized cast-iron stoves
and wall-to-wall carpeting, praised dull colors, Japanese dadoes
and old china, and said that "the most beautifully decorated
house in the entire West belongs to Mrs. Herbert Ayer of Chicago."

This did not endear her to many of Chicago's most influential
wives. But there were other reasons why Harriet was not popular. She was far from humorless and delighted in a funny story
on anybody, but she loathed the malice and backbiting that were
a routine part of the life of the younger members of society. In
fact, she minded less the stories that were told about her than
some that were whispered about women whom she considered
more defenseless. She was no longer the quiet little Mrs. Ayer
who sat in the corner, peeping over her embroidery at the other
matrons. She was the magnificent Mrs. Ayer, at the height of
her beauty, who often walked out of a gathering if she felt that
a friend—or even a complete stranger—was being unjustly criticized. She knew that her name would be substituted the minute
the door was closed, and her reputation ripped to shreds, but she
did not care. "It all seemed so pointless and silly," she wrote her
daughter years afterwards.

She attracted men; many a young bachelor who acted with her
at the Anonymous Club was whispered to be her "slave." Her
ball gowns were cut deliberately low, to display her magnificent
arms and shoulders. One of her favorites, by Worth, was of
cream and green satin, fabrics so stiff they could stand alone,
woven especially for her under Worth's direction. The overdress
was a brilliant green, the underskirt embroidered in small yellow
roses with tiny green leaves. A long train swept out under the
bustle—and Mrs. Ayer was one of the few young wives in Chicago who never seemed to stumble awkwardly over her train—
and the square-cut neckline was very low, though decorously
and flirtatiously filled in with some of Madame Hubbard's price-
less antique lace.

Yet the men she met bored her. Far from being interested, she
often was polite because she was sorry for one or the other of
them—young, tubercular Tom Irwin, madly in love with a pork

heiress whose father had denied him the house; Will Joslin, son
of a soap manufacturer, who hated his father's business and was
hoping to go to Paris and support himself by writing poetry. If
she sometimes flirted with the dull tycoons whom Herbert wanted
to entertain, that was out of kindness, too—or even out of sheer,
frantic boredom, for most of Herbert's friends began and ended
their reading with *Iron Age*. They were interested in politics and
the rest of the world only as it applied to themselves, and although they were shrewd economically, they had narrow vision,
if any, when it came to social responsibility. All opponents of
high tariff were Anarchists, and all working men who attempted
to organize and fight for their rights were against the American
principle of the individual's right to bargain. Although the rich
men who sat down at Harriet's table would fight, and indeed
had fought each other viciously for profit, they were united in
their contempt for the rights of labor.

Harriet heard little except this kind of talk. In fact John V.
talked frequently about the rights of labor to "freedom of con-
tract"—in other words, the right of each man to bargain for himself, instead of in a group.

Many a night, she would go down to the library where she
read until she heard the servants stirring; it was an amazing
room to most of the Ayers' acquaintances, for it was filled with
books that Harriet had selected one by one, from old French
medical books to the modern American poets—in startling contrast to the vast and gaudy libraries of some of the richer citizens, which were furnished with elaborately bound sets, pages
still uncut. And she read, along with the respectable Holmes and
Longfellow and Emerson, the newer Mark Twain and John Hay.
Her happiest times were the long nights in the library; later she
again had her own bedroom when Herbert finally, in pique, admitted that she disturbed him. Then she began to pile her desk
high with books and new magazines, *The Nation, Scribner's, The
Atlantic Monthly*. One day, seeing them, Herbert grew red in
the face and challenged her: "The next thing I know, you'll be
one of these suffragettes running around in bloomers calling for
the vote."

Harriet knew she shouldn't answer. But she had had a par-

ticularly bad time the night before; Herbert had left the guests
to go into the library with a bottle where he had drunk so much
that the servants had to lead him upstairs to bed before the
party broke up. Harriet had pretended not to notice, but later,
pacing the floor alone, she had asked herself what was to become
of her—and her daughters. Was she to go on leading this pointless life until she was too old to care any longer?

So she said, quietly, "At least, the suffragettes are doing something they believe in."

In a fury, Herbert tossed her whole stack of magazines into
the fireplace, where they smoldered and smoked, while he stirred
them furiously with the poker. Harriet watched him, feeling sick
at heart. She was as much to blame as her husband; he had
chosen her, thinking she was an entirely different kind of person, but Harriet herself had not known what she was at that
time. She knew she was making him feel uncomfortable and unhappy by her interest in reading and her desire to do the best
for their children, and that if she could have been satisfied to remain a cipher, he might still love her. But it was too late for
that. At least, she could share the children with her husband.

The children were charming. And they were indulged. Hattie, now ten, had her own apartment on the second floor, a German governess, and a music teacher who was confident she had
real musical talent. The baby had her own huge room, with
bath, which occupied half of the top floor; the maids' rooms took
up the other half. Margaret had a huge carriage lined with
white fur that Harriet had ordered from England, which John V.
nicknamed "Cleopatra's Barge." When Félicie walked out,
dressed in gray silk, with a gray mantle and a huge satin bow on
top of her head, pushing the English carriage with its occupant
wrapped in an ermine robe, the children on the street formed a
procession behind her. Félicie was not unaware of the striking
picture she made. She took pride in promenading at fashionable
hours, and at times when Mrs. Ayer's friends might be on their
way to call—particularly the men friends.

Harriet was quite aware that the display also brought criticism, but John V. and Herbert were delighted, not so much with
the baby, but with the fact that little Hattie often trotted along

beside the "barge," acting and looking like a young princess herself. Hattie was fond of the baby, in an off-hand patronizing way, but she never doubted that she was the important member of the family, and that most of the attention from passers-by was really for her.

Hattie's self-assurance was the direct result of Harriet's insomnia. In one of the books she had devoured during the sleepless nights of her pregnancy, she had come across a discussion of the problem of the older child's jealousy of the new baby. It was a notion that most mothers of the day would have considered ridiculous. But Harriet's own difficulties as a small girl had made her realize how deeply children can be affected and hurt in their own family situations.

She was not so advanced that she informed Hattie of the coming baby, and when the baby was due, she sent the child to visit Grandmother Hubbard, who was spending the spring in Chicago in a parlor suite at the Palmer House.

After a few days Grandma Hubbard brought Hattie home. Although Harriet was in bed, she had been in bed so often during her recent pregnancy and her previous miscarriages that Hattie was not aware of anything unusual. Then Nora came in, with a crying baby in her arms. Harriet pretended no interest, and finally Nora asked Hattie if she would try to keep the baby quiet. Hattie was seated on the low rocker and the blanketed bundle put in her arms; as Harriet had expected, the motion of the rocker soothed the infant, and it stopped crying. Hattie was enchanted. From that time on, she considered that the baby was hers, and she imagined that she had the last word in decisions made about her.

No children can grow up insulated from hurt, but Harriet did succeed in eliminating early conflicts between the two little girls. As little Margaret grew older, Hattie took pride in disciplining her; if sometimes the discipline was a little heavy-handed, Félicie was shrewd enough to know how to distract the older girl without letting her guess that she was being managed. The result was that Margaret grew up happily adoring her older sister, considering that she was perfect, and following her around like a puppy. Sometimes imperious young Hattie was annoyed, and ordered her to "go away!" Margaret never seemed to mind and Hattie, flattered in spite of herself, developed a feeling of obligation toward Margaret which lasted all her life.

She still took first place with her father and grandfather, and enjoyed "entertaining" them with her piano playing. She always was waiting for Herbert, if he wasn't too late, and eager to perform in the drawing room while he sipped a whisky before dinner. But the question of Hattie's lessons had never come up. Untutored himself, Herbert took it for granted that the child's musical talent was more or less spontaneous.

One night, however, he came home unexpectedly and found Harriet sitting on the stairs, listening to her daughter practicing scales behind closed doors in the drawing room.

He made a face. "Does she have to make noises like that?"

"She's practicing. It is the only way she will ever learn to play properly."

Herbert's face grew red. "And why should she learn to play 'properly'? She plays well enough for me, and that's good enough for anybody."

Harriet got carefully to her feet and moved toward the library. The practicing went on. Herbert caught up with his wife. "What are you trying to do? Make her into one of those monkeys that sit up on piano stools and perform for money? She knows all she needs to."

Harriet hurried into the drawing room and told Hattie that her papa was home, she could stop practicing. From that time on, she made certain that Hattie practiced in the morning, after Herbert had left for the office.

Unlike her own mother, Harriet focused her life on her children. Many women with a menage far smaller than the Ayers', found themselves too busy to go into the nursery more than briefly once a day. But Harriet, thwarted in romantic love, found her satisfaction in her children. By modern standards, she would be considered possessive, but not even all her reading warned her about that. She poured her affection out on both girls and saw no reason to disguise its intensity. She did try, however, to do what she felt was best for her children without outraging or antagonizing her husband. John V. was a rock of strength, but she did not like to appeal to him except in emergencies. She was worried about the older man these days, too. His children were all married and he lived alone. He had plenty of servants, it was true, but it was not the same as having a family around him. However, he consistently refused to come and live at Dearborn Street.

Just before Christmas, in 1880, he came down with pneumonia. Harriet insisted that he be moved into the bedroom next to theirs on the second floor of their house and Nora personally took over nursing chores. But John V. did not improve. On New Year's Day, which was traditionally the "at home" day of all fashionable women of the era, she signified that she was receiving no visitors by closing her front door and hanging a small basket for cards from the front door knob.

She urged Herbert to make calls, however, and spent the afternoon with John V. Despite the difference in their ages, she was closer to him than she had ever been to any man in her life, and the thought of his dying was unbearable. She tried not to hear when he insisted that this might be the last time they would be alone together. But he went on talking, and finally she made herself listen. Mostly, his worries were for Herbert and the wrong he had done him. He blamed himself for putting his son in an impossible position in the mills, where he had the title of authority but always had to defer to his father, or his father's friends, in any major decisions.

"He'll be relieved when I'm dead," he told Harriet.

Harriet protested, but she found out her father-in-law had been right.

John V. died early in February. Herbert pretended to be disconsolate. But even at the funeral, Harriet noted a new briskness in his voice. As soon as the services were over, Herbert went down to his offices and became boss in fact as well as in title. Older men soon resigned in protest; only one, a Mr. Higgins, tried to stay on to remind Herbert of John V.'s sound business principles occasionally. But Herbert, tipsy with power, refused to listen. His now could be the last word on business deals, and he didn't intend to let John V.'s cronies stop him. He was going

to be a name to conjure with, in his own right, famous all over
the United States. When his step-brother John tried to make suggestions, Herbert was so unreasonable that John left the business.

Watching this, Harriet felt sick at heart. Even the pompous
strut of his short legs became unbearable to her. Quietly, she determined never to move back into his bedroom. Her husband
seemed to symbolize everything she disapproved of in a man.

She continued to entertain, but now she was less careful to see
that her lists were made up mostly of dull industrialists who
could do Herbert the most good. She invited people who interested her. Her parties increased in tempo and gaiety. She had
receptions after the theatre, with such guests as Adelina Patti
and Sarah Bernhardt. Visiting celebrities who had done something interesting, or had something interesting to say, received
cards. Many celebrities who came out of curiosity became Harriet's good friends, better friends than the Chicago acquaintances
who never turned down a chance to eat Harriet's food and drink
her wines—and criticize her afterwards. But it was an era when
theatrical people were considered freaks or, at least, not socially
acceptable. A decade later, the uninhibited Mrs. Stuyvesant Fish
of New York invited paid performers, the so-called "circus set,"
to her parties as guests. But Harriet was first; moreover, it could
be truly said that she invited actors not as a stunt or to cause
talk, but simply to make her parties interesting and because she
liked them.

John McCullough, one of the great tragedians of the era, would
often come from the theatre where he had played Othello and
tiptoe up to Margaret's nursery to see if she were awake. When
she was, he would crawl around the floor with her, playing bear.
Later, chased downstairs by Félicie, he would tease Harriet by
calling her large-socketed expressive eyes "clown's eyes" and de-
clare that she belonged on the stage.

Clara Louise Kellogg, a soprano who had been invited to sing
before both Queen Victoria and the Czar of Russia, also became
an intimate of the household. She, too, went frequently to the
nursery before dinner, but she was less attracted by the baby
than by the abundance of food offered there, for Margaret always
had choice fruit, especially oranges, and Félicie kept a supply of

beer and black bread and cheese for the grooms who called on her when they were free. Clara Kellogg loved to eat, and she was as fond of the strong cheese and beer as were the grooms. Many an evening, she left her champagne glass in the drawing room and went up to the nursery to enjoy more robust fare.

One night, at dinner, Harriet was uncomfortably aware of a strong, objectionable odor. At last she traced it to the flushed Miss Kellogg, who for once was hardly touching her dinner. Harriet hurried the service along, and finally she and the soprano were able to escape upstairs to Harriet's bedroom to investigate. There, they discovered that a large piece of limburger cheese had dropped inside her dress and was melting among the jewels and laces of her ample bosom.

Harriet never asked her talented guests to entertain; she felt it was unfair and impolite. But occasionally they offered out of graciousness, or gratitude, or simple pleasure in performing. That night, Clara Louise Kellogg, the lingering trace of limburger masked in a heavy fog of Harriet's Parma violet scent, sang the "Jewel Song" from *Faust;* it was the least she could do, she said, after entertaining at dinner with the limburger aria.

Edwin Booth, Richard Mansfield, Ellen Terry and Henry Irving were among other artists whom the Ayers entertained. One night, the entire French Opera Company were invited to supper. She did give musicales for which the entertainers were paid, but these same musicians, famous or not, were always seated with the other guests and treated with equal graciousness. Occasionally, an insecure guest whose husband was aiming nervously at crashing into society, would leave, insulted by being asked to meet someone like Sarah Bernhardt, who was the subject of the current joke: "An empty cab drove up and Sarah Bernhardt got out." But the older people, who had known Harriet's father and John V. and Madame Hubbard, were simple and honest enough to be delighted by so much entertaining and witty company. So, although Chicago's tongues wagged in double-time about Mrs. Ayer, she did not lack for guests.

Later, she wondered how she managed to survive this period. She was sleeping even less than usual. Each minute of each day was crowded, with the children, their plans and parties, the household, and plans for evening affairs. Yet she wanted it that way. "I felt," she wrote years afterwards, "that if I stopped even for one second, something terrible would happen. It was as though I were on fire and running from myself."

In the summer of 1882, the long-feared strike at the J. V. Ayer's Sons plant occurred. Herbert was afraid of violence, and asked for the protection of the militia. Although there was no actual trouble, he spent most of his time at Youngstown. Harriet took the children to Block Island, at eastern entrance to Long Island Sound. She had persuaded Herbert to allow Hattie to enter St. Mary's School in New York in the fall, to finish her last year of general education and to prepare herself for serious musical study abroad. When she mentioned Europe, Herbert's face darkened, but after a minute, he shrugged and said they would wait and see. This, more than anything else, made Harriet fear that the strike might be as ruinous as John V. had anticipated. She hesitated.

"Would you rather have us here? Would it be—any help to you?"

"For God's sake, no! I'll be glad to have you out of the way! Stop acting as though I needed sympathy. When I want your help, I'll ask for it."

Harriet realized that it was too late to try to talk to Herbert. They were virtually strangers—and hostile strangers, at that. She closed the house, gave the servants long vacations, and, taking only Félicie with her, went to Block Island. Herbert came up from Youngstown to take them to the train. At the last minute, he promised Hattie that he would come to see her on her birthday.

Most of the permanent guests on the island were women and children, escaping from the heat and dirt of big cities. But Harriet was the only woman whose husband did not come over, at least for a Sunday. With her beauty, her clothes, and her almost absent-minded air of melancholy, she became a figure of much interest. She was pointed out to the "trippers" who came by boat for big Sunday dinners. One Sunday morning, just before the daily boat was to arrive, the waitresses in the big dining room struck for higher wages. The manager and his wife were in a

near panic, for they expected a crowd; but true to the traditions
of management they refused to give in to a group of "malcon-
tents."

To everyone's surprise, Harriet promptly suggested that the
permanent guests of the hotel dress as waitresses and help out,
for a joke. She looped up a flowing summer gown to ankle
length, put a lace handkerchief on her head as a cap, made another into an apron, and produced a broad Irish accent, borrowed
from the Nora of the early days, that had the other guests almost
in hysterics. While the others manufactured their costumes,
Mrs. Ayer discussed the menu with the decimated kitchen staff
and reduced the elaborate assortment of food to the barest essentials. Then she had a meeting of the "waitresses" and gave them
an elaborate menu to memorize, including French dishes, lobster
and frogs' legs. When the "trippers" arrived, they were greeted
by decorative waitresses reeling off elaborate menus. Before they
could recover from their confusion, the waitress would add:
"Sorry, but all we have left is hash."

Before the last dinner guest had left, many of the impromptu
waitresses had retired to soak swollen feet. Harriet's feet ached
just as badly, but she waited until the dining room was empty
and then went to the manager and pleaded for the real waitresses. She was a very beautiful lady and a very rich one. The
manager shrugged, and agreed that the work was hard; perhaps
he could raise the girls' wages without going bankrupt.

Late in August, just before they left Block Island, Hattie had
her thirteenth birthday. At the last minute, Herbert wrote that
he was unable to leave Youngstown. The letter was so badly
written, so atrociously misspelled, that even schoolgirl Hattie
was shocked. She also was deeply hurt that her father had
broken a promise. Madame Hubbard had come over on the boat
for the party, and the kitchen help—who were now, not unnatu-
rally, devoted to Harriet—had baked a thirteen-tier cake which
was to be cut and distributed to all the children. But Hattie lay
face down on her bed, not caring that she was mussing the lace
and ribbons of her new party frock. Not even her grandmother,
or small Margaret's pleadings, could move her. Finally, Harriet
went in and sat by her bed. Slowly, honestly, trying to explain

the situation without putting any blame on Herbert, Harriet told her daughter that one of these days, she might be forced to leave Hattie's father. Painfully, she explained that they didn't love each other any more, and that it was cruel to both of them to pretend to live together.

"Doesn't papa love me, either?" Hattie asked.

"He does, darling. He will always love you. Better than anybody in the world."

"Then why didn't he come to my birthday party?"

Harriet tried to explain. But Hattie cut her off by jumping up and smoothing out her dress and tying the ribbon in her hair, announcing that she was ready for the party. She never talked about the incident again, but Harriet knew how deeply she had been hurt. When it came time for her to go to school at St. Mary's, she asked her mother:

"When are you going to leave papa?"

Harriet shook her head; she was as confused as her daughter. The one, brief, letter she had received from Herbert had told her that he was not going to give in no matter what happened to the "immigrant scum" and that with winter coming on, and no food in their bellies, the "commies would soon be whistling another tune."

Before leaving New York, Harriet saw her sister Jule, and asked her to keep an eye on Hattie. Harriet was not sure how Hattie's Uncle Lockwood would feel about a visitor, but Jule was so pleased to be of service that Harriet refused to worry about John Lockwood. Then, with a heavy heart, she went back to her husband. He was seldom at home, and when he was, wore such a grim look that Harriet stopped entertaining.

The strike was over and the men were back at work without an increase in wages, but the victory had been an expensive one. Herbert was worried, so worried that not even alcohol could put him to sleep and sometimes Harriet heard him pacing the floor at night. She knew that his holdings had enlarged, that he had taken over the controlling interest in another concern in Youngstown and that he had coal fields. So she could not believe that the trouble was more than temporary, however badly he was reacting. Although she took his tempers and his frequent unexplained absences in silence, she wondered if he would not be happier alone.

In the midst of her emotional turmoil, she wrote a letter to Hattie.

> "362 Dearborn Avenue
> Friday Night—nearly midnight

"MY PRECIOUS DAUGHTER—

"I received such a nice neat little letter from you this morning with every word spelled correctly that it made me quite ashamed of having written you that little lecture on the subject. *Pardonnez-moi et je serai bonne fille!* I have just made up a package of silks for you which will be sent tomorrow. I don't think you will ever sew all the pieces up but I was sure you would like to have them so Félicie and I hunted and we hollered. . . . Margaret says tell Hattie the pink piece is from me 'with my compliments.'

"She grows more cunning and do you know she has learned all her letters and goes around spelling out words all the time. I took her downtown yesterday and she nearly drove me crazy spelling out the signs. Everything is going on pretty well in the house, the old cook is pretty grumpy and poor Lillie the seamstress is very ill, otherwise the *maison* is not changed. Be sure and tell me about the dentist, are his manners as fashionable as his shoes? I was very much impressed by his beautiful clothes, though I don't know as that is all that is needed to make a good dentist!

"Glad Aunt Jule is so kind to you. She is a very lovely woman, I think. You must tell me everything you do for the Guild. I am sure you enjoy working for the poor—only don't in your enthusiasm impose any of your fearful cardboard horrors on the hospital. You would be sorry to learn you had frightened a poor little child into fits or turned an old lady's hair gray in a single night by the sight of one of your own make of cardboard monsters. . . .

"I must stop now, this moment. I have several other letters to write and it is very late. . . . Good night my dear, my own. God bless and keep you ever. Don't forget your poor mother who

misses you every hour of the day and who loves you very, very
dearly

MAMA."

A second letter written after Thanksgiving is more indicative
of her disturbed state of mind, both in its tone and in her handwriting.

"Monday Night

"MY DEAR LOVE:

"I have just received your letter announcing the arrival of the
box and also two from the dead letter office dated the 6th and
7th of November which you mailed with a 2¢ stamp on each—
you little goose! I am so very glad the box pleased you. How
did I think of all the things? My own little darling—*love* makes
one remember many, many little ways and means of pleasing the
one who is so dear. You and your sweet little blue-eyed sister
are my heart's best and most sacred treasures. You came to me
from a good and gracious God. You are *my own*—my blood runs
in your veins and every bit of your sweet little self came from
me. What wonder that I love you? What wonder my sweet
child that I feel you are as near to me as my own right hand or
my two sad eyes? I made your box up with my heart so full of
love for my pretty little girl that if you could have seen it you
would have thought it a better thing than any other gift it contained.

"I am sorry to tell you how wretched my Thanksgiving was,
but I do not want you to worry about it. I will try to bear my
sorrows as long as I can and then my love I shall be obliged to
go away. I cannot tell where—nor when—but unless you choose
it need never be away from you. Nothing can separate us but
your own wish. I think I wrote you I was delighted with your
report. Margaret really is astonishing in her lessons. Miss Mur-
dock says she frightens her she learns so fast. She has written to
Santa Claus for a Punch and Judy and *several books to read*—
Isn't that funny? I hope you had a nice time at Aunt Jule's.
How do you get on with your Uncle Lockwood? It is a very
great comfort to have you write me so often—what about your

music? I shall be on in December to bring you home unless something very unexpected happens. Mail me a list for your party—boys and girls and be sure you think of every one. God bless you my dear, dear love and keep you good and gentle to be a comfort to your

MOTHER."

Hattie's party never took place. In early December of 1882, Harriet had her only violent quarrel with Herbert. It came, absurdly enough, after her husband discovered that Tom Irwin, the lonely young man who used to frequent Margaret's nursery, had given the little girl a ring with a small diamond; a ring which Harriet promptly took away from the child as unsuitable and put among her own jewels for safekeeping. Herbert's blind rage over the incident made Harriet decide to go down to New York with Margaret and spend Christmas there—Herbert thickly told her she could stay as long as she wanted to, he was sick and tired of her extravagance and airs.

She rented a furnished apartment on fashionable Union Square, one of the brightest and busiest sections of the city. Facing on it were the well-known Clarendon, Union Place and Union Park hotels; the Union Square Theatre; the Everett House; the magnificent retail store of the Domestic Sewing Machine Company and other fine stores, including the famous Tiffany's. Some of the finest buildings of the period were located nearby— shops, private homes, apartment houses, churches. The square's broad walks and several acres of grass were filled with crowds by day—and at night the square was lighted "bright as day" by "the dazzling rays of the new electric lights."

Félicie was not happy in New York, however. She missed her beaux, and she found herself swallowed up in the fashionable gatherings around the square. So Harriet sent her back to Chicago, and hired a German governess for Margaret. She also employed a young Negro girl named Lena Raymond. Harriet had never before hired a Negro servant; Herbert, for all his Northern ways, had been dead set against having them in the house, working for pay. Lena delighted her. She was quick and slender and bright. Although she had been able to go to school for only a short time, she had educated herself by constant reading. Her penmanship was excellent, her voice was sweet and cultured, and her standards of personal cleanliness rivaled even Harriet's.

Lena was hired to cook and clean the small apartment. The wages she asked were surprisingly high, nearly as much as Harriet was paying Nora in Chicago, but when Harriet saw how deftly Lena worked, and how beautifully served everything was, she decided she had been lucky. At the time, she did not suspect how lucky she really was, for Lena was to be a true friend at a time when Mrs. Ayer had very few.

Shortly before Christmas, Harriet made up her mind that her separation from Herbert must be final. She wrote Herbert a long letter, trying to ask for her freedom without hurting his vulnerable pride. Then, impulsively, she wrote General Grubb a short note, inviting him to call if he happened to be in New York.

At last, she was starting a new life. Whatever it might hold for her, she thought it could not be worse than the old.

CHAPTER EIGHT

FOR the second time in her life, Harriet faced Christmas with dread. The 1871 holiday in Paris, after the fire, had been somber enough, but Madame Hubbard's elderly friends had at least done what they could to make it pleasant.

The separation from her home and husband was Harriet's fault, and her fault alone. Even Madame Hubbard had been shocked when Harriet told her that she was thinking about divorce, and had said she would not tell any of her friends that Harriet was in New York, in the hope that Harriet would come to her senses. Harriet accepted her mother's attitude. She had learned never to depend on Madame Hubbard for understanding, and she knew that her mother had been running away from her own problems too long to be of any practical help.

Margaret was young enough to adapt to changes easily. She loved the excitement of the city, and she made friends quickly in the park—too quickly, according to the sour-faced governess. Margaret also adored Lena, and would often escape to the kitchen when the German woman was hunting for her.

But Hattie was another story. She never mentioned her father, but Harriet suspected how much she must be missing him. She had maintained the same cool façade after John V.'s death, until

Harriet found her one day in the back of the preserve pantry, smashing jar after jar of jelly and conserve with maniacal fury, and weeping hysterically when Harriet hurried her upstairs, hands dripping with blood and jam.

This time, Harriet caught her clue in Hattie's music. The day before school closed for the Christmas holidays, Harriet had visited St. Mary's, and paused outside the music-room, where Hattie was supposed to be practicing. She heard no scales; instead, she heard a tumbling riot of chords, shrieking out anguish and heartbreak. Startled, Harriet looked at the Sister who was accompanying her. The Sister smiled gently. "It is good when you can express your troubles in music. The child has great talent. We have been hoping that, when she finishes here, she might have the opportunity to go abroad and study music." Harriet had nodded, and gone in to catch her daughter in her arms and stop the sobbing music. But it echoed for days afterwards in her mind.

As the holidays drew near, the streets were crowded, and the stores decorated with brilliant ornaments and wreaths. Huge piles of trees stood on the street corners, and wagons loaded with trees and wreaths and festoons went from door to door. The stores were open at night, sending great shafts of gaslight over the snow, and the streets blazed with the new electric lights invented by Thomas Edison. Boys with penny whistles and young men with tin horns added to the noise of the horses' hoofs on the frozen streets and the cries of the hawkers. And the elevated railways roared overhead, sending down showers of sparks on frightened horses and hurrying throngs.

Harriet had bought a tree, and decorated the furnished apartment as best she could with evergreens and holly, but the beautiful German Christmas ornaments that she loved were packed away in boxes in Chicago. Margaret made little chains of bright colored paper, and Lena baked sugar cookies in the shape of children and animals. Harriet had shopped extravagantly, buying wonderful big dolls for Margaret, and a set of furs for Hattie, but even the sight of the gaily wrapped surprises did not brighten the sad Christmas Eve atmosphere.

Margaret, homesick for the first time in her life, had gone to bed so willingly that Harriet felt sick. Hattie, growing quieter as each moment passed, had fallen asleep in the other half of Harriet's big bed. The German governess was gone, not to return until after New Year's. And Lena was sleeping in the tiny maid's room off the kitchen. Harriet looked out the window; a thin frosting of snow had fallen, making Union Square look like a Christmas card. The gaslights of the stores were out, for the crowds of last-minute shoppers were now on their way home. Through the opened curtains of other houses and apartments, Harriet could see parents, and grandparents, happily decorating trees, loading them with candies and beautiful ornaments. She still had her own tree to decorate, but she could not seem to gather the courage to start. One by one, the lights in the houses and apartments were extinguished. A hush fell over the square, broken only by the sound of horses' hoofs on the pavement as some late traveler hurried home. Harriet, shivering, turned away from the window just as the church bells pealed midnight.

She brought out the box of little toys that she had bought to trim the tree, the huge star for the top, and the yards of tinsel. She looked with shaking tenderness at Margaret's paper chains, and at the sugar cookies which had been Lena's donation. But she could not bring herself to begin. Christmas services were being held in churches throughout the city; she wished now that she had asked Madame Hubbard to attend Grace Church, on nearby Tenth Street, with her. But it was too late now. She had work to do, and she must hurry, or Margaret would be awake before she had finished, rushing out to see what St. Nicholas had brought. Just as she bent to pick up one of the paper chains, there was a knock at the door.

She turned, wondering, a little frightened. She knew no one in New York. Certainly, neither Madame Hubbard nor her friends would come to pay calls at midnight on Christmas Eve. There had been no word from Herbert, but Herbert was not a sentimentalist. She was sure that if he had planned to surprise them at Christmas, he would not have waited until midnight. She thought of waking Lena; but the poor girl had been up early that morning, and would be up again soon, making breakfast for the children. As she hesitated, a wonderful thing hap-

pened. Outside in the snow, the voices of carol singers rang out
in the old hymn, "Silent Night." Her eyes filled with tears. She
was sure that whoever had knocked, had come in good will.

She opened the door. General Grubb stood there, his face
bright with cold, his beard frosted with snow, his arms loaded
with parcels. Harriet stepped back, unable to speak. It had
been six years since she had seen him. She had even imagined
that she had forgotten what he looked like. But his impact on
her was just as strong as ever. He seemed to fill the small room,
and he was still the handsomest man she had ever seen, with
blooming vitality which made other men seem colorless.

It was a perfect Christmas, after all, one that Harriet remembered all of her life. On Christmas Day, he called again and
met Madame Hubbard and the children, captivating them all,
particularly little Margaret who immediately called him "the
Ginger," as close as she could come to "the General." And, in a
last moment alone with Harriet, he told her that his wife had
consented to a divorce, so that he would be free to court Harriet
before long. Meanwhile, he asked permission to write her, and
to call on her again if he found himself in New York. Harriet
was in a glow of happiness when he left.

But the next day, she was restless again. It was going to be
hard to pass the time until their dreams could be realized.

Recently, she had caught herself disciplining the volatile little
Margaret with the admonition: "Darling, be patient. You can't
have everything in a minute. You have to learn to wait. . . ."

Now, Harriet thought wryly, she knew from whom Margaret
had inherited her impatience, her quicksilver urge to have everything accomplished in an instant. Margaret's mother, too, would
have to learn to wait, to be patient.

When the holidays were over, Hattie returned to school and
the German governess came back, with new determination in her
eye to make small Margaret toe the line. There was nothing to
do in the house, for Lena was a jewel of efficiency, so Harriet
looked around for something to occupy herself. She had never
known New York as a city, for she had only passed through it on
her way to and from Europe, or stayed in the Astor Hotel downtown briefly, in order to shop at Sypher's. Now she visited the

museums and art galleries, and took sightseeing trips on the elevated railway in the less crowded periods when the fare was raised to ten cents. The tempo of the city fascinated her. New Yorkers themselves complained that it was too fast, but they complained proudly. They told of visitors from other cities who were more exhausted "both physically and mentally" from the strain of doing a week's business in New York than they would have been from a month's labor in some other portion of America.

Walking around the city, even venturing up into the sparsely populated section above Fifty-ninth Street, Harriet felt revived. She loved Paris, and everything French; going there was like going home. But New York excited her, it was a challenge. She wrote the General: "I find myself walking faster, trying to keep up. Don't scold me and say that the struggle for money is vulgar and that the stupidest people often have the sharpest money sense along with the dullest sense of morals. I know that. But I can't help enjoying my role as a spectator. Chicago is my birthplace, and I love it for its memories of my childhood, but I am glad that I do not have to go back and live there after discovering New York. The contrast would be too great. . . ."

Violets came every day from the General's greenhouses, and long, charming letters, written in his cultivated hand. Even Madame Hubbard, after meeting him, was reconciled to Harriet's divorce. So Harriet wrote a second letter to Herbert, making her desire for a divorce more explicit, and begging him to answer her this time.

To her astonishment, her only reply from Herbert was a telegram informing her that he had sold the house, and if she wanted the rest of her clothes, she had better come and get them. Her horror and surprise were increased by a letter the following day from her friend Mrs. J. B. Lyon telling her that Herbert was in bad business trouble and needed money; that he had not only sold the house but most of its furnishings for $50,000; but that she and Nora had held out what they thought were Harriet's most treasured possessions and were trying to keep them intact. Harriet wired them that she was coming to Chicago. The nuns at St. Mary's agreed to keep Margaret so that she would be with Hattie, and Harriet was able to dispense with the governess.

But she kept Lena on; the Negro girl had touched her by offering to work for nothing when Harriet had felt it necessary to warn her that she might not have a job with her in the future. Harriet was touched. She had had many servants, and she had been sure that most of them were loyal, and that some, like Nora, were personally devoted. But she had never found one with Lena's selfless integrity. She put her arm around the girl. "I hope it won't come to that, but I thank you."

It was, in fact, hard for her to realize what had happened. In spite of John V.'s premonitions, in spite of the fact that Herbert had been increasingly worried about business, she could not believe that he would not survive and prosper again. Money was all Herbert really cared about, with the exception of the drinking cronies and the cheap girls who entertained his leisure moments. She could not imagine Herbert without money.

She had loved the house, partly because it had been John V.'s last gift to her, partly because she had chosen with such care everything that went into it. But, lying in her berth that night, she faced the fact that she would have lost it eventually, anyway, that it belonged to Herbert and that she had no right to it. In addition, there were her jewels, to which she also felt she had no proper right. She had them with her, to give to Herbert to sell, if he was still in financial embarrassment. Her thoughts were trying traveling companions, and she was relieved when the journey was over. She was not encouraged, however, by Herbert's appearance. His face was drawn, his eyes red and bloodshot, and his manner brusque. He hustled her off to their waiting hack, crawled in beside her, and slammed the door. Then he told her that he owed the banks some $100,000 for which he had signed notes, and he was desperately trying to beg, borrow, and sell everything he could for cash.

Harriet gave him her jewels, without regret, but she wrote Hattie:

"I am broken-hearted because my dear old King [her carriage horse] has been sold. I asked especially for him not to be and supposed I could trust them to carry out so direct a wish, but your father notified me simply that he had been sold, he did not know for what sum, and I cried like a simpleton over it, I feel as though one of my few faithful friends has been stolen from me."

She stayed with Mrs. J. B. Lyon and together they went over the few things she had saved from Herbert. They were mostly small pieces, bric-a-brac, crystal, china, some of them valuable but not things that would bring high prices at quick sale. She asked Mrs. Lyon to keep the pieces until she could find some cheaper place in New York to live. Mrs. Lyon urged her to stay on in Chicago with her. When Harriet refused, Mrs. Lyon tried to persuade her to go abroad and move into one of the inexpensive *pensions* where many gentlewomen in reduced circumstances lived in respectable semi-poverty, hoping their daughters would marry well. But the idea of genteel poverty was repugnant to Harriet. Besides, she could not believe that all of John V.'s vast business would be lost; certainly, there would be enough left for her and the children to live modestly in New York.

But as the days passed, so did her hope. She learned that finally even Mr. Higgins had pulled out of the firm because of Herbert's reckless extravagance and unrealistic ideas about expansion. There was a big mortgage on the real estate, in addition to the bank loans. And the good-time cronies and friends of Herbert's prosperity were not so friendly when it came to lending him money. On February 17, 1883, Herbert Ayer failed because the bank refused to cash a paper calling for $15,000.

The headlines blared: "A TOTAL COLLAPSE—The failure of John V. Ayer's Sons Declared to be Absolute and Sweeping." The *Chicago Times* of February 18 said: "Another great failure in the iron trade, the fourth in the list since the suspension of the Union Iron and Steel company, occurred yesterday. The house of J. V. Ayer's Sons, dealers in merchant iron, and as well known throughout the country as any firm or corporation in that line of business, and at the same time one of the oldest in the West, became seriously involved by the refusal of the United National Bank to cash a piece of paper for $15,000 maturing yesterday when presented for payment. . . . It appears entirely probable that the Union National would not have refused payment of such paper unless there were large amounts of it elsewhere maturing early. Indeed, it was ascertained that $15,000 more fell due today, and that in the neighborhood of $100,000 was held by Eastern banks and others, all of which was given on six months' time. . . ."

Herbert had poured everything he owned or could borrow into saving the business, but he had expanded too far, and too fast. His interests had included the firm of Brown & Bonnell, which controlled not only rolling mills but coal fields, blast furnaces and limestone quarries. John V. had been a small investor in Brown & Bonnell; Herbert had bought stock until he had the controlling interest, and then splurged heavily, borrowing money to make it the single largest rolling mill in the West. If all had gone well, he would have become many times a millionaire. But he had gambled and lost. The long strike had eaten into his capital. The market was in bad shape, for Congress was debating a cut in protective tariff on iron, and potential purchasers were holding off, hoping prices would go down. Into all these factors came the whisper of "mis-management." Brown & Bonnell, Herbert's most important holding, was saved by the other directors, who asked that a receiver be appointed. But Herbert was ruined.

His remaining friends said it was only a matter of time until he got hold of something good again, and made a come-back. Harriet hoped so, more even for his sake than her own. She was numb with the shock, but she reasoned with herself that other women had encountered similar problems, and survived. Herbert came to see her the day after the receivership had been announced. He had not even bothered to shave, and his personal linen was soiled. His eyes were red-rimmed and he hung his head throughout their talk, tracing the pattern in Mrs. Lyon's Persian carpet with a dusty boot.

"I've got friends who are looking out for another connection for me," he told her, "don't worry about me. As soon as I get on my feet, I'll send you and the children some money. But in the meantime . . . can you manage?"

Harriet told him she could. What else could she do? She had a little money left in the bank in New York, but very little. Madame Hubbard had written, vaguely promising to help, but Harriet knew that her mother was no longer a wealthy woman.

There had been a letter every day from the General, too; he had repeated in each one that anything he owned was hers for the asking. But Harriet was determined that, no matter what happened, she would not ask anyone for money.

She said, "Don't worry about us, Herbert. I'm sorry it turned out this way. But I wish you all the luck."

He did not ask her what her plans were. He stood up and held out his hand.

"I'm sorry, too, Harriet. I didn't mean us to end this way. You are welcome to the divorce anytime, if you can pay the lawyers."

Dr. Clinton Locke and his wife and their daughter, Fanny, drove Harriet to the train. On the way Fanny, who was a little older than Hattie, chatted enthusiastically about her plans for next autumn. She was going abroad to study in Stuttgart, Germany, under the chaperonage of the talented American novelist, Blanche Willis Howard. Naïvely, she asked Mrs. Ayer if Hattie couldn't come with her; despite the slight difference in ages, they had been good friends.

Mrs. Locke tactfully changed the subject, and no more was spoken of Fanny's trip aboard. But Harriet got on the train with her determined jaw set. She wasn't asking for sympathy; she didn't want it. But somehow, she would find a way to make money. Her children were going to have advantages like other girls.

PART TWO

CHAPTER NINE

FROM Harriet to a Mr. Cobb in Chicago, a friend of her husband's:

"DEAR MR. COBB:

"As your opinion has great weight with Mr. Ayer, will you as a great favor to me take my part when he explodes as he will, about my going to work. There are several arguments to advance, the best of which I consider is the fact that he has constantly endeavored to impress his financial ruin upon us and likewise the failing state of his health which leaves us in the event of his death or illness upon the world at perhaps a time when we should not be able to command the sympathy and attention we do now. . . . I do not wish him to know what salary I get so please say you are in ignorance of it but know I am to get a commission. If you do not mind also saying that I told you in talking matters over that when I begged Mr. Ayer to insure

his life for the children he replied that he was not able to pay
for such a provision and that I thought no one could blame me
if I tried to do something which in the case of his death would
pay for our bread and butter when I know otherwise we should
be left almost penniless and with no resources but our own small
property. When Mr. A. is able to set aside a sum of money upon
the income on which we can live, I shall be willing to fold my
hands but until that time while I am well and strong and have
no legitimate duties to interfere I propose to work. Do not discourage me. It is not as though I wanted to do anything disreputable or absurd like going on the stage or turning lecturer.
I shall incontinently go and drown myself if I cannot have occupation. If I sit and think over my sorrows and trials, what use
shall I ever be to anyone? I depend upon you to stand my
friend . . .

HARRIET HUBBARD AYER"

Sypher & Co. hired Harriet Hubbard Ayer, expecting that her
main value would be in attracting old friends who were sorry
for her, or acquaintances who liked to patronize a society beauty
—particularly one who had not bothered to be polite to everybody—reduced to working for a living. In fact, even the advertising writer, who had seen the publicity value of hiring Mrs.
Ayer, anticipated the worst. If she had appeared to work in a
jeweled stomacher with plumes in her hair, they would not have
been surprised. And the clerks, who remembered Mrs. Ayer's
lighthearted way of buying without even asking prices, winked
at each other and wondered how long she would last.

Since 1870 more and more women were being employed in
shops and offices and factories; by 1890, the figure was to reach
well over a million in the United States. A few feminists were
entering professions which even today are unusual for women:
law, medicine, the ministry. But women who earned more than
a meager living wage were very few. Madame Demorest, who
had created a paper dress pattern, was one. Actresses and singers like Sarah Bernhardt and Clara Kellogg were others; Lily
Langtry had been a court favorite in England before need for
money made her seek out a stage career. Harriet suspected that

she herself might have some kind of a career on the stage, if she cared to use the influence of some of the artists she had entertained in Chicago. But she was nearly thirty-four years old; she preferred a profession with a more certain future.

Sypher & Co. had no idea that her ambitions were serious. They expected her to marry again, or find some rich friends who would act as her protectors. Meanwhile, they planned to capitalize on her presence. The advertising writer ran cards in the papers announcing that "Mrs. Ayer had been added to the sales staff, and would be pleased to welcome customers."

The first morning, Mrs. Ayer rather disappointed the rest of the clerks by appearing quite suitably dressed in a gray merino without a train, and with white lawn collar and cuffs. When she stepped out of the cab—"She'll soon get over that and be using horse cars with the rest of us," the clerks whispered—her manner was as friendly and assured as it had been when she was a valued customer. She handed the porter, Big Dan, three packages. "Wine and oysters and a cold bird," said the office wit. But Big Dan beamed—he had a soft spot in his heart for Mrs. Ayer, who had always remembered to ask after his invalid wife and his boy, Denny—and hurried away with the packages. The clerks' eyebrows went up; but she greeted them all, as innocently charming as though she were still a great lady.

She was not quite as naïve as she seemed. The day she had been hired, she had asked the advertising writer to take her around the concern. Twice a year, when its showrooms became too crowded, Sypher's held a large auction and the advertising man remarked that it was about time for such an event, that they had acquired too many large pieces which were impossible to sell.

"Why?" Mrs. Ayer asked.

The advertising man smiled patronizingly. "The only customers who are furnishing big new houses are the *nouveau riche,* and they are the very devil to sell, if you'll pardon my language."

Mrs. Ayer asked why, again.

"You'll find out soon enough. They don't want any old stuff on the floor, they're only interested in the new things that have just come in from abroad that nobody else has seen. They're afraid they'll buy something that somebody else has turned down. Take that Flemish chest; it's a beautiful old thing, but it has been in stock so long that everybody recognizes it. I don't know what we're ever going to do with it, except use it for kindling wood."

"How much do you want for it?"

He laughed. "What anybody will pay. Don't waste your time on that. Start out with the small pieces. Even the experienced clerks have given up on the big stuff."

Harriet nodded. But before she left Sypher's that day, she sought out Big Dan, and asked him to clear some space around the Flemish chest and give it a good polish. He beamed down at her, but also warned that she'd be wasting her time. Harriet didn't answer, but her eyes sparkled mischievously. Big Dan responded, as she knew he would, for the Irish in him loved even a faint breath of intrigue. When she arrived for work, the old chest had been polished until it shone and set in a prominent spot in the showroom.

Big Dan had had no idea what was in Mrs. Ayer's packages, either, but he did not give his co-workers the satisfaction of suspecting his ignorance. Whistling, he unwrapped the first, which was a pot of beef broth, laced with red wine, for his wife; it wasn't the first time that Mrs. Ayer had given Big Dan something to tempt his lady's appetite. The second was more mysterious: a frail Chinese bowl, of a shade of blue that made even Big Dan catch his breath. And the third was a box of forsythia sprays, which had been cut from the bushes in General Grubb's New Jersey garden and forced into bright bloom in his greenhouses. They had come that morning with the daily bunch of violets, which Harriet wore at her waist.

Mrs. Ayer arranged the forsythia in the blue bowl, twisting the stems as she worked until they reached up in a lovely long line on one side, and swept down to the floor on the other. "A Japanese trick," she told Big Dan, smiling. "Now. This belongs on the chest, so that no one can ignore it."

Then, violets at her tiny waist, a gray hat with plumes on her forsythia-colored hair, gray kid gloves on her small hands, she waited. Shopping hours were usually from ten in the morning until one o'clock; after that, fashionable women lunched and then went calling. Most of the women whose carriages stopped at Sypher's that morning came to see Mrs. Ayer; they drifted casually in and out with no intention of buying. But a few, after they had seen her, were lured into conversation, and, to their surprise, made small purchases. The clerks did not mind the fact that she dominated the scene; before long, pretty Mrs. Ayer would be very bored, and their turn would come.

Mrs. Ayer later said proudly that she sold as much as an average clerk's whole year's salary in the first week. She had the eagerness of a beginner, but she also had the imagination and enthusiasm necessary for success in any kind of business.

In later years, she enjoyed telling her friends and her grown-up daughters about her first sale. Toward the end of the first day, when most of the clerks were yawning and watching the clock, a showily dressed woman got out of a large brougham with two men on the box. She was obviously one of the difficult *nouveau riche*, but instead of running away from her, Harriet patiently took her all over the store, ending with the Flemish chest and remarking, "It's a shame that no one these days has a house large enough for a beautiful piece like this. In any case, I'm afraid it's too expensive for most people."

The woman said nothing, but the next day she was back with her husband, a prominent Wall Street financier, to look at the chest. He was so deliberately rude to Harriet that she raised the price to $1,500 and pretended to be very bored with the idea of making a sale to him. He not only bought the chest, but told his friends about her. Soon she had more customers than she could take care of in business hours.

Sypher's suggested that she work from her own home, and sell on commission, for many of the wealthiest customers did not care to make their selections in stores with the *hoi polloi*. Harriet agreed, delighted. It meant hard work, but it also meant that she did not any longer have to go on looking for a tiny apartment in an unfashionable section; it meant that she could keep Lena who was so devoted—and practical—that she was cutting ruffles off Harriet's petticoats to reduce the laundry bill, and introducing her mistress to cheap cuts of meat that Harriet had never heard of. But most important, it meant that that—perhaps—

Hattie could be sent abroad to study piano. Hattie had taken the news about her father's failure very hard, indeed; she had never known anything but luxury and her standards were far from realistic. When Harriet mentioned the necessity of saving on laundry, Hattie seriously suggested that perhaps it would be easier to economize on matches. Harriet and Lena had laughed but afterwards, Harriet made a promise to herself: her children were to have the best possible education, but she would also try to equip them so that, if the worst happened, they could always make a living. In Hattie's case, her obvious talent for the piano must be cultivated and encouraged.

Harriet arranged to purchase a small brownstone house at 120 West Thirteenth Street. It was like many on the block, with double doors between the parlor and dining room, and a big kitchen with a small yard. Mrs. Lyon shipped on to her the bric-a-brac and other small, but important, belongings salvaged from her Chicago house; the exquisitely embroidered lavender-scented linens, stacks of which had never been used; all Harriet's books, which the new owner didn't care for because they looked "used." With these she created a background against which to display the furniture that she selected from Sypher's. She had her walls painted soft, dull pink and put clouds of ashy pink curtains at the windows so that even on the darkest days, her house seemed gay and pleasant. And the fresh flowers which came every day from General Grubb's greenhouses filled the rooms, so that as the seasons changed, the rooms seemed to be redecorated.

Her clients were often trying, but the talents that had made Harriet a lively and charming hostess made her an excellent businesswoman. She did not mind being patronized or pitied, so long as people bought what she had to sell. And she felt no scorn for the *nouveau riche,* so long as they put money in her pocket to give to her children. In fact, she grew to like some of the women, and sympathize with their frank efforts to break down the barriers of a society made up of people who a generation ago were in their same shoes. For the first time, she recognized a quality of strength and even toughness in herself that had been lacking in Herbert. He had overextended himself out of weakness and he had failed without putting up a fight. She had heard nothing from him personally, but Mrs. Lyon wrote that he was staying with his old cronies who were trying to help him find work.

The only problem was the baby. Harriet was working hard, and small Margaret had to be left more and more to the care of Lena, but Lena was reliable and Margaret adored her, and one of these days her youngest daughter would benefit from her mother's long hours of work. For Harriet was certain that, at last, she had found her proper niche. She was happy and free and sure of herself. Even Madame Hubbard watched her daughter with amazement. "But you don't have to work so hard, surely."

And Harriet answered, glowing, "Mamma, I love it."

One day in early April, Harriet herself answered a rather peremptory knock on her front door, as Lena was busy in the kitchen. She was expecting some pieces from Sypher's, which she had selected the day before for a new client. But a tall almost too handsome, man told her that a friend—naming a famous railroad magnate—had told him to see her. "My name is Jim Seymour," he added.

James Seymour was the first man who had ever come alone to see her. Sometimes bored husbands accompanied their wives on shopping calls, but most of them had no interest at all in the details of furnishing a house, beyond the fact that it be showy enough to impress other rich men.

But Jim Seymour wasn't an average man. He was a multimillionaire with a reputation for being both ruthless and charming. He was charitable to a degree that most rich men thought soft and sentimental. But he was far from sentimental when someone crossed him, or tried to cheat him in a deal. Harriet had heard her women customers mention him in low, timid tones—yet wistfully. He was a man worth fascinating, if only for the sake of one's husband. Yet they also whispered that "he could bow a lady to her carriage as expertly as he ruined her husband in business the next morning."

Harriet found Jim Seymour interesting, with his dark eyes and skin unexpectedly topped by prematurely silver hair. His manners were courtly, perhaps a shade too courtly, for it was obvious to anyone as socially shrewd as Harriet that they came from practice, not from the heart. But she did not worry about that. She was more fascinated by the story that James Seymour knew almost as much about making money as did Jay Gould, his idol, because she had recently become determined to earn a great deal of money herself; and she knew from experience that the better the teacher, the faster one learned the lesson.

However, she found Mr. Seymour's calm assumption of his welcome in her house irritating. So she did not ask him to come in. Instead she looked up at him—even with his rather languid slouch, he was well over six feet, and his showily expensive clothes did not disguise the muscles underneath—and said pleasantly, "I'm sorry, I usually see gentlemen with whom I am not acquainted at the store. If you would care to make an appointment—"

He shook his head. "Wait, Mrs. Ayer. I'm a busy man. I came to your home because I wanted to look it over. But now I've seen you, that's enough. You're hired."

Mrs. Ayer arched her lovely brows. "Perhaps I should have something to say about that."

"May I come in and talk with you?"

After a moment's hesitation, Harriet shrugged and led the way into the front parlor. Lena, hurrying out from the kitchen, stepped aside when she recognized Mr. Seymour. She, too, had read a great deal about "Phoenix Jim" in the gossip sheets. He was supposed to have come originally from Texas but he had made his fortune in Arizona oil. The editor of *Today*, a scandal sheet, called him "P'ison Jim." Lena was younger than her mistress, but she felt as protective toward her as she did toward the baby, Margaret. While Lena hovered reluctantly in the background, Harriet shook her head at her.

"Thank you, Lena, I won't need anything further." Then she sat down in one of the old French chairs that she wanted to sell, and motioned Jim Seymour to another. "Where is your house, Mr. Seymour?"

He sat down abruptly. "I have a place in East Orange, New

Jersey, in the country. But the house is my wife's affair. Right now, I'm having a yacht built. I want you to fix it up."

Harriet looked at him in surprise. "I'm sorry, Mr. Seymour, I don't know anything about yachts. Houses are my specialty. Perhaps I can find someone who specializes in boats for you."

He leaned forward. "I don't want anybody else. I want you to make my yacht something that everyone will talk about, but in the right way. I won't be laughed at. Do you know what I mean?"

Harriet did. The more she dealt with her customers, the more she realized how important it was to them to do things correctly, not to make foolish mistakes. For herself, she had never cared if anyone laughed at her, even criticized her cruelly. But she had come from a background very different from Jim Seymour's.

She said softly, provocatively, "I have very expensive tastes."

And James Seymour looked back at her, smiling, his teeth large and white in his handsome dark face. "So have I, Mrs. Ayer."

In late April, Harriet Hubbard Ayer went on her first of many business trips abroad. She had convinced Sypher's that it would be profitable to send her, for she could show them the plans for Jim Seymour's yacht. So long as he said he wanted the best, and refused to discuss price, she had had an inspiration. She planned to duplicate as nearly as possible the furnishings which had been chosen for the yacht belonging to England's fun-loving Prince of Wales, later Edward VII. She had not yet told Jim Seymour, but she knew he would not quibble. Unlike some tycoons, he was not a miser who ate penny apples for lunch. He had as little respect for cash as Harriet did, and he was almost carelessly generous, especially when his interest was quickened.

Harriet had known from the beginning that theirs was no routine business relation. When he looked at her, she was very conscious of herself as a woman, and she knew that he was interested in more than her taste in decoration. Although their relationship had never been anything but formal and proper, she carefully did not mention his name when she wrote to General Grubb.

The General was off on safari in Africa; it was a trip that had been planned for several years and he felt reluctant to withdraw, although he did not want to be gone from Harriet for so long. She assured him that, with her trip to Europe, and the summer she planned to spend with her two daughters before Hattie went abroad, she would be fully occupied. Actually, she was working so hard that sometimes she had begrudged taking the time for dinner and the theatre when the General made his infrequent journeys into New York. This was ridiculous, and she was ashamed, because when she was with him, she forgot everything else. But she felt a certain guilty relief at his absence. She hoped that when he returned, she would have her affairs in order.

One afternoon just before she was to sail, Jim Seymour had asked her to come down to his office for a final conference. They finished their business and he thrust aside the architect's plans for the 160-foot boat, which he was going to call the *Radha*, an Indian name which meant "Flowering Club." He leaned back in his chair, the smoke of his cigar spiraling toward the ceiling. "These are exciting days, Mrs. Ayer. Everything is changing so fast. There is no excuse for anyone not getting rich, if you have half an idea."

Harriet asked, "Even a woman?"

He smiled at her. "Not every woman. But an exceptional woman, like you, could make a great deal of money."

"In my business?"

He shrugged. "I don't know. Certainly not unless you owned it. Nobody ever got rich on commissions. But I'm thinking of something else, something you could make and sell, a big business with volume. Let the men fool around with mines and railroads. See what you can take out of their wives. What are women most interested in?"

"Their children and homes," Harriet told him. Again Jim Seymour shrugged.

"Perhaps. But I've never found anybody, man, woman, or child, who didn't think of himself first. Or herself. Try to figure out something that every woman in America will want, and give it to them."

"But what?"

"That's your problem, *señora*. But if you ever get a good idea, come to me. I'll finance you."

Harriet had no stomach for borrowing money. She had seen what overextension of credit had done to Herbert. But Jim Seymour laughed at her attitude, warning her that only women and fools insisted on spending only what they earned, that the secret of high finance was borrowing.

"You'll never get anywhere, Mrs. Ayer, unless you think big and act big. Just bear that in mind. And bear in mind the fact that I'd like to help you. I don't take to helping everybody, I guess you know that. But I'd like to help you."

It was with Jim Seymour's words echoing in her mind that Harriet went about her European commissions.

CHAPTER TEN

To THE amazement of the Paris American colony, who had prepared to sympathize and perhaps snub Harriet a little, she had never been so beautiful, so glowing, so sure of herself. If all her gowns were not still by Worth, they were equally fashionable, and Mrs. Ayer wore them with French *élan*. The horse chestnut trees in the Bois de Boulogne were in flamboyant waxy pink bloom, but as Mrs. Ayer rolled through the *bois* in her open *calèche*, she put them to shame. Her complexion was dazzling, her navy blue eyes clear as ever, and her gowns were cut stylishly low to display neck and shoulders that were worthy of exhibit. And, always, there was a bunch of violets at her slim waist, and a chic bonnet perched high on her beautiful red-gold curls.

Now that she no longer had a fortune, Mrs. Ayer received a cool welcome from some hostesses. But French society, more sophisticated than "the 400" in New York, admired a beautiful woman all the more because she could earn a living. She became the current sensation in Paris. Although she was hard at work exploring dusty antique shops by day, at night she went to the brightest balls, and was sought after by the most fashionable beaux. Word soon went around, however, that Mrs. Ayer, delightful as she was as a dinner or dance partner, was *une allumeuse*—a not too flattering French term for a woman who kindled passions without ever intending to go farther than a mild flirtation.

The truth was that Harriet, for the first time in her life, was enjoying an attractive woman's right to flirt. She had already met the one man in the world she would ever marry if he—and she—were ever free. But, like a young girl, she gloried in attention and breaking hearts; she counted the boxes of flowers which arrived each morning with triumph. Although it was the General's violets, which arrived each day from a Paris florist, which she always wore at her waist, that only made her more interesting. Many a bored husband went after her, to try his luck. Harriet teased them all, played them against each other and, even as she admired General Grubb's strict code of honor, wished that he were there to make her other beaux seem dull and cheap by comparison.

The American colony again had reason to criticize her, and some of the older matrons took advantage of their seniority to talk to her seriously. If she had been a shade more humble—or less attractive—they would have sympathized with her valiant effort to support herself and her daughters. But Harriet for the first time was discovering the joy of being able to do something that was worth money, of feeling free. Perhaps she was a little *too* proud—and attractive—for some of the matrons never forgave her. It was they who were quick to remember her "social irresponsibility" and "loose ways," when she was in trouble in later years.

The Paris antique dealers were no less surprised by the change in Mrs. Ayer. Her radiance did not shock or, in fact, disappoint them. Most of the dealers were men and preferred to deal with pretty women even in business. What did surprise them was her new attitude toward money. When she was buying for herself, she had been the most lighthearted of spendthrifts, winking at the ridiculous prices she knew they were charging to her account. Now she was shrewd about every penny, and exacting as ever when it came to quality. Yet she traded so adroitly, and matched wits with them so cleverly, that they could not but admire her.

Her knowledge of French was, of course, her secret weapon. Within a week, she spoke French as well as ever, and was thinking in it when she bartered. She bought some very expensive and lovely things which she felt confident of selling to her clients; several fine bits of china or glass she sent back to Sypher's simply because they were so beautiful she felt she could not resist them. In one day, she bought the paneling of an entire French castle and many of its furnishings, including Empire and pre-Revolutionary portraits which would be snapped up by ambitious clients who lacked ancestral portraits of their own.

The purchases for the *Radha* she left until the last. She had to go to England for what she wanted, and many of the fabrics must be woven to order. The English did not bargain, and Mrs. Ayer was sometimes secretly frightened when she got back to her hotel room and added up the cost of her day's shopping. But the next morning, she would be up and out early, going on. She waited for a protest from Sypher's. But none came, and she was grateful for Jim Seymour's sound money sense, which had made him suggest that perhaps it would make Sypher's happier if she asked her largest clients—of which he was by far the biggest—to deposit a lump sum on account.

She felt even more touched when she returned to Paris and found a letter from him telling her that he had stopped at St. Mary's to see Hattie and little Margaret, who had been taken in by the nuns during Harriet's absence, and that both were doing splendidly. It was a gesture of kindness that she would have expected of General Grubb, but not Jim Seymour. She felt grateful that she had found such a friend.

The last few days, she and the former Mlle. Frochard, now Mme. Duval and the mother of three small children, retraced some of their early walks, and Harriet stopped in the less-frequented shops to buy a few things for herself. They ended their shopping tour at M. Mirault's, where Harriet was greeted as an old friend. She ordered some of her Parma violet perfume and chatted comfortably with him about Chicago and chemistry and her own changed situation in life. M. Mirault looked at her through his steel-rimmed glasses. "But, madame, you cannot

afford my perfume now. You are a working person like the rest
of us."

Harriet shook her head. "I need perfume more than ever now,
for my morale."

Had he ever found, she asked him idly, the formula of the
skin salve his grandfather had made for Madame Récamier?
It seemed he had and by the time he was back with an ancient
ledger, she had an idea.

"Make up several small jars for me, and I will try to sell them
to my rich clients. But don't charge too little; these women don't
appreciate anything unless it is expensive."

Harriet paid M. Mirault well for the salve, then put it in her
trunk and forgot it. She loved perfume, but she had never used
cosmetics in any form—they were associated in her mind from
early childhood with women who were "not nice"—and even face
salve meant artifice to her. In her mind, she knew this was a
ridiculous Victorian idea, but it was one of the few positive ideas
with which Madame Hubbard had indoctrinated her children.

She docked in New York just in time for Hattie's graduation
from St. Mary's. Even a few weeks away from her daughters
had seemed too long, and Harriet admired them with fresh eyes.
She was proud of the number of honors which Hattie won, and
at her "rendering" of the Hungarian Rhapsody as part of the
graduation entertainment. Margaret was beside herself with
excitement whenever her sister's name was mentioned, and insisted on standing up on her chair the better to see "my sister."

Harriet was surprised to see a large hand tap lightly on small
Margaret's head: "Sit down, Grasshopper."

She looked around. Jim Seymour bowed. "The Sisters kindly
invited me to Hattie's graduation. These things aren't much in
my line, but it was a chance to see you."

Margaret was greeting Mr. Seymour enthusiastically. They
were apparently on the best of terms; his nickname "Grasshopper" had not been an inspiration of the moment as Harriet supposed. She accepted his compliments on Hattie's playing with
maternal pride, and quickly switched the conversation to business, inquiring about the *Radha*.

"She'll be finished by the end of June," he told her, adding:

"I've promised Hattie and the Grasshopper here that they can be on board the first time I take her out. Very politely, they said they would have to ask mamma. I told them mamma was invited, too. Naturally."

Fortunately, the ceremony of awarding diplomas was about to begin, and he settled back in his seat. Harriet let Margaret stand up, as the names were being read alphabetically, and Hattie would be among the first. The applause for her was enthusiastic; Harriet glowed. Her lovely little daughter would be fourteen in August; nearly the age at which Harriet had met her father. She didn't want Hattie to make a similar mistake out of inexperience and ignorance. Somehow, the money must be found to send her abroad. That night, she wrote to Mrs. Clinton Locke in Chicago, asking specific details about Miss Blanche Howard's establishment in Stuttgart. Before the week was over, she received a reply which confirmed her earlier fears. In addition to the fees for the conservatory and for Hattie's room and board in the pension for students, Miss Howard charged $150 a month. It was well worth it, Mrs. Locke wrote apologetically, as Miss Howard was an extremely charming and fine personality, an inspiration to young women, but, of course, the steamship fares and the girls' clothes would also increase the cost.

"I wish Fanny had not told you about her plans, dear Mrs. Ayer," Mrs. Locke had ended her letter.

Harriet wished so, too. Madame Hubbard had taken a house in Great Barrington, Massachusetts, for the summer, and Harriet sent the two children up with her, hoping to join them when she could. But Harriet found few opportunities to enjoy the mountains. She wrote Hattie, who was visiting at the home of a schoolmate: "I long to see you, dear, but I offer no inducements at home! It will be very poky for you, I'm afraid, and I do not doubt you will be asking in a very superior manner 'where we are going this evening' and I shall be covered with confusion and shame because we are not in the vortex of Great Barrington 'High Life.' Dear little one, do not wear yourself out and you are certainly possessed of enough consideration not to be too much of a charge to Mrs. Blake. You have always been so waited upon that it is hard for you to remember but try not to leave your things around. I wish I could think of something entertaining to write you of but I haven't, dear heart. I miss you very much but was sure the mountain air was just what you need. Give my love to all from your devoted *maman qui t'aime.*"

She also wrote Herbert a less affectionate letter, a rough draft of which was found among her possessions when she died:

"MR. AYER:

"Your letter of July 29 is at hand, I quite agree with you that it would be more agreeable for you to have the children with you and as it was understood that their time should be divided between us, I desire to inform you that they are in readiness to come to you whenever you wish. Of course you will provide a suitable person to attend to their physical and moral welfare in my stead. The physicians have, as you know, repeatedly said that Hattie's delicate constitution rendered her wintering in Chicago exceedingly dangerous, therefore you must assume the responsibility [she had crossed out 'take the consequences'] of the course you have decided upon. You will find both children in good health, they are considered well behaved and conscientious girls and have no bad habits. I have been very careful of their associates and must beg the same careful supervision. They have neither of them been allowed to make any acquaintances except by permission and I trust the same rule may be continued. Hattie's health is the greatest drawback to her happiness. . . ."

The letter must have intimidated Herbert, who may have been in an easily intimidated mood. For a later letter to Hattie reports: "There is now no need for you to hurry home since your father does not wish you to come to him. . . . I had word from him today."

Harriet's task of furnishing the yacht was finished in September and she received a commission check so large that she thought she could send Hattie to Stuttgart with Blanche Howard. She wrote Mrs. Locke, asking her to get in touch with Miss Howard. And very soon she received a pleasant note from Miss Howard, who had been visiting her home in Maine, telling Mrs. Ayer that nothing would gratify her more than to have Mrs. Ayer's daughter; she had heard such wonderful things about her brave and beautiful mother. Harriet wrote to Great Barrington with the news, and Madame Hubbard hurried home with the excited children.

Jim Seymour waited until they arrived for the formal launching of the yacht. Harriet was touched that he should remember his promise to Margaret, but he told her seriously: "I don't make promises lightly. Some of my enemies will assure you of that. I never let down a friend who has treated me fairly, and I never forget a slight."

When the *Radha* was launched, Harriet expected to meet the rest of Jim Seymour's family. But only his son Lewis was there, together with some business friends of the multi-millionaire broker. Harriet could not help feeling sorry for Lewis. Although he was nearly twenty, and almost as tall as his father, he was completely dominated by him. Alone, he could be pleasant and witty, in a quiet way that she found rather charming. But he had been taught in a ruthless school.

He was immediately charmed by Hattie, who looked down her pretty nose at him. Although she had just turned fourteen, she had the grace and assurance that came from good teachers and proper surroundings. She spoke French and German well— the French from Félicie and her mother, the German from her governesses and music teachers. She had a good understanding of both music and literature. Hattie was far too intelligent to find Lewis interesting, Harriet was sure, for Lewis had been taken out of school at ten and put to work in Wall Street as an office boy, on Jim Seymour's stubborn theory that he "could learn more cleaning out Jay Gould's ink stand than anything the books could teach him."

But Harriet was not surprised to find poor Lewis hovering eagerly over Hattie while she played the concert grand piano in the salon of the yacht. Watching them, Harriet realized the importance of education and a proper cultural atmosphere for a young person. Lewis had had no chance, she thought. Given opportunities, he might have been an interesting young man, for he loved music and enjoyed reading, without understanding much about either. But it was too late now. The pattern was set, and there was nothing for him to do but follow in his father's footsteps.

For his sake, she was glad that Hattie was going away. She didn't want the young man to form a foolish infatuation for a girl who was obviously not for him. She hoped that Jim Seymour could not read her thoughts. For that reason, she made it a point to throw Hattie and Lewis together during the last few days left to Hattie, and urge her to be particularly nice to him.

Letting Hattie go was very hard. The steamer sailed on a brilliant day in early October and the pier was crowded with visitors saying goodbye and sightseers who had come to watch the spectacle. Several young girls, including Fanny Locke, were already aboard and greeted Hattie gaily. Hattie ran below to see the stateroom which she was to share with Fanny and two other girls. Harriet, clutching little Margaret's hand and trying to keep her from burying her blond head in her mother's skirts, found herself face to face with the woman who was to become her most deadly enemy.

Blanche Willis Howard was not a beauty, but she possessed unusual charm, and was far deeper and more complex than people suspected. Her books were enjoying great success, and she told Harriet that she chose to live abroad because she could enjoy the company of so many gifted artists in an atmosphere of culture, free from the money-grubbing climate of America. She made this statement so simply, so modestly, that Harriet could not take offense—yet the novelist with such scorn for money had eight young ladies in her charge from whose parents she received the net sum of $1,200 a month.

Plumpness was fashionable then; a "round, rosy look" was much to be desired. If Blanche Howard was a shade too plump, no one felt it detracted from her fascination. For her face was lovely, pale-skinned with clear, faintly protruding light blue eyes which seemed to compel you to look into them. She was not unaware of the effect of her eyes—one silly young man had already tried to kill himself for love of her—but she was clever enough to create for herself a personality that could command admiration and affection from women as well as from men.

In one of her later novels, *The Open Door,* she gave a clue
to the secret of her fascinations. A character named Frau Major
was much admired. The woman was around fifty years of age;
she was plump, with an unattractive waddle. But she never said
an unkind word about anyone, when she was in society. She was
sympathy itself for all troubles, and when anyone was criticized,
she found some good word, be it ever so slight, to say for them.
"Her manner was simple, sincere, possessed of the rare charm of
perfect repose. . . . She made her home attractive to scores of
gay young men and young girls, all of whom sang her praises
with warmth. There was not one among them that did not cher-
ish the ingenuous conviction that he or she was the special pet of
Frau Major. . . ." Only in such rare moments of honesty did she
stand back and look at herself—and laugh at the rest of the
world. Her farewell to Mrs. Ayer was typically bland and pious:

"My dear, you are very brave to entrust such a lovely child
as your daughter to another woman. But I will do my best to be
worthy of your sacrifice. My sorrow is that I have no children
of my own. Instead, I satisfy the need to help young people
by taking other women's children for a brief time and giving
them all I can of myself to help them."

Harriet was touched. Her only regret was that she had the
selfishness to cry when she said goodbye to Hattie. She wrote
that night to the General:

"I am sure that Hattie is in good hands. Now I can turn my
poor aching heart to my own problems. My next step, when I
can afford it—and you know that this has to be my problem, not
yours—is to go to Chicago and consult a lawyer about divorce.
This, whether you are free or not. We must not complain, but
only be glad that time passes so much more swiftly if we do
not have to sit and count each hour. And I am busy, indeed,
busier than ever."

The General was on his way back from Africa when she wrote.
His wife had become ill and had returned to Edgwater Park.
Her doctor had written him that she was too unwell to consider
divorce plans. General Grubb had cut the safari short to return
to Philadelphia; he was not sure that the situation was as

black as it looked. But he had felt it was only fair to tell Harriet
his fears, to warn her that it might be a long time before he
could be released from his marriage.

Meanwhile, on October 20, 1883, Harriet wrote her daughter
Hattie a prophetic letter:

> "Desolation Corner,
> Lonely County,
> State of Ennui.

"MY OWN SWEETHEART:—

"Your first letter reached me a day or so since. I cannot tell
you how rejoiced I was to know you were safely landed for of
course we knew the steamer had reached *bon port* by the papers.
Lewis saw it first and telephoned me. He has been up twice to
see me to know if I had heard from you. Otherwise, everything
is going on about as usual, I have hardly seen anyone, I am so
busy.

"I think Miss Howard must be a very rare and splendid creature. You cannot do better, dear child, than copy her lovely
qualities seeing how she endears herself to everyone through her
beautiful personality. I am content to have you with her though
no one can know how lonely I am here at night especially.

"Mr. S. surprised me by coming over and spending last Sunday
P.M. We both went up to see Margaret, as I had already planned.
Mother Duffy took the greatest fancy to Mr. S. and I nearly
shouted aloud when I heard him telling her in all seriousness
that she had a stigmatism in one eye *sure* and probably in both.
Of course he made arrangements to send Dr. Stevens to her at
his expense. He bought a lot of trash for M., which delighted
her, of course. He is very sweet to her, always.

"My own dear love, I am so happy to read your bright little
letter over and over again. Do tell me everything. Draw me a
plan of your rooms and just how they are furnished—tell me
about everyone and what you do every hour. I am rejoiced that
you love Miss H. already. I should like to know her better for I
am sure she is something far out of the ordinary. I want to tell
you something which will touch you of the so-called heartless
Margaret. The Sunday I speak of, one of the Madames told me

she had cried herself to sleep three nights after you left and that all they could get out of her was she wanted to see *ta soeur*. Mother Tomé, the Inferior, said she had never felt so sorry for a child in her life.

"Lena is again taking sole care of me, and Frances, the handsome cook, was coolly marched out of the house at the point of the bayonet, so to speak. You know she was a teetotaller, a strict Baptist and altogether a very virtuous person from her own account. Well, the teetotaller got beastly drunk on cooking brandy. This was as Mr. Hamlet remarks someplace twice a paradox but now the times have given it reason. You would have laughed had you seen me discussing ways and means with the burly policeman.

"Dear love, I hope you will enjoy every hour you are away. Be sure I shall come over if I possibly can this winter. It does not look as though I could afford it but we must hope for the best. Meanwhile, I want everyone to love you. Just see how delightful a thing it is to be a really charming woman like Miss H. All who come in contact with her are not only entertained and brightened by her sweet and gracious presence but the world is better vastly for every such splendid woman. It will be a most gratifying thing to me if you absorb some of her generous sunshiny nature. Not that you are inclined to be morbid—that, thank God, you never were—but you have inherited a trait which you must strive to crush out of sight as well as out of existence. You are not to blame for pre-natal influences, but you will be greatly to blame if you do not with such golden opportunities strive with all your might to be entirely unselfish. Do not, my beloved child, misunderstand me. You have no small or petty trait such as selfishness as it is commonly accepted. On the contrary, you are generous and sympathetic—more so than most girls, I think. Your evil demon is your persistency in attaining the thing you have set your mind on, willy-nilly, right or wrong, crooked or straight. If you make up that small mind of yours, nothing short of an earthquake will stop you and earthquakes you must know come high, and even when attained have been known to break up families.

"Enough of lectures, darling. I will close my highly moral

entertainments with a God bless you and God bless us every one. *Je t'aime ma chère petite piggy de tout mon coeur.* Give my dearest love to Miss Howard and *please* ask her to write me as soon as she can. Again my love, my love, I bless you.

Maman qui t'adore."

CHAPTER ELEVEN

D URING the 'eighties and 'nineties, the concentration on making money in America began to be less intense. Money was still important, but there was a growing suspicion that something called "culture" had its place, too. People whose fortunes had been inherited from enterprising grandfathers, or even fathers, looked down on the new rich who had dragged themselves up by their own boot straps. But even the possessors of second and third generation fortunes felt shy and gauche when confronted with Europe. Consequently, it became essential to send daughters abroad to finish their educations and soak up what they could of European culture.

Margaret Hubbard Ayer says, remembering: "Europe was already considered effete, but more and more women felt that what they were seeking could only be acquired on the other side of the Atlantic. Daughter soon saw that there was also the possibility of acquiring a small title, with Papa's money and, of course, Culture. And good American husbands, with prospects, also needed wives who had the Culture necessary to cope with any foreigner who happened to pass through their city, either on business or for social purposes. So a few years abroad were really necessary. They were called 'finishing years.'

"Here is where Blanche Willis Howard came in.

"The girls did not live with her. But when they came every afternoon, they saw a beautiful and well-ordered home set high up on one of the hills overlooking the charming city of Stuttgart. Miss Howard's house was spacious, beautifully run and her staff of servants, butler, cook and housemaid, worked harmoniously and seemingly without a word of direction from their mistress. The meals to which the girls were often invited were small culinary masterpieces over which their hostess had spent much more time and thought than she would willingly admit. The girls got a real look at a perfectly managed household, and they never again would be quite satisfied with ordinary surroundings. They learned to appreciate beautifully kept and waxed floors. They learned to look twice before buying a factory-made rug if it were possible to get a hand-made one, an Oriental. They watched for color harmony. They learned something about draperies, and old and good period furniture. Papa's money was well spent; for, besides learning quite a good deal of German, every girl was taught French, and sat in Miss H.'s loge or box several nights a week at the Hoftheater, which ran a different play each night. Sunday was the great night with Grand Opera, Monday there was a tragedy, a classic play either by Shakespeare or one of the French or German authors; Tuesday was light comedy; and so on, ending with a roaring farce on Saturday. The artists frequently came to America, just as visiting artists like Eleanora Duse came to Stuttgart. There was also a small museum of both modern and old paintings. Each Sunday after church, Miss Howard's young ladies were expected to look at pictures and sculptures, and describe and talk about their reactions at Miss Howard's next luncheon.

"Blanche exposed her girls to art, music and 'Culture' of all kinds. She stimulated their minds and enriched their imaginations. No one knew where the conversational will-o'-the-wisp would land at one of her meals—from 'Could anyone name the nine muses?' to 'What will be the Pope's reaction to the Kaiser's latest move?'

"Some of the girls retired to their *pensions* bewildered, but some learned to look in the *Encyclopaedia*—rarer then than today—to check facts. Some got little more out of their 'finish-ing' than knowledge of French and German. But a few took fire, and these years in Stuttgart were something which they never quite forgot and their excitement and interest in world affairs, in art and music, in literature, remained with them always. And some were inspired and went on to fame and fortune, like Fanny Locke, who wrote delightful plays performed on Broadway later on."

In 1883, when Blanche took Hattie Ayer and Fanny Locke in as "new girls," she was doing very well financially. Her living expenses were much less than they would have been in the United States and, taking into consideration her income from her books and from the girls, she was able to live and entertain well. Stuttgart was the capitol of the little kingdom of Württem-berg, visited by many distinguished foreigners, in the arts and in politics. Whenever Harriet went abroad on her buying expedi-tions, which became more frequent in the years from 1883 to 1886, Blanche Howard urged her to spend as much time as pos-sible with her. And Harriet was glad to accept.

One of Blanche Howard's good friends was the charming, dreamy intellectual, Dr. von Teuffel, physician to the King of Württemberg. Despite the English translation of the doctor's name (*Teufel* means Devil in German), which the American press was to seize on with delight, the doctor was the gentlest of men. But a great misfortune had cast a shadow over what might have been a brilliant career; both the queen and the heir to the throne had died during complications attending the birth of a child, her first. Although the king did not blame von Teuffel and continued to keep him attached to the *Schloss*, the oversensi-tive doctor suffered acutely; and his morale was not helped by the fact that the king's second marriage proved to be childless, which meant that the crown would one day be inherited by a nephew, a Catholic archduke in a Lutheran kingdom. The peo-ple and the court had to have a whipping boy, so they picked von Teuffel. Among the few who defended him was Blanche Howard.

The doctor was often at Miss Howard's house when Harriet was there; he was not only a friend, but Blanche also used his medical services for the girls whom she was chaperoning. Harriet, with her tendency to identify with the underdog, felt very sympathetic and admired the novelist's courage in standing by him.

Blanche Howard had a good, clear mind uncluttered with Victorian sentimentality. Her books—*One Summer, Guenn, The Open Door, Tony the Maid* and many others—were popular in the United States. Although they sometimes dealt with Americans abroad, the backgrounds were usually European, and many were full of satire that was remarkably crisp and salty for the era. Later, she was to write a book with William Sharp, the Scottish author who was to gain fame as a poet, called *A Fellowe and His Wife*, which was, supposedly, a series of letters exchanged between a German count and his frivolous wife who had gone to Rome to study sculpture and "express" herself. Curiously enough, it was Blanche who wrote the letters from the count and Sharp who wrote the woman's letters.

Blanche's motives were never quite free of intrigue and complicity. The darker side of her nature enjoyed manipulating people in real life as well as on paper. Dr. von Teuffel was an admirable subject and her reasons for supporting him were not entirely selfless. Although he was a married man with nearly grown children, his devotion to Blanche was the most important single element in his life.

Blanche wanted Harriet to trust Dr. von Teuffel, and she knew that the easiest way to accomplish this was to throw them together. In Miss Howard's regime, this was simple. Miss Howard often wrote until very late at night and did not get up in the morning until almost noon. She expected the household, guests included, to conform to her rather unpredictable schedule. So, while her maid, Walpurga, listened at Miss Howard's door, trying to determine when she stirred so her coffee would be ready, Harriet would slip out and walk in the woods. Often the doctor joined her. He spoke several languages including English, and his French was as good as Harriet's. Sometimes, when Hattie had no lessons, she would join them. The woods, close at hand, had their own particular magic and mystery. Even when the weather was bad, and rain and fog closed in, Harriet loved

them; she would walk for hours, coming in glowing and re-
freshed. Miss Howard's house, too, had a particular magic of its
own, a serenity, a freedom from clutter. This was as contrived
as the personality Blanche Howard had built for herself, and as
successful. Despite the unpredictability of the hostess, the occu-
pants of her house were encouraged to relax.

Dinner parties were the rule, rather than the exception. Often
some of the girls were included in the guest lists, to listen to
visiting celebrities—novelists, poets, musicians, painters, sculptors, heads of state, diplomats. Sometimes the talk at the table
would go on for hours, brilliant and fascinating. Sometimes there
would be music; Miss Howard was herself an accomplished pi-
anist. Sometimes, after the guests had left, Blanche Howard
would play for hours while Harriet listened, enchanted, saying
nothing. At other times, before dinner was finished, the novelist
would rise from the table, nod vaguely to her guests, go to her
room and close the door sharply. These were the times, Dr. von
Teuffel would explain gracefully, when Miss Howard wanted to
work.

Harriet found all the evenings at Stuttgart delightful—and
stimulating. If the party ended early, she would go in the carriage with Hattie and her friends to their *pension* and then ride
slowly home, through the winding old streets. Sometimes she
would pour herself a glass of Miss Howard's crème de menthe
and take a book from her shelves and read until daylight; these
were the nights when the old insomnia came back to haunt her.
But she did not worry, because Miss Howard did not pry. The
attitude of the household was *laissez faire;* even the girls under
Miss Howard's chaperonage were not badgered or hounded
about their conduct, but Miss Howard was always available in
the afternoon for conferences if they had problems or troubles.

"I wish I could put myself under your guidance for a while,"
Harriet told her one night, when they were sitting up late, after
Blanche Howard had played the piano for nearly an hour with
Harriet as the only audience. "I feel so much better, more re-
laxed, at Stuttgart."

Miss Howard smiled and her pale brooding eyes rested on
Harriet. "You are welcome to come here whenever you like."

Harriet made a small face. "It isn't what I like. I work very hard. Not that I mind, I'm far happier now than when I was useless. But I get cross and ill-tempered sometimes, when I've gone without sleep for long. The doctor gives me powders, but he doesn't want me to take them too often. I'm afraid sometimes I take them more frequently than I admit to him."

"There are drugs in them, I suppose."

"A little morphine." Harriet's voice was impatient. "But what am I to do? I can't stop working and if I work, I have to have sleep."

Blanche nodded. She looked half asleep herself, her heavy lids drooped over her eyes. "Sometime you must talk to Dr. von Teuffel; he's incredibly brilliant. These Germans know things at which our American doctors are just beginning to guess."

"Dr. Schrady says there is no magic cure for my trouble, just more rest and less worry. Half of his patients are suffering from something similar; it's the pace in New York. And yet, don't misunderstand me, I love it."

"What about your little one—Margaret? Does she worry you? You can't be with her very much, when you are so busy. And she seems like a child that needs much care and guidance."

For a long time, Harriet did not answer, although she was aware that Blanche Howard was watching her through half-closed eyes. It was true that small Margaret, small, delightful Margaret, was a source of worry. The nuns at the Sacred Heart convent, where she was now at school, were devoted to her, but they also deplored her lack of application and patience. Although she knew all her letters, and had known them for several years, she would not learn to read. She could not sit down for more than a few minutes at a time—she was always leaving whatever she was supposed to be doing and darting off in search of something new. Jim Seymour had noticed it a long time ago, hence his nickname for her of "Grasshopper." The child was growing up restless and changeable; charming, but unpredictable. Not long ago, during Easter vacation from the convent, she and a young friend had eluded Amelia Queen, the cook, and dashed out the kitchen door on an excursion to see "where the new elevated train went to." They had ridden on it all afternoon, and through the rush hour, until Margaret's wealth of sixty cents ran out. By that time, Harriet had called in the police and was tearfully expecting the worst possible news. When two small dirty little girls crept into the house, she clutched them both to her breast asking: "But why? Why?"

"Why not, mamma? We had a lovely afternoon. I get so tired doing—well, what I'm *supposed* to. Don't you?"

Harriet had laughed, in spite of herself. But she feared that this was not going to be the last time she paced the floor, waiting to hear from the police that her child was dead or badly injured. She wished she could spend more time with the capricious little girl; but even if she could, she wondered if she had the talent and patience herself to help Margaret rise to her potentials.

She met Miss Howard's eyes, and could not look away. It was almost as though Blanche Howard had read her mind and was willing her to speak. Finally, Harriet heard herself say, "But I can't afford it."

Miss Howard smiled. "My dear, she can live right in this house, and have her lessons with me, for the same fee I charge for chaperoning the others. I would love to have her; she's an enchanting child, and at an age when I feel I can really help her. Besides, beginning next year, I am having other children living with me, my niece and two nephews. Harold is about Margaret's age; Howard is nineteen and has great musical talent. Marion, their sister, is eleven; she, too, is a charming girl and I dream that she may become a singer. They will all be good friends for your child; and she will have Hattie nearby until the summer. I suggest that you bring her this spring, so she can have some time here with her sister before the summer."

"It sounds wonderful. But you forget—I'm all alone. My children are all I have that really matter."

"Of course. That is why you must be brave. It is not the children who owe their parents a great debt. You and I know it is the parents who owe the debt to the children they brought into the world. They didn't ask to be born. . . ."

Harriet's eyes filled with tears. "I know you're right. I'll manage, somehow."

But the next day when she boarded the train to go back to

Paris, Harriet was startled by the decision she had made the night before. She had never liked Miss Howard better, or felt more grateful to her. And Miss Howard had embraced Harriet and called her "heroine" and "the bravest woman in the world." But still, Margaret was just a little girl, she would not be seven until the spring. And, in spite of Miss Howard's generous offer, sending a second child to Europe would mean considerable extra expense. Jim Seymour had long urged Harriet to start in business on her own, and she had told Sypher's that this was her last trip for them. But even so, she would still be living in the kind of uncertainty that kept her awake at night. She had given Jim Seymour a little money, which he had carefully invested, but when he had turned over the proceeds, he had smiled ruefully. "You'll have to do better than this. You'll never get rich this way, and even a financial wizard like me can't change wishes into horses."

Halfway between Stuttgart and Paris, she had an idea. Early next morning, she rented a carriage and told the driver to go to an address on the Boulevard Malesherbes. There, sandwiched now between two grander shops, still stood the little place of M. Mirault. She told him: "I would like to buy that Récamier formula."

"But, madame, do not be foolish. I'll make up the cream for you whenever you wish any for your rich clients, and give you a commission on what you sell. If they like it, we can profit. Perhaps we can make up other creams, too, I have many old formulas, some of them quite as excellent, I suspect."

But Harriet wanted the Récamier formula. At last, shrugging, he gave up. His price was not high, but it was a large sum for Harriet at that time, and when, aboard the *Normandie* at sea, she had time to consider, she wondered if she had made a fool of herself. She had no way of knowing whether she could obtain the ingredients for the cream in quantity, and the extravagance of paying considerable money for a formula which might—or might easily not—be old, loomed as a ridiculous mistake.

The *Normandie* (precursor of the modern ill-fated ship) was just a year old, and the most luxurious steamer afloat. It crossed the ocean in only eight days. But that was still too long for Harriet. As always these days, idleness made her unhappy. Through-out the trip, she was dogged by blinding headaches, insomnia, fits of unaccountable apprehension. She took the pills that Dr. Schrady had prescribed, but they only seemed to increase her morbid state of mind.

She was living, she knew, a strange kind of life. The man she loved, the man she knew could make her happy, and make her children happy, did not belong to her, and perhaps never would. Divorce was a long and sordid process; she herself could not quite face the ugly business of starting her own. Perhaps she wasn't meant to be happy. Perhaps she had been too ambitious, both for herself and for her daughters; too vain; too lighthearted. Perhaps there was a punishment waiting. . . .

She was so disturbed when she arrived in New York and found the General was not there to meet her, that she forgot her pride and sent him a telegram. Two days later, he came to see her, looking drawn. His wife was incurably ill, although she might live on for several years, growing gradually worse. Under the circumstances, there could be no question of divorce.

It was a bitter blow for Harriet. Her quick sympathy was for the General, but she had to insist that, under the circumstances, they must stop seeing each other. He agreed reluctantly and Harriet watched him go, half-aware that she was making a mis-take. He was an extremely attractive man, and she knew there were plenty of women who would not have her scruples. But she could not set up high standards for her daughters and then fall short of them herself. She went back to her work. It kept her from thinking during the day. But while the rest of the household slept, there was nothing between her and her thoughts.

Late one night, Lena found her mistress in the kitchen, work-ing with pans and test tubes and a variety of odd materials. After that Lena always came down when she saw the light, work-ing deftly by Harriet's side, until Harriet perfected a salve which was like that she had taken out of the old trunk in the attic. She tested it on her own skin. She had never used, or felt she needed, a salve, but she was sure after a while that her skin was softer and more radiant than it had been since she was a young girl—in spite of relentless insomnia.

She gave a small amount to Madame Hubbard. The older woman pretended to be shocked, but she was back before long asking for more. Harriet's mind was made up. She found a small blue jar, one of her precious collection of blue china that Oscar Wilde had admired in Chicago, and filled it with face cream. Then she telephoned Jim Seymour.

Their relationship had changed during the past year. They were still good friends, but the old intangible tension which Harriet had felt, seemed to have gone. She was glad, for she felt easier in his presence, and more inclined to accept the favors he gave so generously.

He came to see her the same day, as soon as the market closed. She showed him the jar, and explained how she had arrived at the idea. "If both my mother and I find it beneficial, think of other women who might like it."

He picked up the jar and opened it. The salve was scented with Harriet's own delicate perfume. He smiled. "How much will it cost to make in volume?"

"I haven't the slightest idea. I've just managed to get the formula right, I think. I've been working from a very old one that was made for Madame Récamier."

"Who's she?"

"A beauty of Napoleon's time. She never did come over to his side and he feared her influence because of her beauty."

Seymour grunted. "Can you sell this for a dollar and a half?"

"I haven't the slightest idea. I'm not very good at that sort of figuring."

"Hire someone who is. I'll lend you $50,000 to start. Spend all you need. I'm ready to give you up to a quarter of a million dollars. You can call the company Récamier, if you like. You can talk about Madame Récamier in your pamphlets. But there's another beauty whose endorsement will mean more. You must put your own name on the cream, Harriet."

It was the first time he had ever called her by her first name. That was almost as startling as his offer of $50,000.

Harriet insisted that he take stock as collateral, which he agreed to return when she paid back the money. She was always clever at making money, never very good at the details of keeping it. Despite the reputation Jim Seymour had among the "Napoleons" of Wall Street for sharp dealing, it did not occur to her to have the agreement in legal form.

Harriet rented a factory on Sixth Avenue and Thirty-first Street and offices on Park Place. She also continued her decorating service. And, at night, she wrote advertisements:

"How Julie Récamier Preserved Her Beauty for Over Half a Century.

"Julie Récamier was acknowledged to be for over forty years the most beautiful woman in France. Her loveliness was such a power that Napoleon once said of her, 'I fear Madame Récamier's influence against me more than the muskets of a whole army'. . . . For over forty years the women of her most picturesque period marveled and fruitlessly endeavored to ascertain by what means Madame Récamier preserved her transcendentally lovely complexion. The mystery was never revealed and it was by the merest accident I came into possession of the secret. . . . While in Paris many years ago, I suffered greatly from the effects of the sun, and my complexion seemed irretrievably injured. I was stopping at a small private hotel and an old lady (the Countess de C——) sitting opposite me brought me a little pot containing a paste which she had used all her life, a compound made for the celebrated beauty, Julie Récamier. . . ."

Mrs. Ayer hit exactly the right appeal. Within six months, the cream was selling well not only in America, but in Europe. She sent an assistant to England to introduce it. The Princess of Wales herself was enthusiastic and permitted Harriet to use the phrase, "Manufacturer by permission to Her Royal Highness, the Princess of Wales." Harriet then conceived the idea of persuading other famous women of the time to let her use their endorsements in advertising—women like Adelina Patti, Sarah Bernhardt, Lily Langtry, Lillian Russell and Mrs. James Brown Potter. And it was not long before she was lying awake nights planning new additions to the Récamier line: balm, freckle and moth lotion, soap, powder, depilatory, tonic for the blood. . . .

Mrs. Ayer had found the key to making a great deal of money.

Her "cosmetics" were the forerunners of the great beauty businesses of today headed by women, with their names prominently on the shops and products. But in the Victorian '80's, a woman who used her name on any product for sale was immediately declassée. Working in a shop like Sypher's, or having her own decorating and shopping service, was acceptable, because "poor Mrs. Ayer" needed money. She could have been accepted back into society at any time upon a good marriage; for example, to a gentleman like General Grubb. But the use of her own name on a product which was for sale to anybody who put down a dollar and a half, was beyond the bounds of good taste. General Grubb wrote her, sadly and briefly, protesting. She answered him, telling him that it was too late to stop now, she was too involved financially. He did not answer. It was unlike him but Harriet did not have time to worry.

Before the cream was formally launched—the first ad appeared on May 30, 1886—Harriet took Margaret abroad to stay with Blanche Willis Howard. A letter written on March 23, 1886, to Hattie, tells of her plans and includes almost an apologetic mention of her close association with James Seymour. It was on the letterhead of Harriet Hubbard Ayer ["lately with Sypher & Co., artistic furnishings and shopping agency"] and it said:

"SWEETHEART:

"We expect to leave here the 17th of April by *City of Berlin* German line. I have engaged our room, or that is the suite our boss always has. You cannot imagine how good and sweet he is to me, to Margaret and to everyone who belongs to me. You know how I feel about it, that he ought not to depend on me so much, and yet I don't know what he would do without me to come to with his tribulations and sorrows. He seems actually to have no one at home who knows him or sympathies with him except Caddie [his youngest daughter] whom he idolizes.

"I only write to say I love you and that I am up to my eyes in work. M. has come home to stay, until we go. She has just received your letter and Marion's [Marion Smith, Miss Howard's niece] and wishes Miss Smith to understand she is neither a frog-skinner by inclination or profession, simply by accident.

"She is *lovely*. Miss Howard has written me the most adorable letter, will take M. to her home and her heart. Is she not a beautiful creature in every way, and are you not fortunate children? My own little love, I long and long to see you, and I am coming unless some accident—a financial one it will be—prevents. Don't set your heart *too* much on it. You are a bad girl and I will *break your bones* if Miss H.'s measure does not come presently so I can have everything made up for her and finished before we sail.

>   *Addio—t'amo tesoro mio*
>   *Sa Madre.*"

In Paris, one of Harriet's projects was to visit old friends and ask them to let her use their names and pictures in advertisements for the cream.

Adelina Patti was the first person Harriet approached. As she was the foremost singer of her time, perhaps, according to some musicians, of all time, her name meant a great deal. Margaret went with her mother. Today, she remembers the meeting with enchantment. The great prima donna, who was several years older than Harriet, was a tiny child-like woman, with captivating child-like enthusiasms. She was delighted to help Harriet. She was enchanted with her plan to make a balm, and found the face cream *merveilleuse*. The name of Récamier was an inspiration. And the little daughter, whom she had known as a baby, was exquisite.

Harriet insisted that Margaret sing for Mme. Patti. Margaret was not old enough to know how important Patti really was, but she was impressionable enough to feel stage fright. The nuns had admired Margaret's voice and pitch, but Margaret had never sung outside a schoolroom or her own parlor. Worst of all, the instant that she opened her mouth, Mme. Patti's little dog, a white terrier, put its head down on the carpet and howled to heaven.

Patti laughed and told Margaret that the dog only howled when he heard a perfectly pitched voice, that he *always* howled horribly when she sang. The dog was put out of the room and Margaret, comfortable under the great lady's treatment, sang again. Patti tried to persuade Harriet to leave the small girl with her, to study voice, instead of taking her to some stranger in Stuttgart.

But Harriet shook her head. Her friend was kind, and generous. But she did not want to impose. "There will be time enough for her singing later. Right now, I want her to learn to study. Do you know that this great girl can't even read?"

Halfway to Stuttgart, Margaret suffered another attack of stage fright. She didn't want to go to a strange country and live in a German house. The German nurse she had had in New York had been mean; she wanted to stay with mamma and Lena. She promised to work hard and learn to read. She promised mamma anything if mamma would only not make her live with an awful old German woman in a German house. . . .

Blanche Willis Howard changed all that. Within a day, Margaret was captivated, and saw her mother leave without emotion. To this day, Margaret remains grateful to the novelist for many things. She remembers: "The house was on a street called Mörike Strasse, just outside the limits of Stuttgart, near a very high hill which led into a beautiful wood dominated by a high tower. The woods were policed by royal woodsmen and must have been comparatively safe because from the first, I was allowed to go out at any time, even very early in the morning, and roam to my heart's content."

All of Blanche's pupils, even small Margaret, were encouraged to use Blanche's pet nickname, "Wawie"—the Indian word for "white." The cult of Wawie made a deep impression on the little girl. Everyone worshiped Wawie: the wise doctor, the famous guests who came to dinner, the girls who were her pupils, and her young relatives. It was only natural that Margaret should exert herself to please such a marvelous person. And Blanche's enthusiasm for the small girl made Margaret feel rare and important.

The novelist's enthusiasm was not forced. She had plans for Margaret. As she explored the personalities of the young women pupils in her charge, and tried deftly to wean them away from the Victorian attitudes toward home and parents—particularly their mothers—she had been plagued by the thought that too many of these girls had already been shaped beyond her ability to help them. She yearned for a younger child, one who would be more impressionable. Her first glimpse of Margaret had interested her, and Hattie's conversation about her little sister whetted Blanche's interest. She wanted Margaret as an experiment; if, later, she proved to be dull or a bore, she could be shipped back to the arms of her adoring and—Blanche suspected —overpossessive mother. . . .

CHAPTER TWELVE

HARRIET decided to use the Hubbard coat of arms for the Récamier trademark. It was her final gesture of defiance toward "society."

A small number of sophisticated moderns shared her rebellion against the cult of "family." Blanche Willis Howard, in a pleasant little novel called *Tony's Maid*, poked a great deal of fun at the worshipers of name and station. One scene, between two servants in a snobbish hotel in Switzerland, goes like this:

" 'Fam'ly is fam'ly,' said High-Dudgeon.

" 'I don't say it ain't,' his colleague rejoined, disconsolately, 'and when it's all you've got, you'd better make the most of it. But since you've seen so much of it on the market dirt cheap you can't feel as you used to about it. Family! you can buy all you want anywhere. Once you couldn't. Once it was all genuine, your old carved oak, your lozenge panes, your 'scutcheon. But now, when you can buy up a good old name, and even put another pearl on your coronet, and nobody's astonished, or grins, except behind your back, why, all I have to say is, *family's a drug on the market.*' "

In her "artistic furnishings and shopping" business, Harriet
not only had a look behind scenes at the *nouveau riche*, she was
also exposed to those leaders of society who were determined to
shut out "invaders" like the Vanderbilts whose fortunes were
considered too recent to make their owners acceptable. The situation was an extension and exaggeration of Chicago social life,
which Harriet had found ridiculous enough.

The queen of New York society was Mrs. William Astor who
lived at 350 Fifth Avenue, the site of the Empire State building
today. It is said that the term "the 400" was originated because
her ballroom accommodated just four hundred persons, and
only the persons invited to her yearly great ball could properly
be called "social." Not that her parties were particularly exciting: the food was rich and heavy, the music undistinguished,
and the entertainment nil. Mrs. Astor herself, wearing a black
wig (she was losing her hair) and a vast stomacher of jewels,
would preside on a throne at one end of the ballroom with her
favorites of the moment. Mr. Astor was seldom present. His enthusiasm was his yacht, on which it was said Mrs. Astor had
never set foot.

The only other name which held real social magic at the time
was that of Mrs. Stuyvesant Fish, who had a million-dollar man-
sion at 25 East Seventy-eighth Street, decorated in a fashion that
was said to make it "most uncomfortable for anyone without
breeding." Mamie, a tall woman of great poise and little tact,
gave far livelier parties than Mrs. Astor. She once had goldfish
bowls, complete with live fish, on her dinner table instead of
champagne glasses; the fish had to be emptied into other con-
tainers before the champagne could be poured. Her guests
included prominent actors and actresses, a daring innovation, although Harriet had done the same thing years before in Chicago.
But Mamie had position and a fortune so secure that nobody
quite dared say exactly what they thought of her antics, although
Mamie never feared to speak *her* mind. She is reported to have
remarked about Mrs. Theodore Roosevelt, "The wife of the
President, it is said, dresses on $300 a year—and looks it."

It was inevitable, once Récamier Preparations were launched,
that Harriet should come to the attention of the women who

controlled New York society. As a shopper and an expert in
"artistic furnishings," Mrs. Ayer was a few notches above the
butcher or grocer. But as a woman in business, head of a bla-
tantly commercial enterprise, using her family coat of arms on a
commercial product, she was a freak. Women who were unsure
of their social status took great care to pretend they had never
heard of her and would not allow a jar of her cream in their
homes.

Mrs. Fish, however, was secure enough to be curious; she was
a lady who probably would have been curious in any circumstances. With a group of her satellites, she made a trip one
morning to Mrs. Ayer's retail salesroom on Union Square. Mrs.
Fish bought a few jars of the cream. Then she made it plain that
this was not the object of her visit. What she really wanted was
a good look at Harriet Hubbard Ayer.

Mrs. Ayer happened to be in her office. The flustered clerk
ran in with the message. Mrs. Ayer was amused. She swept into
the showroom and let the ladies have a good look. Mrs. Fish was
delighted with her, and never forgot Harriet. Years later, when
Margaret Ayer was singing professionally, Mrs. Fish opened her
home for concerts given by the daughter of Harriet Hubbard
Ayer.

There is no question, however, that Harriet acquired enemies
among both men and women during this period. She was making
a good deal of money, and her beauty was probably at its height.
Hattie remembered that a gentleman in Stuttgart always referred
to her mother as a "full blown rose."

As her business expanded, she found it more and more difficult
to deal with Seymour, who had a tendency to appear in her offices and give orders. She eluded his interferences by carrying a
great many details in her head and keeping some of the most
important papers locked in a closet at home. This was not very
sound business. But what Mrs. Ayer lacked in business sense,
she made up in imagination. She was an instinctive, brilliant advertising writer, and she never lacked for ideas. One of the big
elements in the success of Récamier was her flair for dramatizing.

Here, from a booklet advertising her products, is an example
of her skill. She tells in detail how she discovered the cream,

when she was touring in Europe as a rich man's wife, and how, after the sunburn she suffered from had been improved, she tried to persuade the lady who had given her the cream, the Countess de C——, to sell the formula.

"Finally, I offered her what must have seemed a large sum, and as she was extremely anxious to give something to aid in her church charities and was, like most of the *noblesse* of France just after the Franco-Prussian War, very poor, she consented to sell me the formula and I returned to America with the coveted rule for making the paste which is now known all over the world as Récamier Cream.

"In those days I was a rich woman. I little dreamed that the scrap of paper which contained the directions for an old French skin preservative would be the keystone of a gigantic business. So it proved, for when I found myself absolutely penniless, and in order to support myself and educate my children, I obtained a position in a large bric-a-brac house in New York, often working very late at night. As I have never been a very strong woman, I was under a physician's care frequently.

"One morning my doctor called quite early; he found me at work, having been up all night. After explaining to the doctor, who protested against such a strain 'that it didn't seem worth while to go to bed at 4 A.M.' and listening to a great deal of good advice for wealthy people, but impossible for a woman without a dollar beyond the wages earned by her head and hands to follow, my physician looked at me critically for a moment and said, 'Mrs. Ayer, how in the world do you keep your skin so smooth and fair in spite of loss of sleep, lack of proper exercise and irregular meals? What do you use for your complexion?'

" 'I never use anything,' I replied, 'except a sort of paste or cream which I got in Europe long ago.' I showed the compound to the doctor, who asked what it was composed of, and remarked that it was just the thing women needed, as the ingredients were the best known to science for the preservation and restoration of the skin tissues.

" 'Why don't you make it for sale?' he asked. From this conversation I date the inception of the business which is now known all over the world.

"The success of Récamier Cream naturally attracted the attention of society women and of the most famous professional celebrities. Shortly after it was placed upon the market Mme. Adelina Patti-Nicolini sent to me to know if it were chemically a pure preparation—she feared it might contain lead or arsenic or some of the many poisonous ingredients used in empirical compositions. I called upon Mme. Patti and satisfied the most charming of *prime donne* by showing her the chemists' analysis of Récamier Cream and made her my firm, enthusiastic friend. Mme. Patti was so delighted with the results of using Récamier Cream that she sent again for me and asked me to make a liquid which should be harmless and at the same time take the place of an article she was then using which gave her face an unnatural and whitewashed appearance. . . ."

Woven among the romancing was the harsh truth that her health was not strong, and that her doctor was treating her for a variety of ailments all of which today might be diagnosed as the result of nervous tension. But, like many people today, she found it was impossible to stop. She worked at her offices by day and sat up most of the night writing advertisements.

One of them, which ran in the *New York World,* is interesting because it uses an approach which is still in favor. She also included drawings of the young lady in question "before" and "after" treatment.

"MYSTERIOUS DISAPPEARANCE OF A NEW YORK SOCIETY GIRL

THE ELDEST DAUGHTER OF A WELL-KNOWN FIFTH AVENUE MILLIONAIRE SUDDENLY DIS-APPEARS FROM VIEW—GOSSIP ALONE THE FOUNDATION FOR THE STORY OF HER ELOP-MENT—THE FACTS AS THEY ARE NOW RECORDED

"About six weeks ago Miss Jeanne Roosevelte, eldest daughter of Mrs. Van Rensselaer Roosevelte, suddenly disappeared from society. Her family were absolutely unapproachable. To all newspaper interviewers word was sent that the family 'had nothing to say.'

"Suddenly it was announced that Miss Roosevelte had returned as mysteriously as she had disappeared. It was also stated that during her mysterious seclusion she had undergone some magical process which had transformed her from a noticeably plain girl, with regular features but most unfortunate complexion, into a radiant and faultless beauty. There being, it was acknowledged, but one process capable of effecting such a transformation, a reporter was at once sent to interview the only woman in America who could be held responsible for this seven days' wonder—Mrs. Harriet Hubbard Ayer—at her offices.

"Mrs. Ayer was found at her desk. She paused in her work and said: 'You asked me to tell you the truth about Miss Roosevelte's disappearance and marvelous acquisition of beauty during that time. Ordinarily I should be obliged to refuse to do so, as I never give facts of this kind to the public. Miss Roosevelte and her parents, however, assure me that they feel it but right that all women should know by what simple means a very plain girl has been transformed—for there is no other word for it—into a beauty. Hearing of the success of the Récamier Preparations and reading, not only letters from Mrs. James Brown Potter, Mrs. Langtry, the Jersey Lily, but also scores of unpublished notes from well-known society women, notes from members of the Vanderbilt, Astor, Kernochan, Goelet, Lorillard, Beckwith—in fact, every one of the most aristocratic families of old New York, Miss Roosevelte asked me candidly if I thought it possible for her to be rid of the terrible blemishes on her face. I assure you,' continued Mrs. Ayer, 'when I looked closely at her face I was almost discouraged, I never saw a more dreadful-looking skin. It was coarse, blotchy, and with a dreadful outbreak of little white-headed pimples across her pretty brow and about her chin; worse than all, her nose was covered with blackheads, and they had so enlarged the pores of the skin that they were the size of a pin-head. I felt very sorry for Miss Roosevelte, very anxious to help her, very confident of the merits of the Récamier Preparations, but I must confess I was a little frightened at the undertaking. However, I said to myself: Why, if we but improve such a skin, we shall do wonders! So I agreed if Miss R. would follow my instructions to the letter, I would attempt her cure.

She was but too willing and the next morning she started for the farmhouse of an old friend of the family, accompanied by her maid alone, and carrying with her a goodly supply of the Récamier Preparations. I will not weary you with an account of the treatment, which was aided by fresh air, long walks, plenty of sleep and very simple food; and lo! Miss Roosevelte walks into my office one morning, so blooming, so lovely, and with the complexion of your ideal Aurora.

"'Here,' said Mrs. Ayer, 'is Miss Roosevelte's picture, taken expressly for *her dear friend, Mrs. Ayer.*'

"'That is all there is to it,' continued this busy woman, as she broke the seal of a long letter from Adelina Patti."—*New York World.*

It might be added that, at the time Lily Langtry gave Mrs. Ayer a long letter endorsing Récamier Preparations—"they will remove tan, sunburn, and the many annoying blemishes women, especially in the changeable climate of this country, are subjected to"—she was living in Mrs. Ayer's Thirteenth Street house, which had been leased for her American debut. Mrs. Ayer left no stone unturned—in business.

CHAPTER THIRTEEN

D URING the years when Harriet's products—and Harriet herself—were becoming world-famous, her personal life was far from happy. Her children were in the care of Blanche Willis Howard, and although Harriet saw them frequently on her numerous trips abroad, and gave them holidays in London and Paris, she was increasingly ill at ease about the arrangement. On June 2, 1887, just before Hattie was due to return home permanently, she wrote her:

"Before I forget it, tell Wawie to draw this next month on me at 39 and 41 Park Place, the Récamier Manufacturing Co., through the Bank of New York. I do not exactly grasp it but with all the money I have sent W. she drew $485 in April and now in May, $333, as I understand it, for M.'s expenses alone. You can easily see that this is something appalling. I cannot understand it to save my life. I am so anxious to see you, which God willing will not be very long, and to hear what you say about Margaret. Do you think I *should* leave her with Wawie another year? How shall I *ever* get her away? Is it not awful? This is not a very satisfactory letter but I am nearly beside myself with work, day and night, and weary beyond endurance almost. . . . Kiss the babe for me and tell her I sent her some books and a new coatee for her birthday. I hope she was happy. God bless you both. I long and long to see your blessed little faces once again. . . . Of course, M. will come to London with you when I meet you. I wish she could come back with us all but right now this is the critical time and I am so anxious and weary. . . . Did I write you I had had a final goodbye with the Ginger? I never got over that affair between him and Mrs. L. and I never cared for him afterwards. That is my unfortunate disposition when once I turn against a person, Gibraltar is not more invulnerable than I. I have never been able to forgive him for discussing me with Mrs. L. It simply *killed* me. . . . I long so to see you it seems to me I shall go mad. . . . HHA."

The General's wife had died the year before. If Harriet's divorce had been final at the time, she probably would have married him immediately, in spite of certain differences that had come between them. Friction between them was perhaps inevitable because of the conspicuous part Seymour played in her life and because the General's name had been linked with various other women. Both protested their innocence, but he continued to believe that she was too friendly with Jim Seymour, just as she quite sincerely believed that he was not true to her.

She was also deeply worried about her suit for divorce, which was being treated by the Chicago press as a scandal. In those days, it was a man's world, indeed. Although she had evidence that Herbert had traveled with various women, introducing them as "Mrs. Ayer," she would only be able to obtain the children if he did not contest. When the divorce finally went through, she won the custody of the children by default, subject to a modification of the order in the future, in case Mr. Ayer ever cared to fight the ruling.

While the divorce was pending she persuaded the General to take a trip abroad, with the prospect of entrusting his daughter Effie to Blanche Willis Howard—Harriet reasoned that this would give Hattie and Effie an opportunity to become acquainted, and Effie would be there to take care of Margaret after Hattie graduated from the Conservatory of Music. However, the General came home with Effie after a short trip and warned Harriet brusquely that she had made a mistake in picking Miss Howard as the custodian of her daughters.

Harriet—even before her letter of June 2—was nervously exhausted. She herself was not completely uncritical of Blanche Howard, but the General's cavalier attitude irritated her and when she pressed him for an explanation, he refused to give it. Years later, he told Margaret Hubbard Ayer that Blanche had exerted all her charms in an effort to fascinate him; that one night, after other dinner guests had left and she had urged him to stay for a minute, she had disappeared into her room and come back wearing a revealing pink silk kimono. ("I've had invitations to the waltz," he told Margaret grimly, "but never one quite so blatant. I took Effie and came home. I tried to get your mother to take you two children away—but, of course, I couldn't tell her why.")

Actually, Harriet being Harriet, the General could have told her exactly why he did not approve of Blanche Howard, and Harriet would have understood. She was no prig. But she had extremely high standards, and it would have finished Wawie, so far as she was concerned, if she had known what had happened.

Harriet's letters show how strongly she felt about correct and womanly behavior. One, dated shortly after Hattie went to Stuttgart, reads:

"A good true woman is the most perfect work of God and Nature, a bad one is worse than any devil you can conceive of. You see, whatever people may be themselves, they honor above everything else a good woman—even Mr. Seymour who is a man of the world and, I must say, I have judged as one of not too high principles.

"What you write of L. T. pains and shocks me inexpressibly because I *know* she is taking a mistaken, disturbed way of life. It is natural and right that a woman should attract men, quite natural and right that she should desire to be attractive to them, but in an honest and legitimate way. Be as gracious and charming as you will, my own, and remember always that the perfect sweetness of perfect maidenhood, the exquisite bloom of virginal purity never did and never can outlive one serious or *un*-serious flirtation. A girl who talks openly about exerting herself to fascinate men as L. T. does, certainly cannot understand what she is proposing to do. For, mark you, darling, the man is not injured by anything of this nature—unfortunately (or so I think) the moral code of our day has no article in it requiring purity in men —but it is certain that the basest of them desires a pure woman for his wife, and the only way he can tell a good woman from a vain, frivolous and weak one is by her modesty and chastity. So the girl who sets out to fascinate the other sex plays with a deadly fire and always gets burned, and always carries the marks for all the rest of the world to see for all the days of her life."

At any rate, the General was apparently too much of a gentleman to talk about an attempt to seduce him and Harriet's sense of fairness was offended by what she thought was unreasonable prejudice. She was delighted with the children's progress—Hattie was a charming, cultured young lady and Margaret had not only learned to read, but was wolfing down every book she could get her hands on, even mythology. She answered General Grubb sharply—and more friction developed between them.

The reticences between the two eventually were the cause of their breakup. Harriet never told him of the money she had borrowed from Jim Seymour, but perhaps he suspected more than she guessed, which might account for his bitter objections to her business. Certainly, after being very much in love, they grew farther and farther apart. A draft of an undated letter Harriet wrote to him—and probably sent—indicates pathetically how much she loved him, and how their estrangement hurt her. Written in pencil, on fine-lined paper, it was found among her possessions at her death:

"I do not think you should be perplexed. To me the situation is despairingly clear but you are as blameless as mortal can well be. As to your 'mind' we both know it to be something more than intelligent and for your heart, dear, I will candidly tell you I think it exists warm and human but *not* for any woman I know of. I have known that for a long time. If one could go back three weeks or three days or three hours even! But you and I know we cannot, though we try in bitter anguish, go back one second in this rapid flight of ours toward the forever. One may say 'we will begin all over—these days and nights may be blotted out'—he or she lies who even makes a semblance of belief in such folly. It seems bravest to me to look the thing in the face and to bear it as I may—to pretend that it is not would but make the matter worse—I am not strong enough to do battle against the real and fight phantoms as well. Of course it was bound to come to me sometime, I have always known that, I have even thought it had once or twice but only for a few hours, I have tried time and time again to believe it so, but one can no more woo it than one can drive it off. When it comes it is so much stronger than all else. I smile as I recollect all I have read about men and women who controlled this emotion, whose *principles* would not permit them to love where they knew it to be wrong. Principles are very good things to have in times of peace, but when we meet the one person capable of moving us through head or heart or senses, if we be not utterly crippled and confined by the absurd conventionalities of the mob, we whistle our principles down the wind as we flick the dust from a garment. I know few men and women will own up to this but I also know that every living sentient creature must at times feel it too bitterly true. So far as I myself am concerned I am not sorry. Joys and sorrows may be but sensations and death the one sure thing. Yet I would not if I could forget the few moments in which I have clearly seen Life's wondrous possibilities. I knew they were not for me. I knew it was quite hopeless from the first. It did not make it less dear. I never attempted to fight it, I knew it would be useless. I also knew you must understand it. I have tried to think myself to blame, but that also is absurd. Certainly, I was not looking for this thing and it never started from a small beginning. From the first, it was overwhelming and I could do nothing but wonder and be glad, so though we never see each other again I insist that you must not regret it, for me. Life will not, cannot, be harder for me with the conception I now have of its possible pleasures. . . ."

Already hurt and humiliated, Harriet was completely unprepared for another blow, which fell when she met Hattie in England to bring her home: Hattie announced that she wanted permission to marry Lewis Seymour.

Harriet was flabbergasted. Hattie was almost eighteen, a reasonable age for marriage. But Harriet tried to fight for time. She planned trips for Hattie, entertainments, and spoke of clothes: "You must wear white all next winter—morning, noon and night—white flannels and cashmeres for every day, surahs and silks for evening. I want you to have lots of pretty clothes and happy years of girlhood before you think of marrying."

What degree of rebellion against her mother lay behind Hattie's decision to marry Lewis Seymour, it is difficult to say. Harriet did not dislike Lewis—nor ever did. But she saw more clearly than her daughter that he was very much under the influence of his father; moreover she believed that a marriage between Hattie and Lewis would have in it the same elements of failure that had existed in her own marriage to Herbert. Harriet blamed herself for bringing the two young people together in the first place, and for throwing Lewis and Hattie together in Stuttgart in the fall of 1886, when she had allowed Lewis to accompany her on one of her trips abroad. A letter written from London shows how little Harriet suspected the likelihood of any affection between the boy and her daughter. On Hotel Bristol stationery, it reads:

"DEAR LOVE:

"At last! Here we are, all worn out and total wrecks. Now don't be too cut up because I must go to Paris first—I have commissions which must be filled. The minute I get them started we will take the first train for Stuttgart. Now don't scream when you read this. *Lewis* is with us. Just say a young gentleman friend of Mama's is with her as he was ill and came for a change. I want you to receive Lewis nicely. I have a particular reason which I will explain to you later. . . ."

The "particular reason" for Lewis' attendance was, of course, Harriet's debt to Jim Seymour. While Harriet finished her commissions in Paris, Lewis stayed on in Stuttgart until her return to Germany. She had been surprised when she thanked Hattie for being so kind to "poor" Lewis, to see bright color flood the girl's delicate complexion. But she still suspected nothing. Now she was amazed and hurt that her daughter had kept the secret from her so long.

Harriet said little in front of Blanche Howard about Hattie's engagement for she discovered, to her surprise, that the novelist knew all about it and had encouraged the liaison. But on the way home, on a steamer trip that seemed endless, she tried to point out to her daughter how ill-matched she and Lewis were. She tried to warn her that, as soon as physical attraction between them began to wane, he would seem like a very different person. Like many mothers, Harriet was faced with the impossible task of making an infatuated girl understand the difference between passion and real love.

Hattie paid little attention.

In her desperation, Harriet said things she later regretted. They returned to haunt her a few years later. But she was not able to move her child. Even before they had landed in New York, the Seymours had reached Madame Hubbard and won her as another ally.

Sadly, Harriet accepted a call from Mrs. Seymour. They had almost nothing in common, and Harriet wondered painfully if Lewis' mother liked the match any better than Hattie's mother. But Mrs. Seymour was too afraid of her husband to express herself. "I found her commonplace, but not common," she wrote Mrs. Lyon, damning Mrs. Seymour in a sentence.

Hattie refused to argue with her mother. She simply did as she pleased, living her life in a sealed compartment into which Harriet could not break.

Then Harriet made another mistake—the worst of all. She went to call on Jim Seymour in his elaborate Wall Street office. It had been a long time since she had asked a favor of him, and she knew that he half-resented her independence. He enjoyed doing things for people, keeping them in debt to him. She was not at all sure what Seymour's reaction would be to her request to separate Hattie and Lewis, but she was sure of one thing. If she could bring Jim Seymour around to forbidding the marriage,

for any reason, Lewis would not dare to defy his father. And
Hattie would get over him and some day be grateful.

So, on a humid day late in August, dressed in starched white,
with white kid gloves and high button shoes, and a big white
hat—plus the violets that still arrived each morning from General
Grubb's greenhouse—Harriet went to see Jim Seymour. Walking
down Wall Street, which was already beginning to look like a
stone canyon, under a dull sky darkened by the net of telephone
and telegraph wires that enclosed the business area, she felt suddenly afraid. She tried to tell herself it was the depressing
weather; the lack of sleep these last few nights, fretting over
Hattie; even the powders, which seemed to depress her without
easing the pain of her bad nervous headaches. But she knew it
was something more. After all her pride in being free and self-
supporting, she had been trapped by her own ambition.

At least, she realized what it meant to be "beholden" to Jim
Seymour.

He was looking happy. He came from hot weather country, he
liked to tell people, and hot weather agreed with him. Besides,
he always said he made more money in hot weather because then
other people were apt to be careless.

Years later, she told Margaret about the circumstances of the
interview. But she never would say what happened, or why she
would never see Seymour alone afterwards and threw herself
fiercely into paying back every penny she owed him. In fact, she
gave her consent to Hattie's engagement to Lewis on one condition—that she would wait a year. The purpose of this was not to
try to change Hattie's mind about the young man, although Harriet would have been happy to have had that occur, but to give
her time to be rid of her obligation to his father.

It was only after Harriet's death that Margaret found out, by
accident, some part of what had gone on at that interview between Harriet and James Seymour. Margaret was employed as
a columnist on *The New York World*, and frequently went out
on assignment with a photographer whose named she remembers
as La Grange. One day, after they had worked together frequently, La Grange asked Margaret:

"Miss Ayer, did you ever know why Jim Seymour tried to ruin your mother?"

Margaret told him that she never understood just why, nor had her sister Hattie. Then La Grange told her that he had been working for Seymour in the summer of 1887. He saw Mrs. Ayer go into his office and, a little while later, noticed that the door was closed. He was busy at a desk, going over some papers, and thought no more about it until he saw Mrs. Ayer standing in front of him, leaning on his desk and looking so white he was afraid she was going to faint. He got up and made her sit down, while he hurried out and found a hack to take her home.

Afterwards, Seymour called him in on another matter. But he was in a bad temper and finally he asked if he, La Grange, had seen Mrs. Ayer. La Grange explained what had happened. Seymour blurted out in coarse language that Mrs. Ayer had refused to become his mistress after leading him on, and that he was going to make her pay for treating him that way, if it was the last thing he ever did.

La Grange, who was very young at the time, thought Seymour was merely making angry threats. But what happened in the following years proved that Seymour had meant every word he said, and that probably he had said the same things to Harriet and she, knowing Seymour well, had realized he was in dead earnest.

That autumn, she sent Hattie on a trip to Chicago, to visit Mrs. Lyon and other old friends. Undoubtedly, she still hoped that Harriet would change her mind about Lewis, or meet someone else who would drive Seymour's son out of her mind. But silence followed Hattie's departure and Harriet, in her overwrought condition, was driven to write what now reads like a letter sure to alienate her daughter still more:

"New York, October 19, 1887

"My Dear Love:

"You have been gone nearly a week and I have not heard from you any more than though you had disappeared from the face of the earth. Don't you think darling you might find time to send your poor old mother a telegram or a postal card? I cannot tell you how hurt I have been to know that Lewis was hearing daily from you and that you could not give one five minutes to your mother. I have only two children in the world, and all my life is passed in trying to make you happy. Even now while you are away I am doing double work, furnishing Mrs. Philburn's flat, to make the money I so gladly spend for your pleasure trip. I do not intend to reproach you, my child, for I know at the most you are but thoughtless—but when you are my age you will see how hard it is to feel that the child you have made an idol of— and for whom your greatest pleasure is to toil—the child you have never denied anything small or great if within your power to grant—can forget you while she remembers her lover whom she did not even know three little years ago. Don't think me hard, dear, I am only grieved, I have only you two children and if you can so soon forget me in the name of a pitiful God to whom shall I look for remembrance? There are many letters for you and Granny is inconsolable about you—she says she never missed anything or person so much and looks upon you as the brightest spot in her life. Give my love to all and enjoy every moment.

Maman qui t'aime."

"Remember I am not scolding but I am hurt, and particularly so because everyone asks me constantly what I hear from you!"

CHAPTER FOURTEEN

ON MARCH 13, 1888, the *New York Herald* reported: "A great white hurricane roared all day through New York yesterday and turned the comfortable city into a wild and bewildering waste of snow and ice. . . . When day broke the city presented an amazing appearance. . . . At every turn could be seen these deserted vehicles."

This was the famous blizzard of 'eighty-eight. A great hush fell over the city. There were no carriages, no public transportation moved, and those who ventured out had their progress hampered and muffled by the great drifts. Telegraph and telephone wires had been ripped from the poles and cross-arms; when they were replaced, the city fathers decided to put them underground, which in itself was a great civic improvement. New Yorkers were isolated even from neighbors half a block away. Candles and kerosene lamps were brought out of attics. Households suffered from shortages of food and fuel.

But to Harriet, it was almost a respite. She and Hattie and Lena were shut off from the world. There was no use in worrying about her office, so she and Hattie spent hours talking about themselves and the old days in Chicago, and Hattie's experiences abroad. They were closer together than they had been for years and, despite the hardships, Harriet's health improved. She was sleeping better, and when she had a restless night Hattie would often sit up with her. Wrapped in blankets, Harriet opened her heart to her daughter and told her about her childhood, her marriage, the fire, her reasons for divorcing Herbert. She had never talked to anyone so confidingly before, and she hoped desperately that her own mistakes might point a moral to her daughter.

But when the snow began to melt, and the horse cars and trains began to move normally, Hattie's first step was to pack her bags and go for a visit to the Seymours' in East Orange. Harriet gave up and again used work to push everything else out of her mind. After nearly a month of disorganization, her office was in a turmoil of unfilled orders and canceled shipments. Tempers flared. One assistant—a Mrs. Mason—who had been with Harriet for several years overstepped her authority and then told Harriet that she was acting on suggestions from Jim Seymour. Harriet promptly discharged her, and took over the clerical work she had been doing.

As summer approached, Harriet's health began to grow worse. The feeling of exhaustion "beyond endurance" came back, and her nights were filled with regret for the things she had done and those she had left undone. After Harriet's death, Margaret found among her mother's papers an unfinished letter written during that time to her. If she had received even the fragment, it might have helped counteract the influence of Blanche Howard. For it is Harriet at her most charming:

"My Sweet Little Maid:

"Do you think Mamma forgets her little sweetheart because she is so lazy about writing? You must not, dear heart. Mamma is so sure you are happy and well that she puts off writing, saying to herself 'tomorrow, when I am not quite so tired'. . . . Enfin, Hattie has told you all about the little French baby named for you? It was here to call on me this A.M. and behaved very well only it forgot to ask after you, but its Mamma sent you all sorts of nice messages. I sent it a complete layette from you, and it was all dressed up in its new clothes when it called. It looked just like a little Indian baby all rolled up in a little round bundle, a very convenient way for the mothers to carry the little snips around, but I don't think the babies can enjoy it, do you?

"Hattie and I talk about you and your sweet Wawie all the time and we love you both so much that we really don't see how you can get on so well without us and we ourselves miss you so much and long to see you that if we had wings we should long ago have been hovering around Wawie's castle, if ever you do hear a flip-flop outside your window, open quickly, for I may have turned into a big, big . . ."

The letter ends there. Margaret has no recollection of ever having received it. During the spring, Harriet also wrote a letter to Blanche Willis Howard hinting that she felt it was time for Margaret to come home. She planned to bring her back during the summer, but Margaret came down with scarlet fever and, while hurriedly packing to go to her, Harriet collapsed. Anxiety for Margaret, on top of the long strain of overwork, broke her physically. Dr. Schrady sent her to Montclair, New Jersey, to spend the summer in the nursing home of Dr. J. W. Pinkham. And Blanche Willis Howard wrote so reassuringly of her devotion to Margaret during her illness that Harriet felt conscience-stricken about having warned her that she was going to take her younger daughter away from her care.

Margaret was then nine years old and her illness still remains in her mind as a happy time, one of her happiest with Wawie: "I had never known such devotion. Read to by the hour, told the most wonderful stories, so that ancient mythology seemed to come to life. . . . And in the next room, when I wanted it, the most beautiful music played for me on the grand piano by Howard, Wawie's talented nephew. Every afternoon there was ice cream, a luxury in those days, at least in Stuttgart. I was being tied to Miss Howard by bonds of gratitude and affection and, as the illness lasted for a long time, with some distressing complications, I grew actually to worship her.

"We had some strange conversations, strange, that is, now that I think of them. But at the time, everything she did was perfect, and made a deep impression on me. Once she said:

'You are going to be very tall, Margaret. Strange, isn't it? Your mother and father are both short. Now, General Grubb is tall and his hair is curly, like yours. But your mother's is straight, isn't it?' I had no idea what Miss Howard was trying to imply, until later, but I never forgot her words. . . .

"Mamma wrote every day, but Miss Howard sometimes forgot to give me her letters and, to be honest, I forgot her, since my idol was always there to answer every childish problem. We used to talk about the days when I was a tiny girl in Chicago, and Blanche said: 'Your mother had a great many men friends, did she not?' I answered that she did, indeed, and they were all very nice to me. I can still remember Wawie's sigh and the sad look in her eyes as she said: 'Poor child. Well, perhaps you will be able to act when you grow up.'"

While Margaret was ill, Blanche encouraged her not to use her eyes, and she did not have to write letters. This was a great relief, for ordinarily she wrote her mother every Sunday. "I hated Sunday for that reason. If I made a mistake in a letter, particularly in spelling, I had to copy it ten times. My letters became a chore, stiff and infantile, due to my search for words I *could* spell. Even so, many lovely Sunday afternoons were spent at the writing table, beginning a new letter every time I made a mistake."

After her illness, Margaret felt she owed her life to Miss Howard, and dreaded the day that she might have to leave her. The first time Wawie put her in her room to write her Sunday letter to her mother, she was furious and rebelled violently. Blanche stared at the little girl, smiling.

"I've been hoping you wouldn't see your mother for what she is. But you're growing up, I guess. I couldn't have kept it from you much longer. However, we can't disappoint her entirely. She knows you are well enough now to write to her."

"But what can I say?"

"Sit down, dear, and I'll tell you. We'll get it over quickly and you can be free to play."

Margaret even then realized that Blanche Howard had special powers. Her eyes, slightly protruding, had an hypnotic effect and it often amused her to demonstrate her power. The hypnotism

game became a favorite with her charges at the *pension* and
Blanche Howard did not discourage them. No one was as successful at imposing her will as the novelist, and sometimes she
exerted this strange power over Margaret and the doctor for
other purposes than amusement.

There are some indications that the handsome doctor was emotionally weak; and the small girl was volatile, emotional, affectionate. It was easy for anyone as clever as Blanche Howard to
make her absolutely dependent. Only occasionally was the
strange, morbid side of the brilliant novelist disclosed. One
night, after the sinking of a famous steamship, Miss Howard
came to Margaret's bed at eight o'clock—the child's bedtime—
and talked steadily until eleven o'clock, managing to make
Margaret really believe that the defects in her character were
the mysterious reasons behind the sinking and loss of life.

Hattie decided to be married right after Thanksgiving, and
Margaret would have liked very much to see her sister's wedding. Harriet also longed to have her younger daughter present,
but did not want her to see her father. Not only had Hattie
invited Herbert to the wedding, but the Seymours were paying
his expenses.

After a consultation with Dr. Schrady, Harriet, who was still
far from well, decided that as soon as the wedding was over, she
and Lena would go abroad to get Margaret, and the three of
them would spend the rest of the winter in some sunny spot in
Italy. She wrote Margaret a long, affectionate letter, assuring
her that "you and I will stay as long as we like, and after we are
both strong and well again, we will go back to our little house on
Thirteenth Street and Mamma will never leave her darling
again."

That letter must have startled Blanche Howard into action.
Harriet, in all innocence, was playing directly into Jim Seymour's
hands.

Hattie was married on a snowy Saturday late in November
from the house on Thirteenth Street. It was a simple ceremony,
with only the family present, but Harriet had massed the house
with flowers, much as she had done for her own wedding to

Herbert. Herbert, looking small and seedy, gave the bride away, but kept out of Harriet's way, for which she was grateful.

By pushing herself to exhaustion, she had managed somehow to pay back every cent of the money she had borrowed from Jim Seymour. She was able to look him in the face without flinching. But when Hattie went gaily down the steps of the house, clinging to her brand-new husband and the rest of the Seymours hurried away soon afterwards, gathering Herbert in their wake, Harriet felt utterly alone and bereft. It did not cheer her to know that Hattie and Lewis were expecting to live in a wing of the big house in East Orange with his mother and father. Harriet was glad she had only a few days to wait before sailing for Europe.

The passage was rough, and took nearly two weeks, so she and Lena did not arrive in Paris until December 15. Blanche Howard was there to meet them. Harriet had expected Margaret, too; but Blanche explained that Margaret wanted her mother to come to Stuttgart for Christmas—a big, wonderful German Christmas with a huge tree and presents. Harriet did not have the heart to refuse, although Dr. Schrady had warned her against the German climate, especially in winter. She was terrified when she coughed up blood her first morning in Paris. She cabled Dr. Schrady, who cabled back recommending the famous Paris physician, Dr. Charcot, who specialized in nervous troubles.

Dr. Charcot did not want her to go to Germany, either, but Blanche Howard insisted that she would take the best possible care of Harriet and promised to send her to Italy the day after the holiday. She was convincing, as always, and the doctor was no more proof against her charms than many other people.

The next spring, in a trial heard before Judge Daly in the Court of Common Pleas, which was reported at length in the New York newspapers and afforded Mrs. Ayer's enemies much lively amusement, Mrs. Ayer gave her own version of this incident, as follows: "In pursuance of Dr. Schrady's instructions I consulted Dr. Charcot, the eminent specialist in Paris. He advised me to go south to Italy and gave me prescriptions, medicine and directions. Miss Howard had come up from Stuttgart and was very anxious that I visit her at her home there, where

my little girl has been for several years. Dr. Charcot consented
that I should go there for four days. Miss Howard started from
Paris with us.

"After the train left I discovered that my satchel which contained Dr. Charcot's medicine, prescriptions and directions had
mysteriously disappeared. When we reached Stuttgart, Miss
Howard began at once to urge me to call in Dr. von Teuffel
who, she was sure, would cure me. Dr. von Teuffel had been
an intimate friend and almost daily visitor at Miss Howard's
for eleven years. She had told me so much of his wonderful
skill that I consented to try him for insomnia. Now, mark that
we reached Stuttgart on December 22, and on the same day Miss
Howard cabled her employers in this country: 'Treatment begins
December 26,' which was the day I intended to leave for the
South. I have that message."

At the time, however, Harriet had no real reason to be suspicious of Blanche Howard, and Blanche was shrewd enough
to make sure that she would find nothing suspicious. Harriet
was installed in the charming downstairs guest room which
Margaret had used during her illness. Margaret was overjoyed
to see her mother and sat on the foot of the bed, alternately
chattering and bouncing to her knees in excitement. Smiling,
Blanche sent her out of the room—"You can spend all the time
in the world with your mother tomorrow"—and brought Harriet
a very sweet cup of cocoa. Ordinarily, she did not approve of
cocoa, but she had ordered the maid, Walpurga, to make it that
night for one specific reason: Dr. von Teuffel had told her that
chocolate and sugar masked the bitter flavor of sedatives.

As Harriet grew sleepy, Blanche fixed her strange pale eyes
on the woman in bed and said softly, "You must trust me. People are trying to harm you. Don't ask me how I know. I just
do. Stay here with Margaret and me, where you will be safe."

The warning had exactly the effect Blanche Howard intended.
Exhausted, Harriet put herself in the novelist's hands. She sank
into semi-drugged lethargy, content that she was at last surrounded by people who loved her: little Margaret, Lena, Blanche
Howard, even the gentle Dr. von Teuffel, who came to see her
several times each day. On Christmas night, Blanche Howard

convinced Harriet that she should try his treatment; he had made "several miraculous cures using a drug named sulfonal."

Sulfonal was a new hypnotic drug used in small doses in cases of sleeplessness, in larger doses for insanity. Dr. Schrady had once recently prescribed it for Harriet. She had studied enough chemistry in search of cosmetic formulas to know that in careless hands sulfonal could be extremely dangerous. Its harm lay in the length of time the body needed to throw off its effects; with heavy doses, the effects were cumulative. But the sedatives Blanche Howard mixed with Harriet's evening cocoa had left her listless. The very thought of attempting a long train ride to Italy made her tired. She agreed to start Dr. von Teuffel's "cure" the day after Christmas. That was all Blanche Howard wanted.

It is difficult in retrospect to evaluate Dr. von Teuffel's role in the events that followed. Certainly, sulfonal was a recognized drug, in favor with European doctors, widely used in nervous troubles. A medical book of a slightly later period warns specifically of its danger: "Because the sulfonal groups are absorbed from the intestinal tract, the effects are slow in disappearing. Culmination may occur during continuous administration producing toxic effects and poisoning. Death from overdosage would be due to failure of respiration and circulation."

European doctors of that era were considerably more casual ("advanced" was the word they used) about drugs than American physicians; some were addicts themselves. There is no reason, however, to suspect that of Dr. von Teuffel. However, it seems impossible to deny that he was guilty of a mistaken diagnosis, at the least. But Miss Howard had convinced him that he was dealing with a dangerous alcoholic and melancholic who needed restraint and constant sedation.

Almost as soon as the treatment began, Harriet grew worse. The only person in the household who saw clearly what was going on was Harriet's maid, Lena. Later, Margaret was able to reconstruct the situation and realize how deeply she herself was under Blanche Howard's influence. But while the "treatment" was taking place, the Negro maid was alone in her knowledge.

Blanche Howard had had no experience with Negroes, so

instinctively Lena protected herself—and her mistress—by pretending to be both illiterate and stupid. Her ignorance of German helped so far as the other servants were concerned. With Miss Howard, Lena rolled her eyes and pretended to know "nothin' about nothin'." It was more difficult to pretend to Margaret, because Lena loved the little girl. But Margaret was so disturbed and upset that she paid little attention to her mother's maid.

Blanche, if she underestimated Lena, had not discounted Margaret. Immediately after the treatment was started, Margaret was horrified to find: "Mamma lay in a sort of stupor, hardly knowing me and often incapable of speech. At first, on 'good days,' she was able to get up and come to dinner, but that soon stopped. My anguish was acute, but so was my curiosity. Miss Howard knew me so well that she didn't need to ask questions. One evening, she took me into the dining room and pointed to the decanter of whisky on the sideboard.

"'Poor child, see—it is full tonight. Look at it tomorrow morning and you will know what is wrong with your poor mamma.'

"As soon as I dressed the next morning, I rushed to the dining room. The decanter was empty. It never occurred to me to doubt Wawie. And my mother lay in bed, incapable of speech or movement. I pulled at her, trying to make her get up. Suddenly, she fell off onto the floor and lay there, inert, a horrible sight. I screamed, and Lena rushed in."

In the midst of the horror and confusion, Lena could only guess at all that was going on. She dared not trust Margaret, for Margaret was now completely under the influence of Miss Howard. Nor could she confide in Mrs. Ayer, for her lucid moments were far too brief. Eventually, Lena decided to appeal to Hattie. Hattie had never been as close to Lena as Margaret. But Lena had known Hattie when she was a girl, and she felt positive that Hattie would not stand by and do nothing if her mother were ill in a foreign country.

One afternoon, she slipped out of the house and walked into town. She hunted until she found a shop which she had seen in the ride from the station; there was a sign in the window: "English spoken." A Negro was a great curiosity in Europe in those days. The German shopkeeper and his wife were only too delighted to aid her. They went to the cable office, and helped her send a cable to Mrs. Lewis Seymour in East Orange:

"Mrs. Ayer is being treated by Dr. von Teuffel and growing steadily worse. I fear she may die. Please telegraph what to do. LENA RAYMOND."

Lena paid for it out of her own money and went home to wait prayerfully for the answer. It did not come for three days, while Lena hardly took her eyes off the front gate, waiting for a messenger. Finally she saw him from Harriet's bedroom. She was downstairs running out in the snow to intercept the cable before Miss Howard or Dr. Teuffel could get it. Sure enough, it was addressed to Lena Raymond. She hid it in her pocket and raced up to the tiny bedroom in the servants' quarters which she shared with the cook. She closed the door and locked it. Then, with trembling hands, she opened the message.

It read: "Consider Teuffel treatment excellent and recommend continue indefinitely. GEORGE SCHRADY."

Lena let the cable flutter to the floor. Then she sank down beside it, and read it again. Whoever Mrs. Ayer's enemies were, it was obvious that Blanche Willis Howard was in touch with them, that they were working together from both sides of the Atlantic. It seemed also cruelly obvious that Mrs. Ayer's daughters were, probably innocently, involved in the plot against her, whatever the plot might be. Lena was sure there was a plot, but refused to believe that Hattie knew about it. And, of course, Margaret was too little to know anything. . . .

CHAPTER FIFTEEN

ALONE in Stuttgart with a sick mistress, ignorant of the language spoken around her, Lena was terrified. She prayed all night. And the next morning, as though in answer, she found Mrs. Ayer partially conscious. It was obvious that Blanche Howard had overslept and had not yet given Mrs. Ayer her first dose of sulfonal. Quickly, Lena knelt down by her mistress' bed.

Harriet asked, "What are they trying to do to me? I think I'm dying."

Lena shut her eyes to hide the tears. "Madame, she and Dr. von Teuffel are giving you a terrible drug that makes you unconscious. Please don't take any more."

Harriet touched Lena's hand. "Open your eyes. I want to tell you something. I think Blanche Howard is trying to kill me so she can raise Margaret as her own daughter. Margaret has changed already. Hasn't she?"

Lena did not dare tell her mistress that she suspected Blanche Howard was methodically, deliberately, teaching Margaret to hate her mother. But she did warn Mrs. Ayer that she must get out of the house and back to America if she wanted to save her life. Harriet shook her head. "Lena, what have I done that

184

any woman should hate me enough to try to steal my daughter? Have I loved her too much and been too ambitious for her? Is God punishing me for wanting to make a great deal of money so that Margaret could have everything?"

Lena tried to comfort the sick woman, but Harriet sank back into troubled lethargy. The young Negro, with gentle and loving hands, bathed her mistress and brushed her hair. Then she brought her breakfast, which Harriet seemed to eat with appetite, for the first time in days. Encouraged, Lena again begged Harriet not to take any more drugs. Harriet promised she wouldn't if she could help it—and asked Lena to see that she was not compelled to.

A few minutes afterwards, Blanche Howard hurried in with the morning dose of sulfonal. Harriet refused to open her mouth to take the powder. Blanche grew angry. Then Lena stepped forward and, pretending she wanted to help Miss Howard, switched glasses and fed Mrs. Ayer a harmless dose of chalk which she had managed to prepare and hide. She promised Miss Howard to see to future doses. Miss Howard agreed. In the next few days Lena was nearly always able to substitute chalk for the sulfonal, but occasionally Miss Howard or Dr. von Teuffel watched so closely that Lena was unable to make a substitution of the harmless powder for the drug and Mrs. Ayer sank back into unconsciousness. These periods, however, were farther and farther apart and at last Harriet was strong enough to sit up. As her strength returned, so did her interest in living. She told Dr. von Teuffel one morning that she was not going to continue the treatment and that she was going back to New York as soon as she could stand.

The handsome doctor left the room without a word. But in a few minutes, Miss Howard burst in, her protuberant eyes furious. She hurried to the bed and looked down on Harriet.

"If you won't let Dr. von Teuffel help you, I'm washing my hands of you. Get out of my house."

"Just as soon as I am able," Harriet told her. "And I'm taking Margaret with me."

Blanche Howard smiled and shook her head. "No, you aren't, Harriet. Dr. von Teuffel has taken Margaret away with him.

She is going to stay with Frau von Teuffel until you are out of
Germany. Everyone here knows that you are a dangerous
alcoholic and that I am only protecting your child from your
horrible influence. Even your own daughter hates the sight of
you and wants you to go home."

Lena tried to calm Harriet, but she was in a terribly nervous
state all day and unable to sleep that night. Without waking
Lena, who was dozing in a chair by the bed, she struggled to her
feet and tottered over to the bedroom door, which she flung
open. The guest room was on the main floor of the house, looking into the library. There, to her horror, she saw Blanche
Howard in Dr. von Teuffel's arms. Quickly she retreated, closing the door as silently as she could. She got back to bed by
crawling part of the way. And the next morning she told Lena
that they must get out of Miss Howard's house as soon as possible, even if it meant leaving Margaret temporarily.

"She won't harm the child, I am sure, for she loves her. And
I'm too ill and weak to fight them all now."

Lena hired a carriage and they drove to the station where
they bought tickets to Paris. In the few hours to wait before
the train left, Harriet went to see Frau von Teuffel. But Harriet
was so weak, and the poor woman so frightened, that Harriet
learned nothing.

"She thought she was dealing with a maniac," Harriet told
Lena sadly.

In Paris, old friends like Mme. Duval (the former Mlle. Frochard) joined forces to help her. Dr. Charcot reversed his
original prescription and urged her to return to America and
her own physician. And, to Harriet's pleased astonishment, a
cable from America, signed by General Grubb, urged her to
stay in Paris, saying he was coming to help her. Harriet's first
instinct was to cancel her reservation on one of the French
"ocean racers."

Then she studied the cable again; it had been sent from New
York and it was signed E. Burd Grubb. No one in New York
knew Harriet was in Paris, unless Blanche Willis Howard had
cabled the information after Harriet had left Stuttgart. Besides,
it was highly improbable that the General was in New York; the

last she had heard, he and his daughter were traveling in China. And, a significant detail she had overlooked, the General had fallen into the habit of signing all his communications to Harriet with the nickname which Margaret had given him on that Chirstmas day when they had first met—"the Ginger." No one else knew this. It was possible that he might have forgotten, after their quarrel, but too many other factors were suspicious.

She wired her lawyer, Stephen Olin, to meet her at the pier in New York. Before she left, she told a friend: "I've made up my mind, once and for all. I'm not afraid of Jim Seymour. If I discover he has been plotting against me, I am going to court. Don't look so horrified. I won't let him ruin me without a fight, and live with a shadow over my reputation the rest of my life."

In New York, Harriet found the evidence she needed—and more. Her cook-housekeeper, Amelia Queen, Dr. Schrady and even Dr. Pinkham, had strange stories to report. Another friend volunteered information to Stephen Olin confirming Harriet's suspicion that the telegram from the General had been a forgery. But most significant—and frightening—was Hattie's attitude. She was pregnant, and feeling very poorly, so Harriet understood her reluctance to leave her mother-in-law's house in New Jersey, where the young Seymours were still living. But when Harriet offered to go to East Orange, Hattie seemed terrified and wrote a long, disorganized letter trying to prove to her mother that she was having the best of care, and the doctor did not want her to have "visitors." Harriet wrote a heartbroken letter asking "since when would your own mother be considered a 'visitor'?" But she never sent it. There was no point in persecuting poor Hattie. She was ill, and she was being influenced by a father-in-law who was extremely clever at twisting and hiding the truth. Not yet twenty, and still immature in many ways, she had been caught in the middle of an ugly mess. If there had been any other way out Harriet would have chosen it, rather than drag Hattie's husband into court. But once she knew what James Seymour had done in her absence—and what Blanche Howard had tried to do, in collaboration with him—Harriet decided she had no other recourse.

Therefore on May 20, 1889, Harriet Hubbard Ayer confronted

James M. Seymour in the New York Court of Common Pleas, charging him with conspiracy against her and of trying to rob her of half her stock in Récamier Preparations. Harriet was dressed in the height of fashion, in a black merino gown which was a magnificent foil for her dazzling complexion, with an elaborate French hat on the beautiful red-gold hair. Although she was forty, she had the figure of a woman half her age. And her navy blue eyes blazed when they lighted on Jim Seymour.

Seymour, whom the *New York Times* described as a "prominent Wall Street operator whose success in this city has been almost uninterrupted," sat wooden-faced while Mrs. Ayer's lawyer, Stephen Olin, told the court that Mrs. Ayer accused Seymour of trying to drive her insane in order to steal her cosmetic business. "A crime almost incredible in this century," said the *New York Herald*, with relish, and went on to enumerate the fascinating details: "She [Mrs. Ayer] implicated in the alleged conspiracy against her: Lewis Seymour, the broker's son; the young man's bride, Hattie Seymour, who is Mrs. Ayer's own daughter; a famous authoress, Blanche Willis Howard; and a noted German physician, Dr. Julius von Teuffel. In order to rob her of her money, these people, according to her sworn assertions, wished actually to deprive her of her senses, through the use of a terrible drug administered in such extreme doses that to continue for any length of time meant death. While this horrid plan was being put into effect in Europe, she says James Seymour entered her house in this city and stole many of her private papers."

Jim Seymour was seen to stifle a yawn, politely, while Stephen Olin outlined Mrs. Ayer's charges in detail in the court. Jim Seymour never was a man to be overlooked in any group, with his unusual height and dark good looks, topped by the prematurely white hair. But he managed to convey the impression that his appearance in the County Court House was not only a mistake, it was a malicious miscarriage of justice. His attitude was one of long-suffering patience, mixed with fastidious disbelief. And, if he felt anger toward the beautiful woman who had summoned him to court, he managed to convey the impression that he was too much of a gentleman to display it. After the yawn, he gave courteous attention to Mr. Olin's story.

Mrs. Ayer, Olin explained, had started her cosmetic firm in 1886, with $50,000 she had borrowed from James Seymour. Mrs. Ayer gave Seymour half of the company's stock, five hundred shares out of one thousand, as collateral for the loan, with the oral understanding that he would return the stock when she paid back the $50,000. Over the next three years, as her business thrived and the name of Harriet Hubbard Ayer became as well known in mining towns and villages as it was among "the 400" of society, she had been able to pay back the entire amount. She had received regular letters from Seymour, acknowledging each payment. But, her obligation ended, when she asked for the return of the stock, he made flimsy excuses.

When she went abroad, shortly after Hattie's marriage, to visit her daughter Margaret and to go to Italy for a rest, Seymour had full knowledge of her plans, through her daughter Hattie. Harriet accused Jim Seymour of conspiring with Blanche Willis Howard to "destroy her healthy reason" with large doses of a powerful hypnotic drug called sulfonal. In Seymour's case, she claimed his object was to get her out of the way, either by her incarceration in an asylum or by her death, in order to gain control of her company. In Miss Howard's case, Mrs. Ayer accused her of collaborating with Seymour to steal away the faith and affection of her little girl, Margaret. Mrs. Ayer climaxed her case by accusing Seymour of breaking into her house while she was out of the country, and stealing not only the letters he had written acknowledging payments of the $50,000 he had loaned her, but also the cypher code for the cosmetic formulas she used in making her products.

Amelia Queen, Mrs. Ayer's cook, verified the theft: "About a week after Mrs. Ayer left, Mr. James Seymour called at the house and said she had arrived in Paris safely, but that she had left some important papers which she wanted sent immediately to her, and that she had cabled to him to come and get them that he might send them on the next steamer. I gave him a tin box containing some papers, and he took one.

"About two or three weeks afterwards, he came again, and

said he would finish his search of the papers Mrs. Ayer wanted. He went into her bedroom and remained a good while. As soon as he had left I found that the closet, which I had locked and the key of which I had in my possession, had been forced open and the papers had been removed, many of them scattered over the floor. Mrs. Ayer had given me strictest instructions not to allow anybody to open the closet except in case of fire or, in case of her death, Mrs. Ayer's daughter, Mrs. Seymour, was to be allowed to open the closet."

Dr. J. W. Pinkham, of Montclair, also testified that Jim Seymour had come to him with a forged order from Mrs. Ayer, which asked him to be given access to all the papers that she had left stored with him at the end of the summer she spent in his nursing home. When questioned about the sulfonal treatment, the doctor declared "that the treatment Mrs. Ayer was said to have undergone in Germany, being given fifteen grains of sulfonal every half hour, would weaken her mind and body and ultimately kill her."

A friend, Henry T. Thomas, of Scribner's, then entered briefly and tellingly into the case. He volunteered in an affidavit that: "After Mrs. Ayer went to Europe, Mrs. Seymour called on me at the Clarendon Hotel. I told her I feared her mother was very ill. She told me she feared so, too, but she could not leave New York because her husband was detained by an important lawsuit. Young Mr. Seymour insisted that his mother-in-law was not seriously ill, but that she was suffering from insomnia and 'imagined a great deal—she was then taking sulfonal with an excellent effect and would probably be cured entirely within a few days.' He also stated that Miss Howard kept the family duly advised about her condition and that there was no real need for Harriet to go abroad. He then gave me to understand that Mrs. Ayer was not mentally responsible and that no reliance could be placed on anything that she said or did.

"I replied that this would account for everything and agreed with him that, if true, it would be a kindness to place her under proper restraint. He said then that she had not been physically ill at all, but had feigned illness, including heart failure and fainting fits, and that there had been no trouble with her lungs, no bleeding and no real cough; that her mind was not right; that, among other things, she had accused him of tampering with the stock book of the Récamier Company and also of stealing $7,000 of her money, but that he had succeeded in convincing her that she was mistaken on both points. He also accused her of taking the notion into her head that the wearing of rubber masks was good for her complexion and immediately gave an order for one hundred thousand which, of course, no person in her right mind would have done.

"At another interview, young Mr. Seymour also told me that he did not think Mrs. Ayer would return for some time as he had sent her a cable signed with the name of one of her oldest friends, General E. Burd Grubb, asking her to wait for him in Paris. He also told me that he had seen by the Paris edition of *The Herald* that Mrs. Ayer and her daughter, Margaret, were about to leave for Italy. However, he did not think this was correct as Miss Howard *would fight like a wolf* before surrendering the little girl to her mother, and with the doctors against her, Mrs. Ayer would have a hard time to get Margaret."

Dr. George Schrady testified that Mrs. Ayer went abroad under his advice; that his diagnosis of her case was haemoptysis insomnia, and that he considered doses of fifteen grains of sulfanol repeated at half hourly intervals for several hours hazardous. He said that he himself had given Mrs. Ayer sulfanol, but never more than twenty grains a day, and he always watched her for several hours after she took it.

But Lena Raymond was the telling witness. She testified in detail about Dr. von Teuffel's treatment. "Miss Howard told me she was to have entire charge of the patient, and that as she was responsible to Dr. von Teuffel, I would have to obey her. She gave Mrs. Ayer the medicine, which she told me was sulfanol. One evening, between ten and eleven o'clock, I saw Miss Howard give Mrs. Ayer the medicine three times. She mixed two powders at a time for a dose with water."

The frequency of the doses continued, the Negro girl said, until: "After the third day, it was impossible to rouse her. Several times, I found Mrs. Ayer unconscious on the floor where she had fallen from the bed. I showed Miss Howard the bruises

and asked if I might not sit in the room with my mistress to prevent her hurting herself. Miss Howard said no. . . ."

But Jim Seymour and his son appeared indifferent, almost
bored. Harriet was still not entirely well, but she was enough
of an actress to hold her head high and look her best. Said the
Herald: "She made a dazzling appearance, even the musty maj-
esty of the court could not suppress her animation." Once or
twice, when some particularly telling point was made, she could
not resist glancing swiftly at Seymour. She knew him well
enough to understand how painful any criticism was to him, how
viciously he reacted when he was hurt. His composure frightened
her more than any display of anger. When Stephen Olin finally
finished his case and sat down, and it was time to hear Jim
Seymour's version of the story, Harriet found herself trembling
from head to foot. But she kept a fixed smile on her face.

Nor did Seymour, whatever he was feeling, show any interest
or excitement.

Through his lawyer, the court was told that Seymour had
loaned Mrs. Ayer the $50,000, but that he had received the five
hundred shares of stock not as collateral, but as payment to him
for his advice in organizing and managing Mrs. Ayer's company.
He declared that her story of his entering into a conspiracy with
anybody, anywhere, to drive her insane was only a symptom of
her bad state of health—had she not gone away to regain it?
The court was also assured that, although it was due to Seymour's efforts that Mrs. Ayer's business had become such a valuable property, he had transferred all his stockholdings to Mrs.
Ayer's daughter Hattie. So what was Mrs. Ayer making a fuss
about?

As for his visits to Mrs. Ayer's house, Seymour did not deny
them, nor did he deny taking certain papers away with him, but
he insisted that these had no connection with the money he had
loaned Mrs. Ayer. Then the lawyers quickly asked that a deposi-
tion taken from Dr. von Teuffel be inserted into the record. The
judge agreed. The doctor admitted that his treatment of Mrs.
Ayer was approximately what Dr. Schrady had stated—fifteen
grains of sulfanol, sometimes given as frequently as four consecu-

tive times in the period of one hour—but he defended it as perfectly proper treatment used by reputable foreign doctors for the ailment with which Mrs. Ayer was afflicted. "Her nervous excitement, her extreme loquacity, and every symptom showed she was a slave of alcohol. . . ."

The word "alcohol" was hardly out of the lawyer's mouth when Stephen Olin jumped to his feet and made an objection to giving the physician's testimony without Mrs. Ayer's consent. The objection was allowed and the court was adjourned. Without looking in the direction of James Seymour, Harriet swept out of the room, her back stiff, her color high. This time James Seymour followed her with his eyes. Then, when he was sure her lawyers had also left, he turned to the waiting *Herald* reporter whom he had summoned.

"I think I have some letters which might interest you. Some of them are from Mrs. Ayer's younger daughter, Margaret, written to her sister, Hattie. Others are from Miss Howard, also written to my daughter-in-law, or her husband, who visited in Stuttgart and met Miss Howard. You will find that they give quite a different picture of Mrs. Ayer from the one the lady tried to present in court today."

The *Herald* made the most of the sensational story which ran for columns in the edition of May 21, 1889, with the headline: "CRAZED BY DRUGS—LEFT AT DEATH'S DOOR" and started out:

"Never outside the realms of romance was a more dramatic story told than was set forth before Judge Daly, in the Court of Common Pleas yesterday. A woman whose success in business has made her name famous in every town and city from the Atlantic Ocean to the Pacific, charged a stockbroker, a man whose wealth is estimated at many millions, with a conspiracy to rob her out of her reason and her money. . . ."

But the most sensational aspect of the story—sensational enough without embellishments—were the letters which Jim Seymour had given the *Herald* reporter. They were written to Hattie Seymour for the most part, with only one to Lewis Seymour, and were shocking and damning—if true. Because conspiracy was charged, the two most startling letters were from little Margaret, who had not yet turned ten at the time of writing, and could hardly be accused of deliberately plotting against her mother.

The first, undated, had obviously been sent during Harriet's stay at Stuttgart:

"DEAR SISTER—

"I think you must have had your eyes shut this summer because you must either have seen mamma's hair get black or else you must have seen her dye it. This is the way I saw it:— Mamma said she would send to London for some cream and a lot of balm, but, as she said she did not know the address of her office in London she would write to Roberts & Bros. in Paris, and tell them to send some cream and balm, for she said she didn't like people to know that she didn't know the address of her people in London. The box came and I opened it, and it only had this bottle of hair dye and an enormous bottle of heliotrope (red), which I threw out of the window because she drinks it. When she was ill she whitewashed her face because she was always struggling against us and wanted to make her face white as death. Now, how you managed not to see these things is what I would like to know. It is all a dreadful business, and I will be very glad when she gets out of this lovely, clean, healthy house. She said she would go away with you when you come, and I wish you would hurry up if you are coming, because she is interrupting all our lessons and I want to learn something this year so as not always to be a dunce. But I am very glad I see how awful she is, for I can see what I would do if I didn't have Wawie to help me and to make me see the other road. I tell you, sister, Wawie has had an awful time with me, and she has done more than my mother ever dreamed of doing, and I shall always be loyal to her, for she is trying to make me a good and honest woman—not this other kind.

Love and many kisses
from your sister
MARGARET"

The second letter was dated January 25, 1889, after Harriet left Stuttgart:

"DEAREST SISTER—

"She left this morning for Paris. I am so very, very glad to be once more where the air is not disturbed by so many lies as there have been in these last six weeks, and to be able to begin my studies again. Dear sister, if I could only tell you what a very, very unpleasant time Wawie has had, and what a very unpleasant time all the rest of us have had. You will see how much pains everyone has taken to make this awfully bad woman who (I am very sorry to say) is our mother, get over this dreadful habit which makes everyone hate her. I am afraid you are going to have a hard time when she comes back, for she says she will never forgive you (fancy saying she would never forgive her own child!) for not coming over. How I wish our mother was good. It's awful and the only thing we can do is to try and make ourselves as much unlike her as we can. I don't think she is pretty, either, for if you ever got all the paint, rouge and whitewash and dye off (but you never will) you'd see she was much different than you thought she was. I think it was very mean of her to leave Papa as soon as he lost his money. Love to all. Kisses,

MARGARET"

The package that Seymour had given the *Herald* reporters contained not only the two letters from Margaret, but also a thick sheaf from Blanche Willis Howard who, the *Herald* commented "wields a trenchant pen." They were addressed for the most part to Hattie, and were so lengthy that the *Herald* only published extracts. The extracts were trenchant, indeed, full of passages like the following:

"I consider her [Mrs. Ayer] without any moral sense, morally insane. She lies to herself. She never blames or reproaches herself. She is cruel, selfish and ignoble, I have watched these traits for one month, in which she has not taken one drop of alcohol. I may be wrong in my prognostications, but I believe that only death will cure her excesses or her lies. Her low notions are in her bones, fibre and blood.

"I am willing to attribute much to long use of morphine, although I confess cause and effect are tangled up in this problem, nor can I reason through the very beginning of her career in Chicago and her subsequent conduct to your father and other men, with the shiftless confidence which her little daughter honors an unworthy mother. I simply say from the start that she has no principles, no self-control, no truth, no purity, no unselfish love. She has loved herself, God pity her, for the result is pitiful this day. I pity her with all my soul, for she is loving and unloved. All her brightness and beauty and high spirits and audacity do not change these facts. But this does not alter the facts that I pity and long to help her. I feel most kindly to her. She has an outward veneer of good nature; she has a real sense of humor, intelligence and brightness, with no depth, except for trickery and intrigue. It seems no one ever taught her as a child; no one guided her. There is no self-sacrifice in her generosity. She is capable of the most sordid motives and remarks.

"She tells horrible stories about so many women. One night she actually related five disreputable stories and on the fifth my patience gave out and I said, 'Really, Harriet, I have not been accustomed to regale myself with the history of fallen women,' at which she only laughed and said she did not know how she got on to the subject, but I think such subjects are always in her thoughts and that she cannot bear to admit that there exists a decent woman. She sent her little daughter for brandy, and continually after drank in her presence. She took Margaret into cafés and gave her cheese and beer, told lies and bribed her with presents to deceive, etc., but Margaret is far too keen not to finally connect these scattered facts and draw her own conclusions, especially when she saw her mother drink tooth wash and heliotrope."

"New Year's Eve, 1889
"Last night your mamma, ten minutes after a hearty dinner, feigned a fainting fit. I was alone with her. She said: 'Blanche, I'm fainting,' and then became apparently unconscious. I ob-

served that her face was not pale, her pulse was good, her hands warm, and I didn't run distractedly for brandy, but merely got smelling salts, and bathed her temples in a little water. Presently a drop ran in her eye. She made a funny face and said rather pettishly: 'I'm all right,' at which I, of course, was very glad. I am not afraid now, but I am afraid when she goes away. Someone should be with her. The first taste of wine will rouse her. I am afraid, sadly afraid. . . . Now she sends Margaret, Walpurga, everybody, for cognac, and is perfectly reckless."

> "January 4, 1889
> Stuttgart, Germany

"The siege continues. It is the hardest fight imaginable because her strong spirit pulls the other way. She opposes everything; determines not to sit up; pretends to be wandering, to be fainting; to have a chill; in short, everything her ingenuity can devise to create pity and alarm and consequently to procure brandy. It irritates me beyond measure when she tells me she is fainting to feel her pulse and find it is calm and quite good and have to tell her: 'I don't doubt that you feel uncomfortable, Harriet, you have just taken a good dinner, but you are not going to faint; your hands are warm and your pulse is good.' Then she pretends not to recognize me and calls me Hattie. Do not think we make any mistake about the delirium. She announces she is going crazy from weakness, then mumbles a little but is careful not to say anything compromising. Her favorite statement is 'Lewis, you are an idiot.' Meanwhile her healthy pulse, temperature as warm and moist as a baby's, her large appetite, and the fact that her wanderings cease the instant the door is closed, and she thinks she has no audience, refute her claims. Dr. von Teuffel finds her in a surprisingly satisfactory condition. He has far more noisy and troublesome patients of this kind and expected more scenes with her. Of course, he will have more. I have the scenes in the dead of night. With all her strength and with all her cunning, she fights against sleep. She slyly deposits her sulfanol on her handkerchief. I have consented to one grand deception, that of feigning ignorance of her terrible habit of alcohol, but I do not lend myself to her little comedy."

"January 6, 1889

"Margaret has just run in to tell me she has dropped a great bottle of dark heliotrope, which came from Paris yesterday, accidentally on purpose out of the window. I didn't ask the child why. It seems better not to be precise in anything, but it is very significant. Margaret is the one who first saw her swallow tooth wash. She observed that she put a great deal of cologne water on her lips. Margaret unpacked the box of toilet articles from Paris last night and put the heliotrope on the dressing table. She showed me this morning how much was gone. I greatly fear she knows too much of her mother's habit. She has been acting a part palpably for days now, and Margaret, constantly in the room, sees it perfectly. She bought white liquor (*blanc des perles*) in Margaret's presence. The worst still, Margaret found six boxes of *eau blonde* to make the hair golden in the Paris box. The child was terribly disgusted."

And to Lewis:

"April 3, 1889

"My Dear Mr. Seymour:

"You can imagine how eagerly we wait news from the battlefield. I can't get up any indignation about what she says of me. You see, I don't hear it, and both charges strike me as ludicrous—awful as they are in themselves—because I can't grasp the idea that anybody in his right mind could make them of me. I cannot help believing that if she sits hours in her counsel's offices, as Hattie wrote me, she cannot fail to reveal her cloven hoof. I am involuntarily counting on this. She speaks untruthfully, immoderately, vindictively and coarsely, and whatever role she begins, she must betray herself before long, especially to clever lawyers, it would seem to me. They may undertake a suit for her, but believe in her they cannot; consequently they may give me the benefit of the doubt when she accuses me of murderous intent and low, vicious conduct.

"I am very curious if you have been able to restrain her at all with the facts I suggested and I am anxious to know if she has resumed her brandy. Only an expert can judge, I think, for she certainly can easily deceive ordinary people, her capacity for alcohol is so unusual. I am naturally distressed about the little girl, and constantly expecting some action on her mother's part. Unless Mrs. Ayer should drink so that she could be proved an unfit guardian I don't see what is going to prevent the little girl from being sent for, to return to New York.

"Ah, what will be the end of all this miserable scandal? I cannot believe that she can hurt you permanently, you are so young and courageous. As for me, I can bear her raving patiently. Her animosity does not change the character of my conduct toward her. But my heart aches for her children, Hattie now, but for Margaret later. Hattie is good and brave but has principles, and has suffered before as deeply as she suffers now. But poor, volatile Margaret, so unsteady, with her tendencies, her dangerous temperament! What will she be? If only she need not return! Kindly keep me informed, dear Mr. Seymour. After all, we are all in one boat, and you have personally my deepest sympathy.

BLANCHE WILLIS HOWARD"

The *Herald* had been on the street only a short time before Harriet called reporters to a conference at her apartment at the Victoria Hotel near Union Square, where she was living while the case was being tried. Seated behind a big desk, she told reporters firmly:

"I don't believe my little daughter Margaret ever wrote the letters printed in this morning's *Herald*. I don't hold her in the least responsible for them. They are either forgeries or they were dictated by Miss Blanche Howard. You will notice that the language is very extraordinary for a child. The phraseology is exactly like Miss Howard's and not at all like Margaret's as I can prove by many letters from both in my possession. Margaret never called her sister 'dear sister' or 'dearest sister.' She had a totally different style of addressing her, usually in French or German since she has studied abroad.

"I am told that after the hearing yesterday the defendant's counsel called the reporters into his office and gave them letters to copy. My counsel had never heard of them until they were printed this morning. I understand it is regarded as an extraordinary breach of professional etiquette to publish evidence in that way without notifying the other side of the nature of the material he had in his possession.

"As to the charges hinted at in the letters pretending to be from my daughter and broadly stated in Miss Howard's epistles—they are utterly, infamously and entirely false. I was not addicted to the use of alcohol. I did not drink heliotrope or tooth wash. I did not order six boxes or one box of *eau blonde* from Paris or any other place. I did not pretend to be sick when I wasn't. I did not tell questionable stories; I did not 'slyly deposit sulfanol on my handkerchief.' I did not 'put a great deal of cologne on my lips.' I did not do one of the disgraceful or deceitful things I am charged with doing.

"The charges are so trivial in view of the gravity of my accusations against the other side that it seems hardly worth while to make denials. I charge them with attempting to deprive me of my reason, my children, and my property. Their only answer is that I drink heliotrope and tooth wash. I sue for the restoration of valuable stock illegally withheld from me and the defense is that I bought *eau blonde*. I'm in a poor mood for fooling and it seems to me the worst of folly to waste time in such things.

"This Miss Blanche Willis Howard who writes these false and cruel letters to my older daughter has pretended to be my dearest friend. She has many times called me a 'heroine' and 'the kindest-hearted woman in the world' and other gush of a similar kind. Even since my return she has written letters in which I am smothered in endearing tones. Isn't it singular that if even a single one of her charges is true that she should love me and respect me so highly?

"When I was sick in Stuttgart, she used to tell me how perfectly I could trust her, how much she admired me, and then warned me not to trust the Seymours, as she was sure they were bad persons. All the time she was in constant communication by cable and letter, as I know now. How do I know that? I have the certified copies of twenty-nine cable messages that passed between them, in which she gave them information about me and abstracts of the contents of my private letters and asked for instructions. These cable messages will tell an amazing story if they ever come to be read in court.

"I know the charge of attempted poisoning in my allegations will seem strange and incredible to many persons. Before I began proceedings I put the case in the hands of attorneys with instructions to investigate it thoroughly. If they found there was not ample reason to support all my suspicions many times over, they were to drop it. They investigated and declared that there could be no doubt of the truth and justice of all my assertions."

Harriet was very far from feeling the confidence and vigor she displayed before the press. She was sick at heart. The quoted portions from Blanche Howard's letters had been horrible enough, with the pictures they painted of her as a despicable wanton. But the ones that were supposed to have been from Margaret were unbearable. She had read them until she knew them by heart, yet each time she returned to the newspaper, they hurt her freshly. They danced in front of her eyes when she was trying to sleep and they were the first things she thought of when she awakened, heavy-eyed and unrested, in the mornings. Since the sulfanol episode, she had tried to cut down on her sleeping draughts, but after the appearance of Margaret's letters, she could not even think of going to bed without something to help her sleep.

She could not write Margaret, nor Blanche Howard. Duplicity was never one of Harriet's faults. The only comfort she allowed herself was shopping for clothes for the little girl, and sending boxes of the kind of things she knew Margaret liked best. Watching Harriet, her lawyers and Dr. Schrady feared she might break down, but Harriet realized that was exactly what Jim Seymour wanted to happen. So she held her head high. For the first time in her life, she used rouge on her lips and cheeks. In the courtroom she stared down Jim and Lewis Seymour.

The gossip sheets were delighted, particularly one called *Today*, which supported her both editorially and by innuendo. On the editorial page, during the trial, they noted: "In *One Summer* and in *Guenn*, Miss Howard was accused of making use of her friends, acquaintances and clients to lend her books an extrinsic interest. The limited numbers that were read, were read on this account alone. *The Open Door* is by far the dullest, stalest, flattest and inevitably most unpopular of the series the author has found a confiding publisher for. I question if even the identification of the originals whom the writer has caricatured, lampooned and slandered will help it much. It is a pure piece of pretentions and platitudinous philosophy, borrowed from Jean Paul and other Teutonic sources, and not even cleansed of their flavor of kümmel and beer. . . ."

In the same issue, they printed a poem by Francis Board Yard in which, however, lampoon and slander might also be said to play a certain role. It was called "In Central Arizona—the experience of a New York Tourist on being introduced to a busted old settler at Dirty Dog Camp." And it read, in part:

> "You come from New York
> And you never heard talk
> Of Phoenix Jim?
> (From Texas he kim)
> Jim of Central Arizone?
> Oh, sho!
> Go slow
> We know
> Jim's took you in
> And give you a skin.
> It's not surprisin'
> For Jim's just pizin.
> He's wuss'n a coyote when *he* smell bone. . . .
> Why right out here
> Any day of the year
> We'd hang Jim with a rope without grease
> Never heard talk
> Of Jim in York
> Where's your cussed police?"

And, in their news columns, *Today* editorialized:

"That a mortal woman could write to one child of her mother as Miss Howard wrote to Mrs. Ayer's elder daughter, is very fair proof of her capability of dictating the younger child's infamous creeds, as Mrs. Ayer avers her belief that she did. No woman's heart certainly will ever pardon the cruelty or animus of those extraordinary epistles. In beautiful, dignified contrast are Mrs. Ayer's words: 'It is quite useless for the defendants in the suit I have brought to goad me into a trial of this case by the newspapers. Men have been known to perjure themselves for the purpose of saving a woman's honor and reputation. But men, who, when called upon to explain the gravest charges, resort to the defamation of a woman's character, by the introduction in print of alleged letters, ignoring all rules of legal ethics, are their own worst accusers.'

Public sentiment swayed toward Mrs. Ayer, more after the publication of the letters than before. Harriet honestly tried to keep from trying the case in the newspapers but her lawyers, recognizing the intelligence and sound thinking in her statements to the press, encouraged her to see the reporter from the *Sun* and make a long statement which included the following telling remarks:

"I wish for the sake of my children, who are inexpressibly dear to me, to say that neither of them has ever up to within a few weeks, been other than the dearest, most lovable, and devoted of daughters. As for the alleged letters of a little girl . . . the child is, as Miss Howard says, of exceedingly volatile nature. For the sake of this dear child, now so many thousands of miles away, I deplore the publishing of these letters which purport to have been written by her. If she did write them, she did so guided and directed by another, of that I am sure. . . .

"My little girl has been under Miss Howard's care for three years; during that time Miss Howard has drawn from me, in cash, over $10,000. I left my little daughter with Miss Howard, believing I had placed her in the care of a tender, loving and honorable woman. I have faithfully fulfilled my part of the contract in earning, by very hard work, a sufficient sum to care for my child, at least so far as money can do so. I submit to the respectful consideration of all unprotected women and to all mothers this query: Supposing that all of these statements, as alleged in the letter purporting to be from Miss Howard, were true, what would a tender, loving and honorable woman do under such circumstances? Would she not try in every possible way to shield an erring mother and her unfortunate habits from the knowledge of a little daughter? Is it possible that a ministering angel, such as Miss Howard claims to have been, would soil the whiteness of her wings with an attempt to destroy a child's love and confidence in the mother who bore her, in the mother whose hard labor was enabling this child to be educated without regard to cost?"

"It is not my province, even by implication, to attempt to injure another woman, for all women need to be charitable to one another, and the self-supporting women of this century, it seems to me, can find more ennobling work than a defamation of another's character. . . . I am convinced that the American public and the American women, thousands of whom know me for what I am, will not accept as a counter statement to forgery, larceny and the attempt to deprive me of my liberty and reason the shallow statement that I am addicted to the drinking of tooth wash or extract of heliotrope. My little daughter never heard from me why or how it became necessary for me to leave her father and earn my own living and that of my children. As a matter of record, I did leave my husband in July, 1882, when Mr. Ayer was in the full tide of his financial prosperity, and his failure in business occurred in February, 1883. The animus which must have incited the person who told my dear little girl that I had left her father because he had lost his money needs no explanation. . . ."

CHAPTER SIXTEEN

A S THE trial drew to a close, it was obvious that James Seymour had been beaten. On May 27, the *Herald* ran the uninhibited headlines:

"HOT SHOT FOR SEYMOUR

Mrs. Ayer Carries All Her Points
in the First Skirmish"

The letters which Seymour had given to the *Herald* were never submitted in court as evidence, which gave credence to Harriet's suspicion that the ones written by her small daughter had been forged, and that Blanche's epistles were aimed deliberately at defaming Harriet.

Said the *Herald*:

"Mrs. Harriet Hubbard Ayer has won the first battle in her legal campaign against the Seymours. In a long decision, handed down yesterday, Judge Daly granted her petition for a receiver for her manufacturing company and continued the injunction restraining James M. and A. Lewis Seymour from disposing of or voting of the stock which they held and she says is hers. Judge Daly severely condemns the course of her opponents. . . .

"On the ownership of the disputed 498 shares of stock which James M. Seymour gave to his daughter-in-law, Judge Daly holds that the decision must rest mainly upon the degree of credit to be given to Mrs. Ayer's testimony as opposed to Mr. Seymour's, for the agreement was made without the presence of other people. Mrs. Ayer swears that the stock was pledged as collateral, for a loan of $50,000, which has since been nearly or wholly repaid. Mr. Seymour says it was given outright to pay him for his services in organizing the Récamier Manufacturing Company.

"The plaintiff [Mrs. Ayer] impeaches his testimony by reference to a suit brought in the City Court in October, 1888, wherein he swore he was not a stockholder in the Récamier Company nor in any way financially interested in it. Mr. Seymour replies to this with another official affidavit, in which he says that on April 17, 1888, he transferred the stock he held to his wife, Caroline S. Seymour, and she returned it to him November 17, 1888, so that at the time of the City Court trial he actually held no stock.

" 'This explanation,' says Judge Daly, 'does not relieve Mr. Seymour. Even if he had pledged the stock his testimony was not true that he had no financial interest in the company. . . . He is thus confronted with conflicting statements made by him under oath at different periods in respect to his ownership of the stock, and this is so whatever construction is to be placed on his affidavits. Mrs. Ayer is entitled on this hearing to claim the benefit of this impeachment of his veracity, and upon the direct issue between the parties, I feel bound to hold her unimpeached testimony must, as the case now stands, outweigh the denial.' "

The newspaper story goes on, at considerable length, to point out other indications of Judge Daly's lack of faith in Seymour's integrity. Seymour did not deny that he had fraudulently obtained access to Mrs. Ayer's house. "He contents himself," said the judge, "with swearing that he never took any formulas, recipes, or cipher code, or any voucher, receipts, etc. This denial is merely negative and his admission of gaining access to plaintiff's house makes it apparent that he is deterred by no scruples and renders such positive denials as he does make of the least possible might. . . ."

Dr. Pinkham, of Montclair, had also flatly denied some of Seymour's testimony, and this further damaged the Seymours in the decision. Mrs. Ayer was proved justified in taking the case to court, and had shown that the Seymours had been deliberately plotting to take control of her business. The judge declared that he could not and would not pass on her accusations against Blanche Howard and Dr. von Teuffel, that the evidence was not sufficiently detailed against them, but that it was his opinion that the Seymours "intended to, or believed they could, use Miss Howard."

At the next meeting of the stockholders, Harriet and two others were elected trustees of the company and then Harriet was elected president. But the meeting was stormy. It was obvious that the Seymours still hoped to cause enough friction to hurt Harriet. The minority stockholders who voted against Mrs. Ayer were Allen Lewis Seymour and a man named Watson, who each owned one share. A Mrs. Lottie Mason-Frenzel, who had been in Mrs. Ayer's employ as Mrs. Mason and had been discharged after the 'eighty-eight blizzard, was present with certificates to prove that she owned thirty shares of Récamier stock, which she had been planning to vote with the Seymours, but her qualification to vote was ruled out. There was no question in Harriet's mind that Mrs. Mason had been brought into the picture by Jim Seymour, was perhaps even in his pay, but so long as Harriet had controlling interest in the voting, she saw no reason to investigate Mrs. Mason further.

Again, Harriet made a mistake. But she was determined that she would not debase herself by being malicious.

Said the *New York Sun*: "A VICTORY FOR MRS. AYER— Enabled to Carry the Election by a Court Decision—The Seymours Could Not Vote."

And *Today* crowed jubilantly: "MRS. HARRIET HUBBARD AYER at 10 o'clock on Monday morning succeeded in raising the siege of her offices and took peaceable and entire possession of the Récamier Manufacturing Co. The defendants Seymour decided to come to Mrs. Ayer's terms, which they offered to do through their attorneys. Mrs. Ayer has more than gained all she asked for, including the 498 shares of stock in litigation, and will at once resume active and entire control of the business.

"Her health has undoubtedly been very seriously injured by the medical treatment she received at Stuttgart, and by the long mental strain under which she has been laboring, but she will be at the office as many hours each day as her physicians will permit her. It is a pleasant testimony that, during her fight, she received over one thousand telegrams and letters of sympathy and congratulation and offers of practical assistance from stock brokers, merchants and representative men and women in every profession.

"Mrs. Ayer refuses positively to be interviewed concerning any possible or probable future litigations, and says the courts have settled everything so far to her entire satisfaction. Her friends are jubilant to a degree, while she receives the tidal wave of felicitation with perfect self-possession and dignity. As to the threatened action for criminal libel against all concerned in the publication of the *Herald* of the abominable letters alleged to be by her daughter, there is no special information to be gained. I understand, however, that Mr. Bennett [James Gordon Bennett], who has been communicated with in the matter, has declared he will discharge every man or boy in his employ who had anything to do with the printing of them."

The editor of *Today* also indulged in a little heavy-handed horseplay in the editorial columns, banteringly urging readers who had "some money to gain from the decease of their aged, decrepit and accessible relations" to take stock in "The Great Central Arizona Sulfanol Mines" discovered by a picturesque Texan "Phoenix Jim who was inspired to *seymour* of life than was permitted by the somewhat confined *ayer* of his immediate vicinity. This will undoubtedly put a new complexion upon the question of whether it is wiser to endure your son's mother-in-law, when you have her property in your possession, or get rid of her as quick as you can while your son controls all her assets. Some mothers-in-law might complain. But when you control a Great Sulfanol mine, you need not bother about small details. . . ."

Harriet, however, was far from jubilant. She had won back her stock and proved that Jim Seymour was plotting against her, but at a terrible price. She had not heard a word from either Margaret or Hattie since the trial started. Margaret's silence was not surprising because she was an unenthusiastic letter-writer at best, and she was undoubtedly being directed by Miss Howard. Hattie's silence, however, cut deep. She was no longer a child and, although she had married into the enemy camp, she could not have forgotten how much Harriet loved her.

So it was like a final slap in the face when the lawyer, E. Hamilton Cahill, who was in charge of Seymour's affairs, told the press that Mrs. Harriet A. Seymour was glad to hand over her shares of Récamier stock because "she is sick and tired of acting as a walking advertisement of the cream—now she doesn't have to pretend she owes her pretty complexion to her mother's preparations."

Harriet could not—did not—believe that Hattie had said that, any more than she believed Margaret had written the two terrible letters. But her children were in the hands of her enemies, and she was afraid to try to reach them directly. Jim Seymour, she knew now, was capable of any outrage. And Blanche Howard, if she had written the letters—and she must have, or would she not have denied their authorship?—was either a monster or a sick woman. In either case, she might be very dangerous, particularly if she feared she might lose Margaret.

Harriet's lawyers advised her to let them send a representative to Stuttgart to bring Margaret home. Harriet agreed to this arrangement, though reluctantly. She felt that if she herself could only be with Margaret for a little while, everything would be all right. However, she was terrified of what Blanche Howard might do to Margaret if she heard that Harriet was coming for the child.

In addition, she was having trouble with Mrs. Mason-Frenzel again. It was only too obvious that the woman was a tool of Seymour's and a dangerous one. She brought suit against Harriet for half of the stock of the Récamier Company, claiming that she, and not Harriet or a French chemist, had invented the Récamier formulas. Her story was ridiculous and without proof and Harriet and her lawyers knew they would be able to shoot holes through it within a few minutes in court. But, once more, Jim Seymour was not attempting to try Mrs. Ayer's reputation in court. He was content to blacken it in the newspapers.

The laws of libel in 1889 were much looser than they are to-day, and James Gordon Bennett, the editor of the *Herald,* was not a man who worried much about them. He was glad to print any story that would boom circulation, and he had discovered that Mrs. Ayer's name would sell copies of his newspaper. So, despite his fiery vows to fire "every man or boy" connected with the printing of the letters which Seymour had given to the *Herald,* he was delighted to print Mrs. Mason-Frenzel's side of the case against Mrs. Ayer. On July 2, 1889, the headline read:

"MRS. AYER'S ROMANCES RUDELY SHATTERED
Lottie Lawton Frenzel Says She, and Not the
Beautiful Julie Récamier, Invented the Cosmetics

————

Claims One Half the Stock of the Récamier Company

————

Toilet Creams, Charmed by a New Litigation, Bringing
to Light Many Tricks of the Trade and Carefully
Guarded Secrets."

The story is far too long to quote in its entirety, but the reporter was given free rein:

". . . During the winter of 1884-5, Mrs. Frenzel, then Mrs. Mason, assisted Mrs. Ayer in furnishing apartments and shopping for wealthy women. Early in 1885, Mrs. Ayer spoke about the enormous profits to be made in cosmetics, and Mrs. Mason thought it would be a good idea to try the business. She was urged to start at once, and Mrs. Ayer promised to find the capital, agreeing to take a half interest in any venture she might make. Mrs. Mason says she took to a chemist some French Toilet Cream that Mrs. Ayer had used with good results and had it analyzed. She finally made a cream . . . which Mrs. Ayer suggested be called Récamier. Mrs. Mason then made a model of a pot to sell the stuff in. . . . A powder Mrs. Ayer liked was then analyzed. One of the ingredients was found to be very expensive, but Mrs. Mason found that something cheaper would do in its stead. . . .

"That fall, Mrs. Ayer read to Mrs. Mason with a great deal of amusement an article she had written as an advertisement, ascribing its origin to Mme. Récamier. Mrs. Mason urged the impropriety of any false claims, but Mrs. Ayer insisted that fiction was the best policy. . . .

" 'I know,' continued Mrs. Mason in her affidavit, 'that Mrs. Ayer was getting money from Mr. James M. Seymour, but what proportion of it she used for her personal convenience and what went into the business I did not know.' . . .

"Mrs. Ayer said if a company could be formed she would see that Mrs. Mason was guaranteed a salary of $5,000 a year. But [when it was], she was told by Mrs. Ayer that she would obtain thirty shares of stock for her from Mr. Seymour if she would sign a general release. This was done and Mrs. Mason thought everything stood as represented until a few weeks ago, when Mrs. Ayer began a suit against Mr. Seymour alleging she was sole owner of the formulas used in Récamier preparations. . . .

"Mrs. Mason says she received many letters from Mrs. Ayer, whose effusive style can be judged from the following sample:

'New York, September 19, 1887
'MY DEAREST GIRLKIN: Oh, thanks for my umbrella. It is booful and I carry it like a bracelet every day. Dear old girl you will never know how much I love you, nor how entirely I trust you. Whatever happens, my dear heart, let us stick to each other. My children will have other interests and will leave me, but unless you marry, our lives will never run apart, and in God's name, I beg you always to be true to me, I have had so many hard blows

from all sides that you are all I have left. I know I can trust you, but after you, I know not one human soul who would not be suspicious of me with half a cause. Remember that I am thine always. I have been absolutely loyal in word and deed to you and shall be to the end of my life.

HARRIET HUBBARD AYER.' "

When Harriet's lawyers managed to get the case into court for a trial, the affair became almost farcial. Judge Pine declared in his decision that it was proven absolutely that "Harriet Hubbard Ayer had obtained the formula for making Récamier Cream, as testified by her, in Paris, France, under the circumstances as alleged by the said Harriet Hubbard Ayer." Harriet also obtained letters from three eminent analytical chemists stating:

"The constituents of the Récamier Cream are well-known remedial agents, and their properties are fully described and authorized in the American and French pharmacopoeias.

"They are combined in a way which, while novel, is chemically correct, the resulting preparations being perfectly safe and beneficial for the uses specified. In the proper sense of the word, Récamier Cream is not a cosmetic, but a remedial agent for the skin.

"The average druggist would be unable to put up Récamier Cream from the correct formula, since the operations involved in its successful production require mechanical manipulations for which he is not prepared. Nor, if he had the mechanical appliances, could he make it as cheaply as you do unless he went into the manufacture on an equally large scale and bought the ingredients in large quantities. Prepared in small amount, the selling price must be considerably higher than fixed by you."

The "Girlkin" letter showed considerably less literary skill than the productions printed under Blanche Howard's name. Whoever had written it—Mrs. Mason or perhaps Seymour himself— had not come even close to Harriet's style of writing. After Harriet's lawyers pointed out its discrepancies in style and handwriting, it was not even put into the record.

Again, Harriet had won a court battle—but readers of the sensational press were left with only the memory of the accusations against her. Entirely without justification or proof, she remained in the minds of many persons a loose woman, a drug addict, an alcoholic. Her products had been maligned, even though disinterested chemists defended them.

Jim Seymour knew then what some people are still in process of discovering: that accusations against the moral character or integrity of a person are remembered long after the individual in question has been completely cleared. Therefore, in order to damage a reputation, it is not necessary to have either facts or evidence; all that is needed is no regard for the truth, no conscience and an outlet to the public.

Harriet knew what was happening to her, even as she fought. Unsavory accusations make much better reading in the newspapers than court trials which show they are baseless. But she was completely unprepared for the final blow, which had been carefully prepared while her attention was being diverted.

On July 9, Herbert Ayer went before the Chicago courts to obtain an order of injunction to restrain Harriet from taking Margaret away from Blanche Willis Howard. He announced his intention of demanding a modification in the court order of the divorce, giving Mrs. Ayer custody of the children, as "his former wife is not a fit person to be entrusted with the girl." He accused Harriet of swearing she would be avenged against Blanche Willis Howard because of the letters she wrote "in the late suit regarding Récamier preparations" and "is now preparing to take her daughter from Miss Howard."

The courts granted the injunction, upon his pleas that his wife entertained men at her home in the evening for business conferences; that she took drugs and was a victim of the use of alcohol; that her behavior was eccentric and unwholesome. The proofs against her were Miss Howard's letters; affidavits from ex-employees, including Mrs. Mason-Frenzel; and statements by several completely disinterested persons who had seen Mrs. Ayer come out of her offices "clad only in blue tights" and wander down the street. All of the evidence was manufactured; the woman in tights was later reported to be a model who had been hired by Jim Seymour, a girl who rather resembled Mrs. Ayer and thought she was engaged in an advertising scheme.

Harriet again protested her innocence, gave the reporters affidavits from doctors and business associates proving her sobriety and balance and non-addiction to drugs. But none of her arguments made news. They were the same old thing, buried at the end of the news stories accusing her.

Said the indefatigable *Herald*: "WHO'LL HAVE THE CHILD?"

Harriet told the reporters wearily: "James Seymour is at the back of this whole thing. He has said he would drag me through an ocean of infamy to take my children away from me."

They printed her remark—at the end of their story.

Herbert Ayer won the custody of Margaret. Whatever his faults, he was not malicious and he loved his children. Never had he been so close to Hattie as since her marriage, and his gratitude to her new in-laws further clouded an already confused mind. He sailed for Europe, all expenses paid by the Seymours, and told the newspapers that he was going over to bring back his daughter, Margaret.

Harriet instructed her lawyers to give up fighting her ex-husband. All she asked was that her child be brought back to America. If Herbert did that, she was sure that Hattie would take care of her little sister. Beyond that, Harriet asked nothing for herself. She was too sick at heart to care whether she lived or died.

CHAPTER SEVENTEEN

IN GERMANY, Margaret was oblivious of everything except that Blanche Willis Howard had promised her that—if she did everything she was told to—she could spend the rest of her life with Wawie. The letters she wrote which were printed in the *Herald* were not forgeries, nor were they dictated by Blanche Howard. ("If they had been, I am sure they would have been better written," Margaret says today.) The bewildered child simply put down on paper sentiments about her mother which she had overheard, and which she hoped would please Blanche Howard who read all her letters before they were mailed.

The next thing she remembers is that Wawie told her the courts had granted her father custody of her, and that he was coming abroad to take her back to the United States. She was genuinely terrified. Her father was virtually a stranger, and Wawie cleverly let the little girl build up visions of the stupid, culture-empty life she would lead with him. She knew very little about him, which was undoubtedly largely Harriet's fault, for her instinct had been to protect her children from Herbert after the divorce, to keep her daughters to herself.

Herbert had, it is true, made infrequent trips to New York, supposedly "on business" but actually to see his daughters. Most of the time, he saw only Margaret. Margaret today remembers the luncheons she had with her father at Delmonico's, when he urged her to eat all sorts of fancy desserts. Sometimes they would go to the circus afterwards, or a puppet show, and she would go home with her arms loaded down with presents, dolls, candy, trinkets. She realizes now what Harriet must have known at the time—that these trips had been very important to her father, and that he had saved or borrowed money in order to impress a little girl. But it did not occur to either of them then to think of Herbert Ayer as what he was—a pathetic and defeated man.

She says: "The luncheons were all I remembered about my father, and I got the idea he must be a very important person, the way all the waiters bowed and scraped and came around to see that he was being properly served. I believed he could make people do anything he wanted, and I was terrified for fear he could take me away from Wawie no matter how hard we fought. So when she suggested that it would be a good idea for me to hide from him, I co-operated willingly. I was put on a train in charge of the conductor and sent to Switzerland to a boarding school in Neufchâtel.

"It was Calvinist and every Sunday during the winter and spring the boarders marched off to a white church under the high white mountains. The church was cold, the view even colder and the minister, in deep black, denounced practically everything in cold fury and pictured the warm hell to which we were all to be cast by a God of justice. Sometimes hell sounded downright cosy."

Wawie had little trouble convincing Herbert that Margaret should be left in her care, and she explained the girl's absence by saying that she was on a cultural tour of Switzerland. Herbert was too overwhelmed by Wawie to protest, and before he left she even tricked him into signing a paper advancing Margaret's age four years. He had no idea that the novelist had plans to keep the child and raise her as her own, and that she wanted to hurry the day when Margaret would be of age, and under no one's legal custody.

However, when the girl returned to Stuttgart and discovered

that she was supposed to be fifteen years old, she was startled. In some ways, it was delightful to be so grown up, but in others it was not fair to her, as she was young emotionally even for her real age. But, at first when she returned, she was very happy. She remembers:

"Frau von Teuffel had died, and Wawie had married the doctor. I loved the doctor. He was a man of compassion and understanding, and seemed to know what was going on in my adolescent mind. Wawie had moved into a duplex apartment, still on the Möricke Strasse. On the ground floor was a doctor's office, waiting room and guest room, all flush with the garden. When Dr. von Teuffel's sons (he had three, but I never knew any of them well) came to visit, I would move down to the main floor guest room, and it gradually became my own. As Wawie grew more and more difficult—she had had a miscarriage which upset her greatly—I clung to the doctor. I helped him peel oranges for a mouth wash he invented, using the oil from orange peels. I watched him do cabinet work. He was working on a large chest with inlays of amber, intended for Wawie, whom he absolutely adored, so much so that he obeyed even her unspoken commands. He had reached a point where he didn't assert himself at all except in these two hobbies. But even here, he seemed to be working so hard to please his wife that to me, it almost seemed that he was trying to 'appease' her. Under the amber of the chest, he placed gold leaf. He began to order more and more gold leaf, real gold leaf, which came in large sheets, very expensive. He was determined that Wawie would not see the chest until it was done, but it was very hard for him to hide anything from Wawie, even his thoughts. Gold leaf was in every corner of the waiting room, and I used to help him put it away before the patients came in, from two to four, each afternoon. Mostly they were poor people, who could not pay, but they were the only patients he had except for Wawie's girls, and a few court people who were so insecure socially they felt they had to go to the court physician. He was always tender and gentle with them, as he was with me. But I couldn't help feeling some im-

pending calamity. I loved him, but I knew something dreadful
was going to happen to him."

Sometimes, at the luncheon table, the doctor could be persuaded to tell Wawie's protegées about the fascinating experiments being made in hypnotism. One child, a local German
girl named Tina, was so popular as a "control" that she became
ill and nervous. Her family complained to Frau von Teuffel, and
took the child away from her, blaming Frau von Teuffel's "niece"
as one of the ringleaders responsible. Margaret recalls:

"As soon as Tina's mother left, I was summoned to Wawie.
I admitted everything; quite frankly, I was only depressed because Tina was a better control than I was. I simply could not
concentrate well enough.

"Wawie stared at me. 'That is what I have been trying to warn
you of,' she said. 'Your mind will always be your great curse.
Instability is the reason people fail in life. Remember, the Bible
says: Unstable as water, thou shalt not excel.'

"The words were like stones, falling into my mind. I was
never to forget them, whenever I encountered frustrations for
years afterwards. Anything that Wawie put in my mind, stayed
there."

Although the novelist still acted as a chaperone and advisor to
American girls, a number of parents had been disturbed by the
mention of her in the Seymour trials, and the new girls were not
quite so "well-born" as they had been in Hattie's day.

Blanche Howard's bookshelves contained "something of almost
everything" and Margaret was allowed to read anything she
pleased (until later, when permission was suddenly refused without explanation). At first, when she still had not learned to read,
Miss Howard encouraged her interest in the religions of the
world by reading Clarke's *Ten Great Religions* to her and Harold Smith. Later, the little girl studied on her own, dipping into
the lives of the saints, mythology, the Norse gods, Buddhism,
studying Lutheran sermons with the same avidity with which she
read fairy tales. She had been baptized in the Episcopal Church,
of which Harriet was a member, and she had received some con-

ception of Catholicism from the nuns at school. Later, in Switzerland, she had had her taste of Calvinism and hell-fire. So her experience in religion was almost as diverse as her reading.

This was very much in Blanche Howard's scheme of things. Part of her "modernism" was her scorn for formal religion. She regarded it as an opiate of the people and explained to her young ladies how often it was used as a cloak for the worst immorality and sin. Hattie, when she had first gone to Stuttgart, had listened to Miss Howard's theories with horror and reported them to her mother, who had written back quickly: "Don't let them keep you from church and recollect however much people may use religion as a cloak for immorality and sin, it is the person and not the religion at fault. The same person would use some other cover for wickedness if she had not religion so convenient. The code of morals is just as good as though a lot of hypocrites had not abused it. I should think you had paid a dear price for your advantages in Stuttgart if in return you had given up your belief in God and your hope of Heaven. You know I make no pretensions to religion, you also know I hate hypocrisy but you and I both know we could not be happy an hour here in this world were we convinced there was nothing beyond it. Just think of that one awful fact a Rationalist must accept. Were I to die for instance, what would console you for the knowledge— what would the world be to you if you *knew* we were never never never to be together in Eternity? Ah my love, that sort of belief is all well enough to live by but mighty poor faith to die by, I think. Just avoid discussions in religion, go to church and pray God to keep you from the besetting and most awful peace destroying monster of our generation—the demon Atheism and its brood of ugly children, Rationalism and all the rest. God keep you, my child, safe in every way, from every danger and sorrow until the arms of your mother enfold you once more. . . ."

Small Margaret had no such letters to comfort her and she went through a period of turmoil, with her only guidance coming from a woman who was growing increasingly ill emotionally.

One afternoon, she received a new blow. She came home from school—"a great gangling girl in a yellow dress of Miss Howard's that had been made over for me, and red stockings"—

and found that a stack of gold-leaf sheets had just been delivered and put in the waiting room. It was already past time for the doctor's office hours and Margaret hurried to hide the gold in the laboratory. Blanche Howard stood there, looking at the unfinished chest.

"You weren't supposed to see that," Margaret gasped. "It was to be a surprise. I must cover it up again or he'll suspect—"

"Don't bother," the novelist said coldly. "The doctor has gone mad. Didn't you see it coming?"

Margaret shook her head, unable to speak.

"Well, he's in an asylum. We won't talk about it. Go to your room and study."

Blanche Howard never mentioned the doctor or the asylum again, at least in Margaret's presence. But the servants told the little girl in hushed voices that the man she had been fond of was quite mad, frothing at the mouth, and had been put in a padded cell. Margaret shuddered, but she understood the rules by now—you were not supposed to mention anyone who was in an insane asylum.

A few months later, the doctor died. The novelist told Margaret about it, coldly and briefly. However, Blanche seemed to be genuinely heartbroken. She went into mourning and the whole household joined her, including Margaret.

"I wore my first black dress, and there was a hat and shoes and stockings to match. When I went back to school, and walked on the street, even the boys looked at me in surprise. For a long time, after Mamma stopped writing, she had continued to send me boxes of lovely clothes, and silks from the best stores in New York. Miss Howard always said the clothes were too old for me, and the silks too dressy and gave them to other people. In the meantime, Wawie had her own old dresses cut down to fit me. I looked so strange most of the time that I took to walking alone in the forest, and going down the back streets coming to and from school.

"But the black must have set me off. I wasn't beautiful, but I had reddish blond curls, cut short like a boy's, and a complexion that was like Mamma's, rosy and clear. The shock of Dr. T.'s death had sobered me, subduing the nervous vivacity which

made some people think I had St. Vitus's dance. I was completely thrilled when a kindly old lady, wife of a distinguished
general, called me 'pretty.' But Blanche Howard deflated my
excitement by telling me: 'You look all right when you are behaving properly. Your features are too large. Just remember
that old people are often foolish about young people.'"

The doctor's death was the beginning of trouble for everyone
connected with Blanche Howard. The novelist had undoubtedly
counted on his affection and devotion more than she realized.
He had left a small estate but she had to share it with his three
sons, which annoyed her unreasonably. Money became an obsession. She had always been extravagant and insisted on living
luxuriously. Her fees had been high and she had drawn heavily
on parents for "expenses," but now the parents were less reluctant to complain of her charges, and many girls were transferring
to more fashionable and less expensive finishing schools in
France.

Moreover, her writing was going badly. When the girls left to
go home for the summer, Blanche took Margaret to live in a
small inn in the Black Forest. When they came back, they
moved into a small apartment in Stuttgart, on the ground floor
of a large building guarded by high, grilled gates. Blanche still
kept two servants, Walpurga and a man named George, but she
was bitterly ashamed of the smaller quarters and her temper,
which formerly had been so placid, at least on the surface, became uncertain. She was cross and strict with the young ladies,
and the luncheons which used to be delightful, became nervous
ordeals, with the guests watching their hostess to see what her
next reaction might be. One by one, the girls left Stuttgart.

Blanche Willis Howard was to die of cancer. Margaret today
suspects that it was during this period that the novelist began
to suffer and to use alcohol immoderately when she was in pain,
which accounted for much of her eccentric behavior. There were
still periods when she could be charming and lovable, but there
were many more when she was cruel and difficult.

Once Margaret found a black-bordered envelope addressed
to her in her mother's handwriting lying on Miss Howard's desk.
She opened it up and read:

"My dear love: I do not know if you care to hear from your poor sad-eyed mother who still holds you dear above all living things, but I feel you must know that your Grandmother Hubbard was finally released from her suffering. She—"

The note was snatched out of her hand before she could read more, and thrown into the fire. She gazed at Miss Howard in astonishment.

"What do you mean reading my private papers?"

"But it was addressed to me—"

Miss Howard's eyes blazed. "From this day on, you are not to read anything in this house—a book, a newspaper, a scrap of anything—without asking my permission. This is your punishment for being untrustworthy. Do you understand?"

"But—"

"Leave the room and don't come near me for the rest of the day!"

Those were the bad days, when Margaret fled from the apartment, and ran into the wood where she roamed for hours alone. But there were good days, too. Sometimes Hattie, who now had two babies, would write and tell Margaret she thought it was time for her to come back to America, it was too much to expect the Seymours to go on paying her expenses in Germany. . . . When these letters came, Wawie would put her arms around Margaret and say the money didn't matter, that she was all she had left, and make her promise not to leave her.

Margaret's love for Wawie had been too strong to die easily. She didn't want to go back to America and live with the Seymours. But she was terribly unhappy much of the time now, and Blanche's worries about money made her long to find some method of earning her own living. All she had was a strong, sweet voice. During the old days, when she had first come to Stuttgart, and shared a room with Marion Smith in Wawie's house on the Möricke Strasse, she would always sing while they changed their clothes for dinner. It was about the time when workmen came home, and the other side of the street would be lined with laborers and passers-by who had stopped to listen. But Blanche had soon put a stop to that, saying it was unladylike. It was a long time since Margaret had sung anywhere except when she was alone in the forest. So she busied herself learning to cook and wash and iron, helping the servants, planning that if the worst came, she could hire out as a servant. . . .

Blanche's instability kept her constantly in suspense. One incident in particular left an indelible impression:

"I was coming home from school one day, gay and lighthearted, probably because I had done well, or somebody had said something about my looks—I don't remember now—and instead of pushing the bell at the gates with my finger, I gave it a push with the end of my umbrella. Alas, it was the wrong bell; not the gate, but one inside the house. There was a great to-do in the house. Miss Howard rushed out crying out about how upset her nerves were and how her work was ruined for the day, then returning to her study in high dudgeon. I felt sorry, but I didn't see how it was such a terrible thing, and neither did the servants, although of course they said nothing in front of Miss Howard.

"That night I was sound asleep when Wawie entered my room and dumped a pitcher of cold water over my head. I woke up, frightened terribly, with Miss Howard's face close to mine: 'That shows you how I felt when you rang the wrong bell this afternoon. Haven't you any consideration for other people at all?'

"She went on and on, upbraiding me for my unstable nature and my ignorance. I jumped out of bed to try to plead with her and fainted—I guess from fright. When I came to, she was gone. But I think she was frightened, too, when she realized what had happened. For it wasn't long before she decided that it was no longer necessary to keep up the household and the two servants. She had an idea for a new book and she was going to take me to England with her, where we would visit some old friends of hers, Mr. and Mrs. Wilfred Meynell. We left without sending anyone our address—papa or Hattie or anybody. It was a new life and, for a while, a delightful one. Mrs. Meynell was the famous Alice Meynell, the writer and poet, and, although she and her husband had very little money and lived in one of those narrow, spinsterish houses on Palace Court Gate, it was always filled to overflowing with fascinating guests including George Meredith, Chesterton, and many others. Wawie stayed with the Meynells, but I was given a small room down the street, although I took my meals with the Meynells. It was great fun but I began to worry because I wasn't earning any money. I had sung for the Meynells and they had said nice things about my voice, so I tried to get into the D'Oyly Carte Company. I was turned down because of my height—five feet eight inches—even before they heard my voice. I was wondering what else I could possibly do when Blanche Howard came to my little room very early one morning, while I was still asleep. I woke up, startled; she was staring at me in the old intense way, willing me to do what she wanted.

" 'Your mother is insane. They have put her in an asylum. I had a cable this morning.'

" 'Where is she?'

" 'We'll talk no more about it. We are going to move away from the Meynells'. I don't want them embarrassed because of your mother.'

" 'But—'

" 'Not another word! Your mother is dead, so far as you and I are concerned. Your father and sister had to have her sent away. My duty is to see that the same thing does not happen to you, with your inherited weakness.'

"She looked at me so fiercely that I dared say no more. But after she left, I buried my head in my pillow and wept. Although I was such a great tall girl, I was only fourteen and, although I had not heard from my mother for so long or written her, I had always held the thought that if I really needed help, she would come to my rescue. But now she was lost to me forever. She was insane, which, in my experience, meant that I would never see her again.

"I decided there was no hope for me. Even Hattie, whom I still loved very dearly, seemed to have gone away into another world. I thought of killing myself. But, somehow, Wawie had defeated herself. Her desire to dominate my thoughts and mold my mind and personality was shattered by the religious training she herself had given me. I had come to believe not in one single creed, or church, but in the existence of a soul which would go on after it had left the body, and a life hereafter in which all people, all races, all groups would go forward together. When all else failed, my belief that courage was found only in the knowledge of God, gave me strength."

PART THREE

CHAPTER EIGHTEEN

ON THE cold, bright morning of February 9, 1893, Harriet Hubbard Ayer was taken in a horse-drawn carriage from her home on Fifth Avenue and Thirty-first Street to an insane asylum in Bronxville, New York. Three people went with her: a woman detective; Dr. W. J. Morton, one of the two doctors who had certified her insane; and Lena Raymond, her devoted maid.

It was done so quietly and quickly that no word leaked out, although the papers would certainly have seized on it, for Harriet Hubbard Ayer was always news. But New Yorkers read in the morning *Times* that plans for the inauguration were under way in Washington; Grover Cleveland of New York had been elected President and Adlai Stevenson (grandfather of the present Adlai) of Illinois had been elected Vice-President. They saw that Queen Victoria was thinking about Irish Home Rule, and J. Pierpont Morgan about acquiring another railroad. And Steve Brodie, the man who is supposed to have jumped off the Brooklyn Bridge, got into print again by stopping a street brawl between a prizefighter and the editor of a sporting paper who wasn't much with his fists but who "happened to be carrying a revolver."

The weather, however, was so fine that many fashionable New Yorkers of leisure put aside morning coffee and newspapers to don fur-lined overcoats and extra flannel petticoats to go skating on the frozen pond in Central Park. And that turned out to be a small piece of good fortune for the unfortunate Harriet Hubbard Ayer.

For later Dr. Morton testified under oath that Mrs. Ayer had been in a coma throughout the trip, and that he had been so concerned about her condition that he went all the way to Bronxville in the carriage, although he had originally planned to get out at Forty-second Street. But Mrs. Ayer, over a year later, used the skating pond to refute his testimony and was able to convince alienists not only that she was sane, but that she had been the victim of a plot—a sequel to the earlier conspiracy against her.

No word of what had happened slipped out until almost three weeks later, February 27. The next day the *New York Herald* printed the sensational news that Mrs. Harriet Hubbard Ayer, "known on two continents as a shrewd business woman, the proprietress of a widely advertised cosmetic, and formerly a social leader of great beauty," had been confined in Dr. William Granger's private asylum at Bronxville . . . "the result of a petition by her divorced husband, Herbert C. Ayer, and her daughter Harriet, the wife of Allen Lewis Seymour of East Orange, New Jersey."

The old charges were rehashed—"addiction to morphine and alcohol are said to have unbalanced her mind, making her incapable of conducting the business of manufacturing the cosmetic with which her name is associated and which was, therefore, in danger of being wrecked to the detriments of her daughters." The divorce from Herbert Ayer, his failure, her lawsuit against Jim Seymour and his son, even the trouble with Mrs. Mason-Frenzel were brought up again. Although the reporter did not identify the sources of his information, he dwelt with relish on her symptoms: "Her most pronounced form of mania is said to be the hearing of mysterious voices, at times threatening her, at others making overtures of a friendly nature, and again inviting her to improper conduct. . . . For hours, it is said, she will sit crooning to herself or answering the voices in the air. Or for a whole afternoon, she goes about singing to herself, occasionally stopping to call gently to her daughter Margaret, whom she imagines is in an adjoining room, or for her divorced husband, toward whom she has no sense of bitterness."

When interviewed by the *Herald*, Dr. Morton was quoted as saying: "But that this painful matter has come out in the courts, I would not discuss it. It is true, however, that Mrs. Ayer is undoubtedly suffering from melancholia. I am not prepared to say whether she will entirely recover. . . . From what I know of Mrs. Ayer, I believe her to be a good woman, not now addicted to morphine or alcohol. I am convinced that the action of her former husband and her daughter are most kindly intended. Mrs. Ayer has long needed the care and attention which can be had only in a private sanitarium."

He told the newsman that Mrs. Ayer was aware that she was to be taken to Dr. Granger's asylum and was willing to go. The reporter, however, had less luck with the others involved. He wrote: "I called on Mrs. Allen Lewis Seymour in East Orange, New Jersey, last evening, but she declined to give any details of her mother's insanity, or even to admit that she had joined with her father in asking for the commitment. At No. 305 Fifth Avenue the apartments formerly occupied by Mrs. Ayer (over her luxurious gold and white cosmetic salon) were locked up. When the application for Mrs. Ayer's commitment was made to Judge McAdam, it was stated by Mr. Ayer that he had no desire to have any interest in her property, but was acting solely on behalf of the children, whose names and reputations he wished to protect, as well as their property rights. Mrs. Ayer has two sisters, Julia A. Lockwood, living at Elizabeth, New Jersey, and May Wetherill, who resides on Bedloe's Island."

However, in Chicago, Herbert Ayer was somewhat less discreet with a reporter from the *Chicago Tribune*:

"When I went to New York, I found Mrs. Ayer in apartments at 305 Fifth Avenue dying from the effects of morphine and other stimulants, with no one to restrain her. I have known for twelve years that she was insane, but to save my children I bore the knowledge secretly. I received a letter yesterday from Dr. Granger that she is regaining her normal appetite and slept well, though she still believes my daughter Margaret is in the next room and strange voices in the air are talking to her. The appointment of a guardian by the Supreme Court will settle the whole matter regarding the disposition of her property. I could not possibly receive a dollar in any way, being her divorced husband. I do not know anything about her affairs and do not believe my daughters are inclined to profit by succeeding in her business. The last year I lived with Mrs. Ayer it cost me $96,000 to pay for her extravagances."

On March 11, a little more than a month after she had been taken to the asylum, Dr. Granger and an attendant brought Mrs. Ayer to appear before a jury in the Supreme Court of New York to determine whether she was incapable of caring for her own interests.

The *New York Times* reported: "Mrs. Ayer was dressed in deep black and wore a heavy black veil, the many folds of which could not, however, conceal her deathly pallor. She kept her eyes cast down. Mr. Stephen Olin, her former counsel, and so best acquainted with her, asked her various questions.

" 'Do you know why you are here?' questioned Mr. Olin.

"The woman gave no sign of having heard the question. Then Lena, the colored girl, asked the same thing, but got no reply. Mrs. Ayer lifted her veil long enough to wipe away a few tears that had started down her cheeks, and showed her face, which was hardly recognizable as the same one that was known for its beauty a year or so ago.

" 'Do you want to stay here?' asked Lena.

"Mrs. Ayer shook her head and was led out of the room. By common wish of the jury, she was not recalled.

"Dr. Granger then testified, saying that he had been connected with Bellevue Hospital and made a specialty of insanity. He said that Mrs. Ayer's stay at Bronxville had been one continuous examination, as it were, and that she had melancholia was beyond a doubt; she was probably incurable. The chances of her recovery were very small, but her case was not hopeless.

"He said that Mrs. Ayer had never spoken while in his institution except to answer questions, and then always in the briefest possible manner. Twice she had sent him a message—once asking for medicine and the other time for her daughter. She was always listless, and when he told her of the proceedings of yesterday and asked her if she wanted to attend them or not, she said she didn't care.

"Dr. Granger said his patient's face showed signs of mental pain and depression of spirits. He had also heard her complain about the voices. There had been no improvement since the present attack began. . . . He had no idea of the cause of Mrs. Ayer's mental condition, but he had never observed anything that would lead him to believe that it was due to the use of alcoholic stimulants. She had never asked for anything of the kind, and nothing of the sort had ever entered into the treatment.

"Dr. George Hammond, whose name was also on the commitment papers, was asked about the causes of her melancholia. He answered: 'Many' and said that overattention to business was undoubtedly one. Asked about the others, he declined to state them. He thought that the chances of Mrs. Ayer's recovery were small, but were better with institutional confinement.

"Lena Raymond, the colored girl who said that she had been employed as Mrs. Ayer's maid for ten years, stated that her mistress had always been very cheerful until last summer, but had been less so since then, and thought she was 'gradually going down.' Mrs. Ayer had, she said, translated a book about a year ago, and looked after her business affairs, all of which was, of course, a strain on her nerves.

"In reply to questions, Lena said that she and a trained nurse had taken Mrs. Ayer to Islip, Long Island, to spend the summer of 1891.

" 'Do you remember hearing Mrs. Ayer talk about suicide?'

" 'Yes, before we went down.'

" 'And while you were at Islip?'

" 'No.'

" 'Did she ever threaten it at any other time?'

" 'No.'

"Lena thought Mrs. Ayer had changed considerably. But she was better two years ago than she was four years ago, but had not been so well during the past year. . . . Mrs. Ayer's private secretary, Miss May S. Morrow, and her general manager, Frank J. Sprague, testified as to her Récamier property. . . . Mr. Olin, representing Mrs. Ayer, said that she had given him a box, the contents of which were known to nobody but herself, but was supposed to be jewelry, in charge of his firm, which he had placed in safe deposit. Between Mr. Olin and Mr. Sprague, it came up that Mrs. Ayer's real estate consisted of a house and lot in Florida.

"The jury was out some twenty minutes. After declaring Mrs. Ayer insane, it appraised her property, besides the mysterious box, at $55,000, of which $10,000 was for the Florida house and $5,000 for personal property.

"The court will appoint a guardian for Mrs. Ayer at once."

In the weeks that followed, the newspapers gradually lost interest in the wrangle between Mrs. Ayer's friends and her lawyer and the relatives who had committed her, over the appointment of a guardian to administer her estate. The items grew smaller and smaller and were buried farther back in the paper.

But a bitter quarrel was going on. Miss Morrow and Mr. Olin, supported by several unnamed friends of Mrs. Ayer's, were determined not to permit Herbert Ayer or Mrs. Harriet Seymour to come into unquestioned control of Mrs. Ayer's person and property. On March 26, the *Times* (on page 10) said:

"Mr. Olin stated that it would be a great injustice if the court should permit the family of Mrs. Ayer, who had caused her so much trouble and sorrow, to come into control of her affairs now when she was helpless to defend herself. For years, he said, they had done everything to make her unhappy. They had made war on her, in and out of the court, and he went over the various lawsuits in which Mrs. Ayer was arrayed against her husband, her daughter, and the latter's husband and father-in-law. Mr. Olin then read from Miss Morrow's petition as follows:

" 'The peculiar loneliness of Mrs. Ayer's position, and the nature of her malady, which permits her to recognize those about her, make it cruel to suggest that her friendships should be wholly ignored and forgotten in the appointment of a custodian of her person. To entrust the property or person of Mrs. Ayer to those who have made unsuccessful attempts to deprive her of her property and have attacked her reputation and rendered her life miserable would be a very great wrong.' "

The family which was aligned against Harriet now included her sister May, whose husband was stationed at Bedloe's Island. Just how the Seymours managed to get her signature, and not that of Jule's, is not known today. Herbert Ayer was being supported by the Seymours, and was installed in a luxurious suite at New York's fashionable new Holland House. This diminishes the highmindedness of the statement which he signed for the court:

"I was suffering so yesterday that I hardly knew what to say, but what I wish and hope the court will do is to appoint some good strong businessman who will have the courage and honesty to have the affairs of the Récamier Manufacturing Company thoroughly examined, and if this is done, I think you will find that those affairs have not been managed in the interest of Mrs. Ayer and that they will show any amount of rascality has been committed."

Her employees, Mr. Sprague and Miss Morrow, answered these accusations with cries of "fraud" and Mr. Sprague wrote a letter to the *Times* protesting the accusation of Herbert Ayer.

The impartial referee appointed by the judge decided against the family, and a businessman (an Alfred Bishop Mason, no relation to Mrs. Mason-Frenzel) was given charge of Mrs. Ayer's affairs.

No more was heard from Mrs. Ayer for over a year. The diagnosis of Dr. Granger, reported in court, that she was probably incurable, was accepted by her friends and acquaintances. No one was permitted to visit her, except the family, and the family did not take advantage of the privilege. Even her lawyer apparently had been convinced of her illness. Herbert Ayer was sent back to Chicago, Mrs. Seymour stayed home in East Orange (she was undergoing another difficult pregnancy) and teen-age Margaret remained silent in Europe. The old friends who wrote to Harriet received no acknowledgment of their letters; gradually they became resigned to the verdict of the family that Mrs. Ayer was a hopeless case. Even her closest business associates—Miss Morrow and Mr. Sprague—gradually gave up, fearing the worst. She was relegated to the limbo of the "living dead" and even talked of in the past tense.

Then one quiet Sunday in August, 1894, when the newspapers were deploring the absence of most of the clergy during the summer heat in New York, sandwiched between stories of the "finest August in the chronology of South Hampton" and reports of the "Catskills gay with life," this headline appeared in the *New York Times*:

"HARRIET HUBBARD AYER SANE AGAIN

JUSTICE TRUAX SIGNS AN ORDER RESTORING TO HER ALL HER PROPERTY"

And the article went on to say: "Mrs. Ayer remained in the institution until April 8, 1894. Even before that time she was allowed more privileges than the other inmates of the place, because it was noticed that she was recovering. . . . She was supported in her application by affidavits made by Dr. William P. Granger, owner of the asylum at Bronxville; Dr. William A. Hulse of Bay Shore; Dr. A. A. Smith of No. 40 West Forty-seventh Street; John L. Lockwood of Elberon, New Jersey, at whose house Mrs. Ayer was guest recently for some weeks, and Captain A. M. Wetherill of Company A, Sixth Regiment, United States Army. . . ."

But the Mrs. Ayer who was released from the asylum, wearing a tattered moiré house dress that had once been fashionable, and worn-out high shoes that were almost falling off her tiny feet, was very different from the beauty of the 'seventies or the dy-

namic business-woman of the 'eighties. Her hair had turned gray
during her incarceration. It fell dry and lifeless from a tiny little
"monkey cap" with a black veil that had been her only head-
covering in rain, snow, or summer heat for fourteen months. Her
eyes were dim and misty behind a double set of colored glasses
and she walked uncertainly; months behind locked shutters, constant weeping, and poor food had weakened her eyes until she
was almost blind. The trim firm figure, so admired by artists and
sculptors had wasted away. She looked like an old woman.
Actually she was still in her middle forties.

For once in her life, Harriet was forced to accept aid. Her
business had not prospered in her absence, partly because its
success had largely depended upon her personal drive and inspiration, partly because the damage to Harriet's reputation had
in turn damaged the value of the Récamier Company. If she had
been physically or emotionally able to go back and rebuild her
business, she might have saved it. But she was too hurt, too sick.

While awaiting the final sanity verdict, she stayed with her
older sister Jule and her husband, John Lockwood. But John
was still a Victorian tyrant in his home and Harriet soon found
the situation there intolerable. She was grateful when May
Wetherill urged Harriet to come out and live with them at her
husband's new army post in Oklahoma, which was then still Indian territory.

The post was very primitive. It reminded her of Chicago during her childhood. The roads were unpaved and, when it rained,
became bogs of thick, dark muck. The frightful heat of the Mid-
western summer was not yet gone when Harriet arrived. And
the bad times with the Indians were so recent that the wives of
army officers never went out without poison, which they were
supposed to take if captured. May was used to seeing Indians
circling the house in order to get a glimpse of her . . . "thinking,
no doubt, what a pretty scalp my red hair would make."

Harriet never intended to live with May any longer than necessary. Despite the warmth of her invitation, Harriet well knew
that a "crazy" sister was not a welcome addition to any household. But she used the months in the West to regain her health,
setting about that task with the same purpose and thoroughness

that characterized everything she did. She aimed at gaining exactly forty pounds, in order to attain the "perfect" weight of 136 pounds recommended for women five feet four inches in the booklets she had written to advertise her products. She exercised in the open air, walking, even working with dumb-bells. She drank cream, cocoa, and a tonic of her own concoction. She ate potatoes, cereal, starchy vegetables. And she heeded her own advice, with which she had closed the "How to Get Plump and Rosy" chapter in her beauty book: "Cultivate calmness and try and disprove the old axiom, 'A sweet temper and a bony woman never dwell under the same roof.'"

During this period Harriet thought hard about her future, and prayed about it. The result was that on April 15, 1896, she stood on a lecture platform of Central Music Hall in Chicago, before a paying audience of society women, to deliver a lecture entitled, "Fourteen Months in a Madhouse."

She wore a long white evening dress which revealed shoulders that were again shapely. Her tiny waist was emphasized by a wide sash of multi-colored brocade. The only visible effect of her ordeal was her gray hair, which she had cut off in order to get rid of the dry, broken, straw-like texture, and which was now growing again in a soft halo of ringlets all over her head. The good food, the rest, the happiness of being welcomed and loved again by her sisters, had helped her eyes. She had discarded her glasses, and with her gray hair and her dark eyebrows and lashes framing the again brilliant eyes, Harriet Hubbard Ayer was almost as beautiful as people remembered her.

She told them: "I am not here to ask your sympathy for that woman known as Harriet Hubbard Ayer, and I would if I could, divorce her from my identity when I present her story. I have not one unkind or vindictive thought toward those ill-advised persons who are responsible for my commitment to an insane asylum. If they honestly thought me insane, and the Bronxville institution a fit place for a disordered mind, it was a sad blunder. If they had other motives, God forgive them, for I certainly do. I have no malice toward the physicians or attendants of the Bronxville institution, though I shall without fear depict them as officers and servants of that house of despair. And when I shall have spoken I hope most earnestly that the tiny stone I pray I shall have the strength to throw into the sea of your thoughts, will make its increasing circles until you are all brought within the radius of my heart's desire, the legislation and enactment of proper laws for the protection of the insane and alleged insane."

Later she went backstage and changed into the tattered black moiré dress and veiled "monkey hat" she had worn for fourteen months in the asylum. She brushed out her curls so that they stood out in a fair imitation of her stiff gray hair during asylum days. Her bedraggled old shoes were tied with tattered bits of vari-colored string, as they had been in the asylum after her knotted laces would no longer hold together. And, with her natural dramatic skill, she seemed to shrink, grow tiny and pitiful under the black veil and the worn dress. Without the story she told, her appearance would have seemed incredible, but in conjunction with the story the tattered costume lent credence and added horror.

One morning, she said, when she lay sick and miserable in the Fifth Avenue apartment to which she had moved after she was alone in the world, she was visited by a strange man who introduced himself as her new doctor, sent by the family.

"Which members of my family?" asked Mrs. Ayer bewildered.

"Your daughter Harriet and your husband," she was told. "They feel that Dr. Schrady is not helping you. I am now in charge, and I have brought my nurse with me."

"But Lena waits on me," Mrs. Ayer protested. "She loves me and knows what I need."

"She is not a nurse," she was told. "I want to make sure you get the best care. I will see you again. My name is Dr. Morton."

The nurse came in after he left, and Lena was sent to the lower floor. Said Mrs. Ayer, "There is no question in my own mind that I was in anything but a normal state. I was so weak I was quite helpless. I could not raise my hand. Everything terrified me and the inexplicable desertion of my physician, my servant, and my friends and the authoritative manner of these strangers no doubt greatly aggravated my condition, for I grew rapidly worse. I concede I must have presented symptoms of Melancholia; but I protest that the treatment I was then receiv-

ing was eminently calculated to make them worse, and that in-
asmuch as I can today relate every incident connected with that
part of my illness, I must protest that I was not a fit subject for
cruel deception and imprisonment in a madhouse."

A few days afterwards (the date was Tuesday, February 7,
1893, according to the doctors' bills and legal documents among
her papers), Dr. Morton appeared with another man, whom he
introduced as Dr. Hammond. They asked her questions. She
was not told it was an examination for insanity. No one else was
present, except the nurse hired by Dr. Morton. And it was all so
brief and perfunctory that Mrs. Ayer was mystified afterwards
and asked her nurse what it was about. She was told that Dr.
Morton would explain everything very soon.

On February 9, the nurse did not appear. Lena took care of
her mistress again, and Mrs. Ayer, although even weaker than
before, was glad to see her and begged her not to let the nurse
return. Lena promised, and told her she had more good news—a
servant was downstairs with a message from Mrs. Hattie Seymour.

The servant was pleasant and what Mrs. Ayer, thinking as an
employer, tagged immediately as a "sensible-looking" woman.
She told Mrs. Ayer that she was Mrs. Seymour's personal maid,
and had been sent to conduct Mrs. Ayer and Lena to Mrs. Seymour's new country place outside East Orange for a fortnight,
where Mrs. Ayer could get "good country air and the joy of seeing her grandchildren." Mrs. Ayer, weak with happiness, turned
to Lena, and found tears in the girl's dark eyes.

"You see, Hattie hasn't forgotten me. I never believed she had.
Now that I'm ill, she is going to take care of me. I'll be well
in no time, now."

Lena pressed her hand. "Do you feel strong enough to go,
ma'am?"

"I feel strong enough to walk to New Jersey, now I know Hattie has sent for me."

With the help of the other woman, who seemed capable (and
"probably very useful to Hattie in the country," Harriet thought),
Lena dressed Harriet in a black moiré travel dress and put a
veiled hat on her lovely bright hair, a chic little "monkey cap"

that Mrs. Ayer had bought before she fell ill. But the trip downstairs was too much for the invalid; she fainted in the vestibule
and had to be carried out to the waiting brougham. Recovering
quickly in the air, she was startled to see Dr. Morton sitting opposite her in the carriage. He told her politely that he was
accompanying her at the request of her daughter.

Harriet held tight to Lena's hand. The day was cold, even for
February, but the sun was bright. It was pleasant being out-of-
doors again. She managed to smile at Lena, and Lena's dark
eyes again filled with tears. Harriet leaned forward for a glimpse
of the vital, fast-growing city of which she had been an eager
part until this recent illness—an illness which had come upon her
slowly at first and which no one seemed to understand. She
turned her head to the left. . . .

That was when she saw the skaters. Her first impression was
one of delight—what a charming picture their bright costumes
made against the background of ice and barren trees in Central
Park. Then she realized a startling fact. This wasn't the way
to New Jersey! They should have turned toward the Hudson
River ferry.

She gasped: "This isn't the way to Hattie's!"

No one answered. For the first time the suspicion that she had
been trapped came to the surface of her mind. Terror choked
her and she sank back in Lena's arms. But she was too weak to
escape. Even Lena, the only one in the carriage she trusted,
could not hold her own against a man. Besides, Lena had another great disadvantage. Less than fifty years ago her people
had been slaves. Bright and loyal as Lena was, she still had reason to fear the power of white people.

The rest of the trip was a nightmare. Sometimes Harriet lost
consciousness and fell into a fitful doze, after which, in her fever-
ish state, it seemed impossible that this trip was really happening. She prayed that when her eyes opened she would be safe in
her bed, with Lena taking care of her. Once she wakened,
seemed to come out of a dark, enveloping tunnel, and found even
Lena gone. She cried out in terror. But Lena was there, after
all, cradling her in her arms.

"Where are we?" Harriet begged.

"Nearly there," Lena answered. But that didn't answer the questions that were hammering in Harriet's tired head. Dozing in Lena's arms she knew it was all right; she was really going to Hattie's. But shocked into flashes of wakefulness she saw only the menace of the country outside. As it grew darker the houses disappeared. They were traveling on bumpy roads between bare fields, and then at last they stopped in front of a dark house and she heard a voice shouting, "Bring her in. . . ."

She felt herself being lifted, and she went down, down into the blackest tunnel of all.

When she opened her eyes again, she was in a bare, furnished room with closed shutters, a smoking kerosene lamp on a table by a bed. She felt herself dropped on the bed, not too gently. An unfriendly voice said, "Undress. I suppose I'll have to find some dinner for you."

Harriet could not move. She lay limp on the rough blanket which covered the bed, her eyes closed. Then she felt tender hands unfasten her dress, take off her shoes and underwear, slip a nightdress over her head. Hot tears fell on her hands. She opened her eyes to see Lena bending over her. Before they could speak to each other the door opened and a coarse, heavy woman in a soiled uniform came in, carrying a worn japanned tray. On it was a dish of cold stew and a pitcher with a broken spout.

"That's all," the woman told Lena. "The doctor said you could say goodbye. Get out."

Lena kissed Harriet on the cheek and left, weeping. The woman locked the door behind her, sat down on the chair and motioned toward the tray.

When Harriet hesitated the woman snatched up a soiled towel and pinned it around her throat. "Then," Mrs. Ayer told her audience, "she seized me by the neck with one hand, and, holding the broken pitcher to my mouth with the other, she poured the disgusting liquid down my throat faster than I could have swallowed it had I been famishing with thirst. And, as I was choking with tears, and frightened beyond expression, the dreadful stuff was emptied all over me, and I was told that I would learn to eat and drink or be 'learned' in a way not to my liking."

That was the beginning of fourteen months of horror, a large part of it spent inside a sunless room with padlocked shutters, lighted only by a malodorous kerosene stove. A woman attendant stayed with Harriet night and day. To add to this indignity, Dr. Granger, the superintendent of the asylum, broke in on her at his convenience, no matter what intimate personal ritual she was performing. She was given coarse cotton underwear and, only after several days of pleading, her own comb and brush—which some of the attendants also used when it pleased them.

During those first paralyzing weeks Harriet made up her mind to die. This was her state of mind when she was taken to New York for the Supreme Court hearing to determine whether she was capable of managing her own interests. She was too depressed and discouraged to care where she was or what was happening to her. She wanted only to be released from a world and a society that had done these things to her. But even that was not permitted. When she did not sleep, she was drugged. When she could not force herself to eat, food was poured down her throat and over her garments—"which I found was the usual method of feeding the insane. I have seen it done time and time again with the doctor looking on or actively aiding in the operation."

One day was much like another. Only the attendants changed, for the pay was poor ($14 to $16 a month). They were usually recruited from the vast army of immigrants pouring into New York, looking for any kind of job. As working in an insane asylum was not considered even as pleasant as being in the "sweatshops," and as Bronxville was miles away from the city and their own people, only the lowest type of worker stayed long on the job. The Irish immigrant who was Harriet's keeper for the longest time could neither read nor write, and had no desire to learn.

Harriet said, "I never had a cook in my employ so ignorant, yet I was compelled to live every hour of my life with this woman and to obey her smallest bidding."

One of her attendants had been a thief and in order to avoid the police for a while was, she told Harriet, "doing the asylum-attendant game." Another male attendant who took a fancy to Harriet told her confidentially, "Ye's got to have dis*si*plin. I've had great success sence I ever tuk up this business, and all account of me dis*si*plin. The first thing I does when I takes a new case is to lairn that case that I'm master and he must obey me or he'll get punished. That way, I have no further fuss. It's dis*si*plin they need and it's dis*si*plin I gives them."

Throughout her months in the asylum, Harriet wore the same dress and shoes she had put on for the journey. When her shoe laces wore out, she had to beg for bits of string which she knotted together. Once every two weeks she was allowed a bath in a tub. As spring approached, she was taken out to walk occasionally, as the attendants pleased, wearing a ragged sweater if it was raining or snowing. There was no other recreation. Finally, in despair when her pleas for books were rejected, she begged the attendant to let her help in some of the work in the household. After consultation with the doctor, she was given sheets and pillow cases to mend.

"I timidly asked for a thimble and thread and needles and I was given a crushed brass thimble, a needle so coarse that it made great holes in the cotton at every puncture, and a spool of very fine and very poor white thread. The thimble fell off constantly, the thread broke every few inches, and the needle made great wounds in my fingers. . . . Other attendants with other charges would come in to watch me at work, it seemed so amusing to them. I could sew only a little each day, because the room was so dark, but I looked forward to that little. . . ."

It was a situation which might have driven any ordinary sane person over the border into madness. But Harriet Hubbard Ayer was no ordinary woman. After the first period of apathy when all she longed for was oblivion, she began gradually to take an interest in the other poor inmates, even in the attendants. Horrible as her own situation was, she discovered that the really insane in the institution were in a far more desperate case. The attendants kept them in such a state of terror that they had no chance to improve. A young girl who was sometimes noisy and troublesome was handcuffed night and day for three weeks, until her wrists were so raw and bleeding that one of the house servants, out of sheer pity, wrapped the steel cuffs in cotton. Another old man, who was so weak he could not walk, was literally dragged around the grounds by two indifferent attendants so that his relatives could be told he was getting his "exercise."

Harriet had thought before this that she had reached the depths of despair. The Chicago fire and baby Gertrude's death had been blows from which she had never recovered. The loss of General Grubb, the alienation from her two children and then the death of her mother after a long painful illness, had made her feel that she had very little to live for. But now, as she looked around her at all this human misery, she was stricken with remorse. She had been vain, and frivolous, and selfish. She had thought only of her own happiness. She vowed that if she ever got out of the asylum, she would spend the rest of her life helping people.

Later she confessed to her good friend Dr. Morgan Dix, pastor of Old Trinity Church, that she had been ashamed to ask God to help her, she felt so unworthy. But her unspoken prayers were answered. One day as she and her Irish attendant were returning from their routine exercise along the stony country roads —a walk which Harriet dreaded in one way even as she looked forward to it, for the stones hurt dreadfully now that her shoes were so worn—a young man spoke to her. He was too well-dressed to be an attendant, far too cultivated in manner and accent to be the kind of doctor she had seen in the institution.

Frightened, Harriet looked away and did not answer.

The young man then spoke to Harriet's attendant, asking her if she would get him a bottle of mineral water from his supply in the cellar—and take one for herself. The Irish girl looked gloomily at Harriet and said she wasn't supposed to leave her, especially outside the asylum.

"I'll watch her until you get back," the young man promised. "The doctor won't mind. I'll explain if he sees us."

After she left, the man told Harriet that he too was a patient, but since he had committed himself, he had special privileges. He added swiftly, in a low voice: "Mrs. Ayer, I am disturbed

mentally. But I am not so disturbed that I don't know there has
been a grave injustice done you. You don't belong in this dreadful place. Please let me serve you."

His voice and his words were kind. But Harriet had been so
long under observation, so long accustomed to brutality and deception, that she was still afraid to talk to him.

He went on: "I know about your case. So long as you can tell
no one what is being done to you, there is no hope. Letters from
outside are intercepted before they reach you; the letters you
write are opened and destroyed. The doctor in charge has the
right to do this by law, if he sees fit. Please try to believe me,
will you?"

Keeping her head down, Harriet said, "No, I cannot believe
you. I believe no one. It must be another trick."

But he persisted: "I know you have been deceived abomina-
bly. But if I promised you on my word as a Freemason to post a
letter to your friends for you, would you write it?"

"I have no friends," Harriet told him.

"You are wrong. I know your lawyers will help. I would
write them myself, except that the information comes better from
you."

When she still looked doubtful, he bent and whispered, "The
attendant is coming back. Tomorrow I will meet you here again.
I know you speak French. I'll pretend to recite a French poem,
to test you, and I will tell you what to do."

The next morning he met them as they were returning from
their walk and told the Irish girl that he did not believe Mrs.
Ayer spoke French, that he would like to test her with a risqué
poem he knew. Amused, the girl agreed. Then he said quickly,
in French:

"Pretend you don't understand. I drive the assistant doctor to
the post office in my carriage every day and mail my own letters.
Write one tonight to your lawyer and smuggle it to me."

That afternoon, for the first time in months, Harriet asked for
paper and pencil to write letters. Her attendant got the supplies
readily; when a "loony" was busy writing letters, it was often
possible to steal away for a few minutes' gossip or a cup of tea

in the kitchen. Harriet wrote a quick scrawl to her daughter Margaret. Then she wrote a careful letter to Stephen Olin, describing what she had been through in the past months. When the attendant returned she handed her the letter for Margaret. The other letter was tucked in her bosom.

She slept that night with the envelope under her pillow. The next day, when the Freemason appeared during her walk, Harriet stooped down, pretending to repair her tattered shoestrings, and dropped the letter on the ground. The Mason picked it up before anyone else could notice and slipped it in his pocket. Harriet went off on her walk, expecting nothing, hoping for nothing, yet somehow impressed with the Mason and his promise. She knew little about the brotherhood, though she had heard that George Washington and Benjamin Franklin had been members, but for the first time in many months she had met a human being who was going far out of his way without any thought of self, simply to help another human being. The thought gave her comfort.

She told the audience: "The following days were stormy. But one afternoon the weather cleared and my attendant told me to get ready for a walk. It was quite late as we returned, and we met the man-of-all-work with the mail. He had been to the train for Dr. Granger, who had failed to arrive from New York, and he had picked up the evening mail, which the doctor usually took care of. My attendant asked if there were any letters for her (she had a beau in Ireland who could write, and I always read his letters to her), and he carelessly handed her the parcel. I took it from her and glanced through the letters. Suddenly I saw one addressed to 'Mrs. Harriet Hubbard Ayer,' with the imprint of my attorney's firm in the corner. I picked it out, as though it were hers. Then I saw another letter, with my attorney's imprint, addressed to Dr. Granger.

"I took my letter, saying, 'There are none for you today—this is for me,' and before she could recover from her absolute stupefaction I tore it open and read it. I think I must nearly have swooned, but I got to my room by will power, with the letter still clutched in my hand. It told me that my friends were ready to

serve me to their utmost capacity and that I would soon have
visitors."

The next day, as soon as Dr. Granger arrived and had had time
to read the mail, unprecedented things started to happen. Mrs.
Ayer was moved suddenly to a front room flooded with sunlight
—"as she was now so much improved." Dr. Granger announced
she would take her meals at his table, with his family. And in
the afternoon, instead of going for her usual walk with the attendant, Dr. Granger himself would take her for a drive in his
carriage. Harriet was still so unnerved and bewildered that she
tried to refuse the drive, but he insisted. She was afraid that
somehow her enemies had heard that she was getting help and
had instructed Dr. Granger to transfer her to another asylum.
But the doctor warned her that riding in a carriage was part of
her rehabilitation, and that if she was afraid, he would have to
report that she was not yet well enough to leave the asylum.
Meekly she agreed.

When they returned from the drive, Dr. Granger made another unprecedented suggestion. If there was anything Harriet
needed, he said, he would put a request to the committee which
had been placed in charge of her property, "although her illness
had been a great expense and her committee had been obliged
to keep her very plainly attired."

Trembling, Harriet looked down at her clothes. "If my committee can bear the expense of a pair of dress shields and one
pair of shoestrings to replace the fragments of string I am now
using," she said, "I should be duly grateful. But the only thing
I really need immediately is a Bible."

A few minutes afterwards there was a knock at the door and
the man-of-all-work handed Harriet's attendants a worn black
book. It was an old-fashioned book of Psalms, written in verse,
with the first Psalms missing. The handy man was apologetic.
The book had belonged to his mother, it was the nearest thing
to a Bible he could find.

Harriet thanked him with tears in her eyes and sat down in the
chair by the window, holding the book in her hands. It was the
first book she had seen or held in over a year. She turned it over

and over, and then at last opened to a quaint version of the Twenty-third Psalm:

"The Lord's my shepherd, I'll not want;
He makes me down to lie
In pastures green; he leadeth me the quiet water by.
My soul He doth restore again; and me to walk doth make
Within the paths of righteousness ev'n for His own name's sake,
Yea, though I walk in death's dark vale . . ."

Her eyes burned. She tried to read on, but she could not see the faded print. Even the brightness of the failing sunshine was unbearably painful. The sudden transition from dark shadows to hope and sunshine had been too much for her. She dropped to her knees and prayed: "Dear God, if it is Thy will that I be blind, give me the strength to bear it."

It was at this point in her lecture that Mrs. Ayer excused herself, left the stage and put on her white evening dress again. When she returned, she was holding three certificates.

The first was a certified copy of the medical certificate of sanity, by the New York State Commission of Lunacy, dated August 12, 1894.

The second was a certified copy of her certificate of insanity, dated February 7, 1893, committing Harriet Hubbard Ayer as a lunatic to Vernon House, Bronxville, New York, and signed by Dr. W. J. Morton.

She said, "No physician can legally sign a certificate of insanity in New York State unless he is qualified by the law to do so. He must, according to the law, have received his certificate as a qualified Examiner in Lunacy, but it is unlawful—I quote the Statute, Chapter 273, Laws of 1890: 'It is unlawful for any medical examiner in Lunacy to make a certificate of insanity for the purpose of committing any person to custody unless a certified copy of his certificate has been so filed and its receipt in the office of the commission [New York State Commission of Lunacy] as above provided has been acknowledged.'

"I have here a certificate copy of Dr. Morton's application to be qualified as an Examiner in Lunacy, dated New York, February 8, 1893, one day after he had, in violation of the law, signed my insanity certificate; and a certified copy of the receipt of his papers at Albany, which were filed and endorsed March 22, 1893, six weeks after he took me bodily to Bronxville and incarcerated me on his illegal certificate.

"If Dr. Morton honestly believed me a lunatic, there were at least a score of world-famous alienists in New York, duly qualified by law to examine cases such as mine was alleged to be, and to sign commitments.

"Why did he not secure the services of qualified men?

"Why was my own doctor not told?

"Why were my friends and attorneys not notified of the intention to remove me bodily from my home?

"What was the need of trickery and deceit if I was really insane and the asylum the place for me?

"And why did Dr. Morton testify at my insanity hearing that I agreed cheerfully to go to the asylum and was in a coma during the entire trip, when I was able to convince five reputable alienists when they visited me at the asylum that I was never told I was being examined for insanity; that both my maid and I were tricked into thinking I was being taken to the country home of my daughter Hattie; and that, far from being in a coma throughout the trip, I was sane and alert enough—although weak—to cry when I saw the skaters in Central Park: 'This isn't the way to Hattie's!' "

The audience at Central Music Hall was so electrified that they could not move for a moment after Mrs. Ayer stopped talking. Then they broke into wild applause—as much a tribute to the woman as to the drama of her story.

CHAPTER NINETEEN

H ARRIET was forty-five years old when she came out of the asylum. It was an age when most women of her era felt they were finished. She had no money of her own. Every cent she had made, every keepsake she had treasured, every bit of property and jewelry she had bought as a protection for her old age, had been sold. Her estate had paid the asylum bills, which had been expensive, and the Récamier Company, without her, had gone deeper and deeper into the red.

What was she to do?

She no longer had the energy, or the enthusiasm for money which had made her work long hours at her cosmetic business. Quite willingly, she faced receivership. Her friends were kind, but none of them were so rich that they could support her indefinitely. And the idea of going back into the business of decorative furnishings, of buying costly treasures for people who did not even see their beauty, was repugnant. She was too keenly aware of the many poor and suffering in the world for her to cater to the heedless rich.

During the years after her case against James Seymour, and before her time in the asylum, Harriet had felt that she was the loneliest woman in the world. Her children no longer loved her.

The father of those children had been seduced by her enemies into signing statements which Harriet knew he was incapable of writing. Even her sisters and old friends no longer seemed close, for they lived in a world which Harriet was trying to escape. The final blow had been the marriage of General Grubb. He had written her in 1890, before he left America as Ambassador to Spain. The letter had been friendly, and he asked her to let his housekeeper know if she still would like to have flowers from his greenhouse. But Harriet, although she had started scores of letters in reply, had never been able to finish one. Not long afterwards, the General married. He was fifty-seven; his bride was twenty-six.

She was deeply hurt, although later she came to see that most of the trouble lay in herself, in her own attitudes. She had rejected the only man she ever really loved, out of a combination of pride and insecurity, just as she had rejected friends and her own sisters.

Then in addition to everything else, she had made up her mind to stop taking any drugs or medication. There is considerable doubt that she ever should have been considered a real addict, although she herself believed she was, and a periodical of the period referred to her as one of the few people who had cured themselves of morphine addiction. Probably she was one of a number of cases on record of Victorian women who were given morphine for pain and, feeling that they were beginning to lean on it, gave it up before they became addicts. Nevertheless, withdrawal of this kind was trying, hard on her nerves and her health. For the rest of her life, except for the period in the asylum when she was drugged by force, she never touched drugs or alcohol of any kind.

There is no question but that she was physically and probably mentally ill when she was put into the asylum, but there is also no question but that James Seymour, who had never forgiven her for scorning him, seized the opportunity to get her permanently out of the way. In those days, asylums were for the sole purpose of confining and restraining, not curing, the mad; few people emerged from these institutions and a tag of insanity was next to a death sentence.

The ignorance of the public regarding mental trouble was of course even more abysmal than that of the medical profession. Blanche Howard's attitude was far from unusual, and Hattie and Margaret could not be blamed for accepting the fact that their mother might as well be dead. Hattie was merely a tool; in later years, she confessed that she had not only been tricked into signing the papers that put her mother away, but that letters and cables addressed to her had been intercepted, and even answered, by her father-in-law. She had been protected all her life, and it did not occur to her that people she knew and loved could be capable of evil.

Her doubts about the whole situation must have been resolved when her father-in-law, James Seymour, suddenly took all the available cash he could gather together and left his wife and sons, to live in California with a married daughter. His drive to punish Harriet for not accepting him as her lover would today be considered psychotic. Certainly, he gained nothing by persecuting her, not even emotional satisfaction, and was the one who suffered most from his own machinations. By the time that Hattie suspected what the Seymours had done to her mother, she also realized what she herself had done. She felt that she could never face her mother again. She could not believe that her mother would ever want to see her.

Harriet, however, was not the same woman she had been. She no longer suffered from a feeling of rejection, or even of false pride. She welcomed the help of her sisters with delight; they became closer than they had been in years. She accepted financial help from Stephen Olin and Mrs. J. B. Lyon (who financed the Chicago lecture and put Harriet on the road to earning her living again). And she kept in touch with the Mason who had helped her escape from the asylum, followed his advice and accepted the friendship of his friends, although she never told anyone his name. After Harriet died, her daughter Margaret wore the Masonic emblem he had given her mother, but neither she nor Hattie ever had the faintest idea who he was, or if he ever returned to his place in the world.

Harriet's feelings toward her daughters were changed, too. She was humble, as well as loving. She realized that she could

not ask them to come to her, that she had to wait—and pray.
And she was able to do this because her whole standard of values
had changed. The frustrations that had made her ill no longer
existed. She told a Chicago reporter after her lecture:

"I have no personal grievance whatever against the proprietor
or employees of the Bronxville establishment where I was confined, as I do not think I was treated any differently than the
average patient. It is in order to decry the system, or lack of
system, in such establishments, that I make my own experiences
public.

"I have not the slightest malice in saying what I have said
and what I shall continue to say. I would suspect even a philan-
thropist who was . . . willing to charge $50 a week (and often
much more) to consign a delicately bred woman to attendants
paid $14 a month for their services. We all know the sort of
nurses obtained at that price. I claim no man in the world has
such a high moral attitude that he should be allowed the absolute control of lives placed so helplessly in his charge as is Dr.
Granger. As for the conduct of the attendants, I believe that the
class of people who take such positions naturally abuse their
opportunities in a place where they are allowed full sway. . . .
I think it was an absurd blunder from beginning to end and that
Dr. Granger was looking for patients and perhaps too eager to
keep them. . . ."

Asked about her husband, she said: "I cannot lead myself to
believe that the father of my children would do such a dastardly
deed for money.

"My former husband and I had our differences. We were
wretchedly unhappy together and we separated. Until Mr. Ayer
fell under the influence of my avowed enemy he never slandered
me. When he did attack me as I said, as I repeat now, Mr. Ayer
was a tool in the hands of another man, and was undoubtedly
drinking when he made his absurd charges against me. That is
the charitable construction to put upon a gentleman who had
many splendid attributes, and who reached a sad depth indeed
to contemplate seeking to destroy and degrade a woman, his
children's mother."

She wrote an exposé of insane asylums which was printed first in the program of the Chicago lecture, and later copied many times in newspapers. Her old magic touch was evident in her plea for "those unfortunates whose sufferings go on day after day, unknown to the world, unheeded by brute keepers whose business it is to be heedless, and unhopeful of any human help: —legally deprived of friends, voice and rights, guilty of no wrong to anyone, merely ill of mind. . . . That those weeping, groaning and shrieking, unheard voices, muffled behind thick walls, should find in mine outside an echo that would resound end to end throughout this liberty-loving land, has been a purpose to me infinitely dearer than the life so blighted by the hideous experiences to which I was subjected, owing to the iniquitous laxity of the lunacy laws. . . ."

Immediately after the Chicago lecture, she began to get letters from all over the United States from people who had had similar experiences in institutions, or who had beloved friends in asylums, and asked for her help. The newspapers took up the cause, and numerous incidents were brought out into the open where people had been "put away" in private institutions by greedy relatives or enemies, simply to get rid of them. She was invited to lecture by groups in New York and New Jersey. And, most pitiful of all, she received letters smuggled out from behind asylum walls.

Whenever possible, Harriet charged a fee for her lectures, ranging from twenty-five cents to one dollar, which she used to obtain legal help for the victims she heard about. But before long she realized that the organizations and aroused groups which were forming, were far better equipped to do that work now. Her chore was over. She had used herself as a means of publicizing the terrible situation, and she later had the gratification of knowing that she had inaugurated the revision of New York laws governing the treatment and rights of the insane.

It had not been done without personal sacrifice and harm to her already damaged reputation. Even some people who loved her best were hesitant about recommending her for jobs, and tried instead to give her money. But Harriet would not accept more charity. She felt she must have work, not only so that she could support herself, but so that she would not waste the years of her life that had been almost miraculously given back to her.

One spring afternoon, when she was more discouraged and depressed than usual, she slipped into the half-dusk of Old Trinity Church and sat in one of the back pews to catch her breath. For a moment, she saw herself as a figure of pity—nearly forty-seven years old, alone, rejected by the children she had loved so much—perhaps too much—laughed at by some as a "loony." She bowed her head.

Suddenly, the tears of self-pity which had been smarting in her eyes were gone. She felt rested, encouraged. She was alive, she had her health again, and she had her two hands and her head. Wasn't she perfectly equipped to help other people, she who had herself touched the depths of suffering so that she could not, and would not, stand in judgment of anybody else?

After a few minutes, she got up and stepped out into the pale spring sunlight. She had no idea where she was going. It was a beautiful day, bright with promise. She looked up at the sky and the sun just then was reflected on the dome of one of the highest buildings in the city—Joseph Pulitzer's new home for his newspaper, the *World*. Joseph Pulitzer was in many ways a difficult man, but he was a great editor, and he drew sparks from the people who worked for him.

Harriet walked slowly toward Park Row where the Pulitzer building stood. It was almost as though she were being drawn there through no will of her own. Inside, she asked the uniformed elevator operator whom she should ask about a job on the *World*. He stared at her curiously.

"Doing what ma'am?"

"I—I guess I would like to be a reporter."

The operator's Irish face creased in a grin. "You don't look like one, ma'am, if you don't mind my saying so. Some of these young blades are pretty tough. The rest are—but I tell you. Go and see that young Brisbane, Arthur Brisbane. He has a lot of crazy notions and he's riding high with the old man right now."

Harriet thanked him. It was her kind of fate—or luck—that young Arthur Brisbane was still Sunday editor of the *World*, for he was soon to be offered a much more tempting salary to join Hearst's new *Journal*. Brisbane was yet to become famous, but he had already injected into journalism a new note which was considered sensational—"yellow"—and depended upon the bizarre, the twist of novelty. Brisbane was also the son of a social reformer, which gave him a breadth of sympathy and interest which other young newspapermen often lacked. When Harriet Hubbard Ayer sent in her name, his first thought was that he wanted to meet this famous—or notorious—woman. He said, "Of course I'll see her."

When she told him what she wanted, his second thought was that of a sound newspaperman. If he, more or less cynical, interrupted a busy day to get a look at Harriet Hubbard Ayer, wouldn't his readers have the same curiosity?"

"Can you write?" he asked her.

"I've written a book, and considerable advertising. And I do know what interests women."

"Such as?"

"Good looks—and health, incidentally. For health is very important to good looks, although some young women won't admit it. And you have a whole new audience which needs that kind of information, the typists and clerks who are discovering that good looks get them further in the world of business than ability—as long as men are the employers."

Brisbane smiled at her, and Harriet smiled back. Half an hour ago, if anyone had told him that he would be considering hiring a woman recently released from an insane asylum, a woman nearly fifty years old, he would have laughed. But Harriet had something that he recognized, for he had it himself. Later, he said that it was the printer's ink in both of their veins.

He said, "Write me a trial column."

She nodded. "I'll bring it in tomorrow."

Brisbane slammed a hand down on his desk. "Tomorrow? This is the newspaper business, madam! You can't wait until tomorrow. Everything has to be done now. Go in the city room and sit down and write me a column."

Harriet went into the city room, where the reporters turned and stared at her. There were a few women reporters, like the famous Nellie Bly, but men still resented their presence in what they liked to think of as a male world. No one offered to help

her. Not one man got up from his desk. Finally, she stopped a
small boy and he supplied her with paper and pencils. Standing
up, her back to the rest of the room, shutting out the noise and
laughter, she wrote her first beauty column on the windowsill.
She took it in to Brisbane, and he hired her on the spot.

So she began the last chapter in her life—the busiest and
happiest of all.

From the first, her column was a success. In the beginning,
her name at least had publicity value and her writing attracted
attention for that reason. But soon it became apparent that Mrs.
Ayer not only could write, she had an eye for the things women
were interested in. She took care to point out that women's
pressing desire to make themselves attractive was not based only
on natural vanity, but also on the great economic upheaval that
followed the Civil War.

"Up to that time, our lives had been relatively simple," she
wrote. "The young girl with just the sweetness of youth needed
no cosmetics to get a husband, and when she captured him, she
needed beauty aids even less. After her children were born, she
settled down into middle age with grandchildren at her feet and
a frilled cap on her head and lapsed into old age before she was
forty. Then, according to the income of the family, she either
helped with the housekeeping and the children or worked for
the church—no need of beauty helps *there*.

"But after the war, which took such a large toll of men, the
picture changed. Women were forced to leave home which
could no longer support them, and contribute to the support of
parents or dependents. . . . Not all of them liked it, but they
were quick to find out that youth and good looks gave them an
advantage over plainer rivals. . . ."

Harriet talked to office workers, in the beginning. Like all
instinctive reporters, she had a knack of making contact with
her readers, and she discussed problems that were hers as well
as theirs. She had a desk now in one corner of the city room and,
as her mail multiplied, she was allotted first one and then two sec-
retarial assistants. Although one of her secretaries insisted to the
end on wearing Sunday dresses to the office—flowered challis and

huge flopping rose- and lace-trimmed straw hats—Harriet worked hard to persuade working girls of the smartness and suitability of the jacket, skirt and shirtwaist. She never wore anything else, while she was at work. In summers, she changed to all-white suits, but they were always tailored, and always meticulously fresh. She joined a small group of working women and feminists who called themselves the "Rainey Daiseys" and who cut off their long skirts full four inches from the ground, sometimes eliciting on the street whistles, cat-calls and even an over-ripe vegetable aimed at their shockingly visible ankles. The wasp waist corset, which caused fainting spells and weakness in so many young women typists, was severely criticized by Mrs. Ayer, who confided that she herself wore a comfortable straight-front corset, and maintained her figure by exercise.

She received almost twenty thousand letters a year. Some of them were answered in the newspapers, the answers to others were dictated to her hard-working secretaries, but there were still sheafs of letters which she took home to answer in longhand, and in privacy. She also experimented at home, working out formulas for cold creams, anti-perspirants, and anti-kink preparations for the curly hair of colored people. The demand grew for these formulas, until she had them printed on long slips a thousand at a time, and stored on office shelves behind her to send to her readers.

It was not long before she was writing for the *Evening World* as well as for the *Sunday World*, doing interviews and feature stories in addition to her regular column and her Sunday page. She covered everything from murder trials to exposés of working and living conditions in the tenements, and because her own experiences had deepened her innate sympathy for the underdog, her stories were often extraordinarily moving.

To a woman who had earned huge sums of money from her own business, and who had once spent $150,000 a year in Chicago on household expenses, a newspaper salary did not look very large, yet she could not resist making impulsive gifts to friends, relatives and even strangers who came into her office. She was broke most of the time, and complained cheerfully about it. But her office door was never closed, not even after her department grew until she and her secretaries were moved into their own private domain in the World annex.

Strange visitors came through that door: women on the verge of childbirth, for whom ambulances had to be ordered immediately; girls in trouble, thinking of suicide; women pursued by drunken husbands; women suffering from drugs, beatings, mental sickness. Not all the visitors were women. An occasional male, sometimes sober and sometimes not, would drop in to ask for advice—or help. An old man once appeared and begged Mrs. Ayer to print in the paper that it was all right to eat peas off his knife so that his daughter-in-law wouldn't yell at him for his bad table manners. "It *is* all right, isn't it?" he added, suddenly dubious.

While Harriet's secretaries ducked their heads over their work to keep from smiling, Harriet also had a struggle with herself. "You're very clever to be able to manage it. I can't—I spill when I try. Most people do. That's why it is considered more polite for them to eat peas with a fork. Don't you think it would be kinder to do what other people must do, because they aren't as adept as you?"

Another morning a huge not-so-sober ruffian swaggered in and demanded the price of a cup of coffee. Harriet gave him five cents. When he left, Harriet's secretary scolded her. Harriet said, "Perhaps he will spend it in a bar. But I've learned through terrible experience that anyone who is without dignity and self-respect, as that man was, needs help. I don't know whether I did any good, but I would hate to think I might have passed him by when he needed me. Besides, he was bigger than I was."

Her sense of fun, her energy, and her unfailing interest in people, made her popular with the staff. She was also a trouper. When she had been with the *World* only seven months, Hearst, who was engaged in a bitter professional feud with Pulitzer, hired most of the *Sunday World* staff at large salary increases on condition that they march out in a body, without notice. Harriet and another reporter worked all night and, with the help of an office boy, got out the edition. It was hard work, but it was exciting, too.

When Harriet's group was dignified by the title "Woman's

Department" and moved to the second floor of the Pulitzer Building annex, many of the regular staff still visited her daily. She soon found herself giving advice to the "lovelorn" reporters on the newspaper, and she was always good for a small loan, even if she had to borrow the money from someone else. For the benefit of these visitors, the rather unglamorous furnishings of the Woman's Department included a spittoon, an American invention which at that time appeared everywhere from the back room of the corner saloon to sitting rooms at the Waldorf-Astoria.

Miss Phoebe Annan, one of Mrs. Ayer's three secretaries, would watch with horror while the advertising manager, a burly Southerner, took aim at the spittoon from the farthest possible distance. One day she complained to Harriet.

Harriet smiled impishly. "I only worry about the others, the ones who miss and make more work for the scrubwomen. Now, Mr. C. is a perfect gentleman. *He* never misses. Think how the scrubwomen must bless him."

Her concern for women was intense, and this was the period of her life when she could be considered a feminist. Men liked her and she still enjoyed their flattery and their company, but her major interest was in women—and women in all walks of life. She interviewed society leaders and the wife of the President of the United States as calmly as she talked to inhabitants of murderers' row. In one breath she writes: "How I do hate to ask a lovely woman of the social world for her photograph! It is the exquisitely painful moment which I know I have before me and I put off until the very last instant." And in another, interviewing a woman accused—and probably guilty—of heartless murder: "I don't know when I have felt so sorry for a woman, for after all she is a woman and not many years ago, a pretty innocent girl. With all my heart I hope she may be able to prove she is innocent." In 1902, when she visited England to do a "Harriet Hubbard Ayer Abroad" series, she interviewed Florence Maybrick, an American woman convicted of murder who had then served thirteen years of her life sentence. Harriet wrote: "Florence Maybrick's fate has always lain heavily on my heart. Her face is an absolute blank except for that terrible sort of dumb protest felt in each feature."

Some of Harriet's newspaper writing was in the sob-sister tradition, moist with anguish. But for the most part, her genius lay
in her ardent and genuine interest in everything around her,
and in her insatiable curiosity. Her attitude kept her young, and
she was regarded as a contemporary by men in the office who
were half her age.

Her newspaper writing also benefited from her strong maternal
sense. She loved to take care of people—which meant her readers, of course—and she enjoyed telling them what to do, for she
never was so soppily maternal that she could not recognize flaws
and itch to correct them, even in those she loved best.

One day, when she had been working two years at the *World*,
she was sent to interview a man who called himself Cheiro, who
claimed to have power to foretell the future. Part Irish and part
Greek, a man of unusual good looks, he was having considerable
success with New York society women. Harriet was fascinated,
but she had acquired enough newspaper skepticism to refuse to
take him seriously when he asked to see her hand. Finally, however, she gave it to him.

He told her: "Your bad days are over. Your children are coming home."

She shook her head, suspecting that he remembered her name,
and situation, from the sensational scandals in the papers.

"You don't believe me?" he asked. "Then make note of this
date. Your youngest child is on her way to you, right now. She
will soon be on the seas. I can see her plainly. You will be very
happy and take her in your arms one of these days, Mrs. Ayer.
Do not doubt me. I am sure."

That night, for the first time in many years, Harriet dreamed of
her younger daughter. It was a frightening dream. Margaret
was standing on a high rock, with waves breaking below. Harriet tried to call her, begging her not to jump. But the wind
carried away her voice, and Harriet awakened exhausted and
nearly sick with a headache. She called the office to tell Phoebe
Annan that she did not feel well, and would be late coming in.

"Your friend Cheiro called up this morning," Miss Annan said.
"He said to tell you not to worry about your daughter, she is safe."

She'll be on the high seas soon, and you are not to worry. Do you know what he's talking about?"

Harriet clung to the telephone, unable to speak. It was the first of numerous mysterious ties and communications which she was to have with her younger child for the rest of her life.

CHAPTER TWENTY

Blanche Willis Howard loved Margaret as deeply as it was possible for her to love anyone. However, in her love, there was a mixture of jealousy and hate. Since her husband's death, she had no one but the girl. Yet even as she forced the fifteen-year-old into pretending she was older, Blanche was quick to resent and resist any indication that Margaret was growing independent. Margaret was made to learn to sew and cook and shop to "pay for her keep." But Blanche still treated her like a child, correcting her table manners, poking fun at her adolescent awkwardness. When Blanche was working on a book, she would lock Margaret out of her room. If they were staying in a small hotel bedroom, as they were more and more often these days, it meant that Margaret had no place to go but the streets or free museums. Yet if a man—or a boy—glanced at Margaret with admiration and Blanche saw it, she would fly into a violent rage.

Part of the trouble was money. Finally Seymour had rebelled and told Blanche that he was through paying such high fees and to send the girl back. When Blanche refused, he wrote that he would send not one cent more. In a way, that was a victory, for it gave Blanche complete control of Margaret. But the novelist sorely missed the money.

She had to write from financial necessity now, which improved neither her temper nor her writing. Her drinking increased. She spent money on liquor when they did not have enough to eat. She borrowed from old friends and acquaintances, and seldom could repay. When her credit was exhausted in one place, she moved to another, each time lowering her standard of living. Soon they were traveling third class, living in cheap hotel rooms, eating in grim little restaurants. Margaret was hungry most of the time. Occasionally, when old friends of Blanche's invited the pair to a meal, Margaret would not be able to control her voracious appetite—in spite of the humiliating reprimands which always followed.

Margaret today estimates that Blanche Howard had received over $23,000 from Harriet and, later, James Seymour for her education. In return, the girl had acquired a cultural background far richer than that of most girls, even those who had been abroad to school, and she was grateful for this in later life. Yet in other ways she was neglected and abused. As Blanche grew more disturbed, she found it necessary to use Margaret as her whipping boy.

Margaret says: "Only a psychiatrist today could understand what had happened to my will and mind. I was actually dominated by this forceful and resourceful woman with almost hypnotic powers. She had loved me when I was little, but as I grew older, I think she wanted me to suffer for all the things that were happening to her. Yet I was so much under her control that I did not dream of rebelling. I learned later that my mother used to write me at Blanche's old address, and send me gifts on my birthday and on holidays. If Blanche Howard ever got those letters she must have destroyed them, and kept the gifts for herself or threw them away. But I doubt if I would have left Blanche then even if my mother had found me, and begged me to come home with her. By that time, Wawie had not only poisoned my mind against her—she had warned me that there was bad blood in my veins, which was from my mother, and only her harshest discipline and watchfulness could save me."

Margaret lost touch with her sister. Hattie, busy with her own family and Lewis' increasing financial burdens, seemed worlds away.

In addition, Blanche had done her best to turn Margaret also against the Seymours now they no longer were sending money. She referred to them as cultural boors; she laughed at Lewis and poor little Hattie; she made Margaret feel that they regarded her only as a burden. So Margaret seldom answered her sister's letters, and then only with stiff, superior little notes.

From the time Margaret was fifteen until she was eighteen, this situation continued, growing steadily worse. Blanche was writing feverishly, but little money came in. Gradually, the young girl realized that she could not go on. Once in Munich, Blanche Howard had insisted that Margaret attend a municipal costume ball with her. Margaret was only interested in the supper which was served. She ate so hungrily that her supper partner, a masked stranger, became curious. When he heard her story, he warned her: "You must get away from that woman you are living with. Never mind who I am. Tomorrow go to the North German Lloyd office and ask for the man in charge. Tell him your name, and you will be given a ticket to New York. But leave—before it's too late."

Margaret didn't dare to follow his instructions, but some months later, back in Stuttgart, Blanche left Margaret with a baker's family while she went on a tour of the Holy Land with his son, a young army lieutenant. Although Blanche was then close to fifty, she could still attract men, even younger men, and persuade them to finance her on brief trips. The lieutenant and Blanche returned long before Margaret expected them and the young officer gave Margaret a piece of earnest advice: "Don't stay with that woman or terrible harm will come to you."

Frightened, Margaret promised to leave Blanche, but she was uncertain what to do. Her father had stopped writing her years ago; she didn't even know where he was. So far as Margaret knew, her mother was either still in the asylum, or dead. After years of rudeness and indifference to Hattie, Margaret hated to ask her for money. But her sister was her only hope. While Wawie was getting ready for their next trip to the Isle of Guernsey, where she planned to spend the summer writing a book, Margaret wrote Hattie begging her to send her steamship fare to the United States. She gave the post office at Guernsey as an address.

At Guernsey, they stayed in a small inn, very cheap but clean and with plenty of plain food. Blanche Howard tried to write in an abandoned inn nearby, leaving Margaret to her own devices. She haunted the post office, and as day after day passed with no word from Hattie, she would roam the high cliffs of the island, desperately wondering if she should hurl herself into the breakers below. She says today: "Something stopped me always—no matter how miserable I was, how sure that everyone had deserted me, even Hattie. I am now convinced that it was my mother who managed to sense my misery and who kept me from killing myself. There was always a bond between us which nothing or nobody could break."

Blanche's persecution intensified, as though she sensed that Margaret had decided to escape. She warned the other guests at the inn that Margaret was not stable. One night at dinner, she spent most of the meal tabulating Harriet Hubbard Ayer's faults and "vices" in language far rougher even than that she had used in the letters printed by the newspapers during the Seymour trial. Then she turned to Margaret. "You are very like your mother, Margaret. If I wished, I could have you committed right now. You had better not do anything that would make me angry."

There was a carving knife on the table. Margaret reached for it, blind with hatred for the woman she had once loved. She stood up with it in her hand. Suddenly, she was aware that she was playing Blanche's game. She had just enough control left to drop the knife and rush upstairs to their bedroom. That night, while Blanche slept, she lay awake plotting her escape. Her only possession of value was a gold watch which had been her mother's present to her in Stuttgart on the last Christmas they had spent together. She determined to pawn it immediately and get at least as far away as London.

The next day, she had a letter from Hattie telling her that she had given money for her passage to America to Blanche Howard's niece, who was starting on a tour abroad with Augustin Daly's Shakespearean troupe. She suggested that Margaret write Marion in London. But Margaret could not wait. She pawned the gold watch and got enough money to take her to London, where she told her whole story to the Meynells, who helped her locate Marion. Then, with a meager wardrobe, mostly hand-me-downs, she sailed on the first ship she could get from Liverpool. She learned later that Blanche Howard had traced her to the Meynells', but they had told her nothing about Margaret until the ship was safely at sea.

It was a dazed and frightened girl whom Hattie and Lewis met at the pier in New York. She spoke English with a faint German accent, and she was nervous almost to the point of hysteria. Although she was just nineteen, she had a confused idea, the result of Blanche's suggestions, that she should act older. Hattie and Lewis took her home with them, to New Jersey. As they had no spare room for the newcomer Margaret stayed with Hattie's mother-in-law in the old Seymour place next door to Hattie's small house. It was not a satisfactory solution. Although the older woman was kind, the young girl must have been a constant reproach and an unwelcome reminder of her mother. Jim Seymour had been neither a good nor a faithful husband and when he went west he had left Mrs. Seymour only the house and a small income. Lewis, who had inevitably shared with his father in the unpleasant notoriety of the trial, lacked the business judgment which might have pulled him through the muddle into which his affairs had fallen. The ill-at-ease stranger added to their worries by making remarks which seemed gauche and even vulgar in the proper atmosphere of East Orange, for poor Margaret's cosmopolitan education was wasted on the Seymours and their friends.

Hattie was quietly taking piano pupils, already exhibiting the teaching genius which was eventually to make her famous. Margaret knew she must get some kind of work. She thought of teaching German, but her knowledge of English grammar was so slight that she feared she could not get any kind of a post in a reputable school. Singing was her only other talent, but she had no idea how to start a career. So she finally wrote to her father. But his fumbling reply, long in coming, only told her to go to her mother:

"Palmer House
Chicago, June 6th, 1898

"MY DARLING DAUGHTER:—

"I would have answered your letter before, but have been ill. We must look at things as they are. If you wish to please, and do as I think best, you will make friends with her at once. I mean your mother. I have seen her. She has been to see me. She is a splendid good woman, and can do you more good than anyone living, and wants to. She is your mother, and one of the brightest women in the country, and will be the making of you, and will take pleasure in being your true good mother. She has a splendid head and good heart, and will go to any extent for your good. Hope you will decide to go to her at once, and am sure you will be very happy with her. She can help you in your art more than anybody, as Mrs. A. is very popular with everyone in that line.

"My health is so bad, and does not seem disposed to improve. I would be much happier if you were living with her, and under her good advice, and am sure you would have a good home and a happy one. With your voice and talent and energy you cannot help but succeed. I ask you with all my heart to go to her. She has the best position on any paper in this country. Please go at once. . . ."

Margaret faced the inevitable: her mother was the only one who could help her. Months ago, when she had discovered that her mother was neither insane nor dead, but alive and an important person, she had longed to throw herself on her mercy. But she was terrified of being rejected and Hattie, who also was estranged from Harriet, offered no encouragement.

Just as she was wondering how she could possibly approach a mother who might not even recognize her, a visitor arrived who

had been sent by Herbert. She was Tante Marie, the French girl
whom Harriet had befriended back in Chicago, who was married
to Herbert's oldest stepbrother. A lively and charming person,
she volunteered to tell Harriet that her youngest daughter
wanted to see her.

The meeting was arranged. Even though Tante Marie assured
Margaret that Harriet would be overjoyed, Margaret insisted on
going alone. She felt she could not bear having anyone there if
her mother chose to turn her away.

Harriet was living on 113th Street in Manhattan, in a small
fourth floor walk-up apartment overlooking Morningside Park.
In contrast to the many luxurious homes she had occupied, this
inconvenient uptown flat cost only $17 a month. She had none
of her old furniture, for it had all been lost in auction sales while
she was in the asylum. But the walls were painted her favorite
pale pink, and light flooded in the big windows.

Margaret had seen her mother's picture in the newspapers, but
she was unprepared for the shock of her beauty in person. Harriet's hair was gray, but her skin was fresh and lovely as a girl's,
her blue eyes dark and clear. She was wearing a white linen
dress with insets of lace, her only jewelry a 33rd Degree Mason's
emblem, gift of the man who had saved her from the asylum,
which she wore around her neck on a black velvet ribbon.

Margaret felt clumsy and ugly in her made-over clothes. She
hung her head, afraid to speak for fear her mother would make
fun of her German accent, unwilling to meet her mother's shining dark eyes. Then she smelled a wonderful scent that took her
back all the years to the days when she was a small child, happy
and secure in her mother's arms.

"Your violet perfume," she murmured. "I'd know it anywhere."

Harriet put a warm hand under her daughter's chin. "Let me
look at you, my darling. If you only knew how I have prayed,
night after night, year after year, that I might once more hold
my baby in my arms again . . ."

Margaret lifted her head. Not until she saw Harriet's tears did
she realize that she was crying, too. Harriet opened her arms.
With a sob, Margaret ran into them. Neither of them could

speak, but when they separated, the chain of Harriet's eyeglasses, which she wore pinned to her bosom, caught on the buttons of Margaret's dress. They both laughed shakily.

"We're chained together, Margaret," Harriet said softly. "I hope that's the way it's going to be the rest of my life."

CHAPTER TWENTY-ONE

MARGARET and Harriet did not live together at first—they were still too shy with each other to suggest that. But they were never really separated again, for they wrote each other daily. Soon after their first meeting, Harriet made plans to bring Herbert Ayer to New Jersey where he could be cared for in a rest home for elderly men. She wrote Margaret on June 28, 1899:

"I have waited all day for a telegram about papa and it just occurs to me that he will send a night message in which case I shall of course not get it till morning. I have written the 'Newman Villa' people today making arrangements for a room. I imagine he will arrive in Jersey City at 6:45 Saturday. I shall be there and will go with him to the Villa which is straight from Dickens and just like a stage performance. The proprietor is such a dear old fellow, an ex-theatrical manager with a heart three times as big as his pet 'villa.' He will be kind to papa and already has a few blind and halt friends of better days 'visiting' him. I have written him Mr. Ayer is my brother-in-law and if papa can only recollect it we shall have no difficulty but he doesn't remember anything five minutes. However, it was the best I could do as I decline to make explanations to anyone. I

will write you at once if I get a message in the morning. I
thought possibly you could come down to the Villa. Herbert
[Jule's younger son] will come with you I am sure. I will write
Aunt Jule about it now. Of course darling I do not know how
you are situated and perhaps you would rather wait and see your
father with Hattie. Only I grasp at a chance to see you again. I
enclose you a letter received yesterday from The Ginger who
wants to see you. I wrote him not to come till next week. The
heat is really awful. I hope we shall have a change soon on account of the sick and the babies that are in the slums. . . . *Maman qui t'aime.*"

And the next day, she wrote again:

"Office, Friday

"MARGARET, DARLING

"I rec'd the message saying papa would arrive tomorrow morning when I reached the office. An hour later I rec'd the one saying he would not leave until next Wednesday. I fear he really
never will get away. My theory is that he thinks he is going to
be well enough to start but when it becomes really necessary for
him to make an effort he is unable to do so. . . . This puts my
dreams of seeing you at Newman's Villa beyond realization so I
must be as patient as I can till next week.

"I am so thankful for this cooler weather but my writing hand
is on a high horse and so I have trouble before me as I am so
dependent upon my braw right arm. Louis Lockwood has just
left my office. He was going out with me to help me with papa
tomorrow morning, and we both hoped to see you and Herbert.

"I fear sometimes you will never see your poor old father again
and it does not seem right. I don't think I ever felt so sorry for a
human being as I did for papa. He is *so* helpless, so poor, so
alone, such a wreck of all that stands for manhood and strength.
Send me a little line, dear . . .

Maman qui t'aime"

Herbert Ayer finally arrived. Margaret saw him go down on
his knees, weeping, to thank her mother. Margaret and Hattie

visited him often until he died, which was in less than a year. Harriet never visited him after his arrival, although she paid all his bills until the end, and saw that he was never in need of anything. She had deep sympathy for her ex-husband, but she did not want to explain why she was taking care of him. Only a few intimate friends in Chicago ever found out what she was doing.

Meanwhile, Margaret screwed up her courage to ask her mother if she might come and live with her . . . "if you want me." The answer came like a flash:

"If I want you! My darling, I want you more than anything in the world. You will be as welcome as the birds in the spring, and I hope with all my soul you will be as free as a bird that has found a nest but not a cage. Just say you are coming home, and after you get to me we will arrange the spacious flat to suit ourselves. You will find the most primitive housekeeping in effect, but we can live just as we please. You have made me so happy I can scarcely write, I long to see you but I will be patient. . . ."

She had rented a piano for Margaret—"although I don't know any more about pianos than I do about clothes wringers"—and bought a "little bed." Margaret recalls: "There was no special celebration the first night I slept under my mother's roof. Some things cannot be talked about. The years of separation could not be bridged by words and there was too much in both our minds to be able to discuss anything. I continued to be frightfully nervous, and any sudden noise would make me start or jump up, and, at a loud banging sound, I would occasionally cry. Mamma called in her doctor, who was wonderfully kind. Mamma had told him about some of the things that had happened to me, and he encouraged me to talk more about Blanche Howard. Ever since I had run away from her, I had suffered with terrible nightmares, in which I was always being pursued—I don't know by what, but I would awake soaking wet with perspiration, and trembling. I also told him about the night that Blanche Howard had wakened me by throwing the cold water over me, and how I had not really slept peacefully since. The doctor advised Mamma to go slowly with any plans she had for my future, and let me readjust to the new life into which I had plunged so abruptly.

"Mamma insisted that I rest and read, and go to museums and concerts while she was working; then in the evenings, we often went out to see her friends, or attended the theatre or other functions, part of her assignments. One thing constantly amazed me —Mamma was such a wonderful companion, gay and laughing, yet her laughter was kind, never malicious or cruel. I told Hattie about Mamma, and how good she was, and one day Hattie went to see her at the *World*. I don't know what was said—neither of them ever told me—but afterwards Hattie wrote mother frequently, and we were invited to East Orange and even Lewis seemed delighted."

When Blanche Howard died toward the end of the century, the Meynells wrote Margaret, and from that time on, her health improved and she never had another nightmare. Early in 1901, she went out and got a job in the chorus of an operetta called *Miss Bob White*.

Miss Bob White was put on in Philadelphia, with an eye to moving it to New York if it had a good run there. This method of testing a show was the forerunner of the custom today of opening in Boston or Philadelphia, for audience reaction. At the turn of the century, however, few shows ever made New York, and *Miss Bob White* was no exception.

Harriet and Hattie went down to the opening night and Harriet spent the night at Hattie's house in New Jersey afterwards and saw the children—"the little baby is too sweet and Carolyn came to my room while I dressed and talked like an old lady." But *Miss Bob White* was not much of a play—Harriet wrote: "It seems to me that no one outside of a chorus girl's mother would want to go the second time to see it!" After it closed Margaret spent the summer visiting friends and relatives—Aunt May, whose husband had been killed at the battle of San Juan during the Spanish-American War, and a few of Harriet's old friends—including Clara Louise Kellogg, and General Grubb. The General now had small children of his own, but he had retained his fondness for Margaret.

One evening Margaret told him the whole story of her life

with Wawie. After hearing what she had gone through, he felt he could tell her of his own experience in Stuttgart. Suddenly, Margaret decided that she had to clear up, once and for all, the hints Blanche Howard had dropped, suggesting that Margaret was illegitimate. As a child, Margaret had never taken seriously any of the "other men" that Wawie had talked about, but she was sure that her mother had loved the General—and loved him still, for that matter, although only as a dear friend. In spite of their bitter quarrel and his subsequent marriage, they had never forgotten each other. (When the time came, Margaret had his old love letters buried with her mother.)

She says: "Even at the turn of the century, when he was over sixty, he was a magnificent-looking man, and a great gentleman. I could understand how any woman could fall in love with him. I wouldn't have been sorry to have found out that he was really my father, but I had to know. Wawie had burned her suspicions into my mind so that I couldn't help wondering and worrying that I was illegitimate.

"So I asked the General bluntly: 'Ginger, how long have you known me?'

"He looked at me as though another world were unrolling before his eyes. 'It was Christmas Day, just after your mamma had left your father and come to New York with you and Hattie. You were a charming little thing with a snub nose.'

" 'How old was I?'

" 'You were going on four. I remember well, because we talked about it very soberly, you and I, as though it were a very great age.'

" 'Had you never seen me before at all?'

"He shook his head. 'I met your mother at the Philadelphia Exposition in 1876. Then I never saw her again for six years. I was in love with her all the time, but she was living with your father and trying to keep her marriage together, and you know your mother's principles. She would not even answer my letters, so I stopped writing. But I never stopped thinking of her and I loved you and Hattie because you belonged to her.' "

While Margaret listened to the General, the last tiny shred of

Wawie's influence vanished. She was free of her poisons, ready to think of her with pity instead of fear. So in the autumn of 1901, Harriet sent Margaret back to Paris to study voice with the woman who had taught Mary Garden, a Mrs. Robinson-Duff. This was a heavy financial burden on Harriet, but she wanted Margaret to be trained to earn her living, even though she could almost not bear being separated from her again. A letter written after the ship sailed said:

"October 10, 1901

"Miss Ayer:—
Paris, France:—

"It was a pretty hard pull, wasn't it? I am congratulating myself on my valiant behavior. If I had ever broken down, they would have carried me to a hospital. When I let go, I do not get easily together. It was well I had so much work to do, as the little flat seemed empty, awfully so.

"Early Wednesday morning *unannounced*, Aunt Jule and Herbert appeared, the latter having sent for her as a *surprise*. Which it truly was. Of course Aunt Jule's flat is damp and not fit to live in, and of course she and Herbert are living with me.

"When I go to Heaven, I am going to ask for a little room all by myself, with nice windows looking out on the pearly streets, and permission to stay quiet until my soul gets rested. I believe there never was a human being who so hated turmoil and chattering and who had such a continuous dose of it day and night, as your mommer. This seems to be nasty of me, and as a matter of fact, I love Aunt Jule, and am glad to do everything I can for her. But I am going to run away over Sunday because they will be here, or I am afraid I shall be like Miss Fanny Squeers, jump up and down and scream out loud. Hattie has written me a letter every morning—very sweet—asking me to come out there.

"I do hope, my blessed, that you have not been sick. I know you have felt I was thinking about you, for I have been conscious particularly towards night, that your thoughts were with me. No, we never can be really separated again. It is your place and mine now to bear this parting with courage and to work, work

and work. It will be over with one happy day, and if you get
what you are going for, we shall never regret it. . . ."

Margaret was away eight months. During that period, Harriet
wrote her daughter twice a week, long, out-going letters which
reveal her ability as a writer. She never regarded herself as anything but an "accidental" journalist, but her position on the paper, and her standing with Joseph Pultizer, who demanded the
best of his people, prove her ability. Her description of the arrival of a distinguished visiting journalist in one of her letters is
typical of her reportorial vivacity:

"Pearson, the English magazinist, is here and we are all doing
fancy turns. The Sunday room is simply funny. The people are
running around like caged animals trying to look gifted and busy
so as to make a good impression. Mr. V.'s desk is piled to the top
and he has an expression on his countenance that President Mc-
Kinley need never strive to emulate. And H— throws out his
chest and looks grieved and over-worked. If it weren't such a
nuisance, it would be certainly irresistibly funny! Pearson has
goo-goo eyes, over which he is kind enough to place spectacles:
this dims his gaze and we are able to bear it. I tremble to think
what might happen were we to catch the full effulgence of his
beaming orbs. . . ."
But her warmth and feeling for people in trouble show
through, too, in a passage urging Margaret to be kind to a boy
whose family had been involved in a trial Harriet covered as a
working reporter:

"Mrs. Fosburg, the lovely mother in the terrible Fosburg case
which you remember was tried in Pittsfield last summer, came
to see me the other day. She is one of the most charming women
and that trial the most horrible perversion of the law, I have ever
seen demonstrated. The son James who was such a splendid fellow at the trial, and such a magnificent witness for his brother, is
in London, associated with the Westinghouse's. I gave Mrs. Fosburg a letter of introduction for him to present to you, if he
should go to Paris. I think he is about twenty-one or twenty-two,

and a perfectly delightful boy, a Yale 'grad,' and if he calls upon you, I want you to be especially nice to him. I suppose people will talk about his brother's having been accused of murdering his sister, but if there ever was an innocent man, it was Robert Fosburg. You recollect the judge ordered the jury to acquit without leaving their seats. The trial is of course a terrible shadow on the family, but I shall at all times emphasize my standing by being just as nice as I know how to, to any member of the Fosburg connection."

Harriet had no longer the desire to force herself or her opinions on her daughters—she had learned better. But she was a woman of strong character. She could no more help giving advice or small "roasts" than she could stop breathing. For example:

"If you will permit the Editor of the Home Page to make a few remarks, she would like to say that it is not so much the corset as the way Miss Ayer had fallen into of standing, that made the young girl's stomach protrude. Miss Ayer's mamma had noticed this mannerism of her daughter, but having suggested it several times, concluded to desist. I am glad you have got a new corset, but you will certainly have to stand differently. You must look out for this—it is awkward! Just the very reverse of correct. Now, how do you like your roast?"

"I am sorry to hear what you tell me about M. G. and her love affairs. No one can be more liberal, I think, than I am in my views, and I have the most intense sympathy for even an irregular love episode where people are in earnest, but I do loathe intrigue, and I hate the atmosphere of it.

"You will have to try to keep your moral vision unobscured. I knew when you went to Paris that you would get into that set, where the men and women are idle, rich, and more or less wanton.

"There are two things I despise, one is debt, and the other is licentiousness. A great many people confuse love and the latter, and a great many people who consider themselves honorable are, from my point of view, thieves, because they buy things which they have not money enough to pay for, and take the risk of getting the money, and meanwhile defraud working people. I don't want to preach, and you know perfectly well how I stand about these matters, but the man or woman who cheats his tailor or dressmaker are individuals I have no use for. This is apropos of nothing, except in a general way, of the people you are apt to meet in Bohemia or artistic life. Individually, you and I *haven't got to keep up an appearance* which our very modest bank account cannot explain or justify."

"If you have your white dresses made, will you please say that I *wished* to have them made plainly. You must *not* wear elaborate clothes. My income practically everyone knows is limited, and it is in very bad taste for either of us to dress as though we were rich. You know I am not in the habit of commanding you to do anything, but if you will look upon this in the light of an order I shall be gratified. I am not willing that people should say, as they certainly will, that you are overdressing, while I am here earning the money. How do you like the scolding from mommer? But you know how much I love you, and that I am not willing to place you in a position where comment would be unkind. . . ."

And: "Do you manage to get a good bath every day? Everything will depend, so far as your looks go, upon getting a bath, keeping your stomach in order and securing plenty of rest in a well-ventilated room. Dr. Edison told me the other night that my habit of extreme cleanliness enabled me to throw off disease in a marvelous manner. He said: 'If you were not a temperate woman, and so clean a woman, nothing could keep you from an attack of pneumonia; as it is, your skin throws off secretions in an extraordinary way.'"

While Margaret finished her voice training, Harriet managed to secure a roving assignment abroad, so they came home together on the *Pennsylvania* in August. Just before she sailed for

Europe she had written: "My darling, I can hardly wait to see you. Dress anyway you like. But if I were to meet you with sixteen flounces on your skirt, a bear garden and a peck of violets on your hat, and forty seven chains around your neck, it *would* be a shock."

CHAPTER TWENTY-TWO

HARRIET once wrote Hattie: "I have just come from a long chat with Mrs. de Wolfe [mother of Elsie de Wolfe, a good friend of Harriet's]. She is very sweet and seems to be happy, but her situation is not without pathos. The helpless mother dependent upon her child is always to me pathetic. When I get there, I hope I shall be able to stand it."

She never had to be dependent on her daughters, for she died at the age of fifty-four, a little more than a year after she and Margaret came back on the *Pennsylvania*. The last year of her life, however, was in many ways her happiest. She and Margaret lived together, and she had the satisfaction of seeing Margaret play a featured role in a Florenz Ziegfeld extravaganza called *The Red Feather*. Hattie and the children also lived nearby and Hattie had advanced to a position of importance in the music world with her own studio at Steinway Hall. Harriet's early determination that her children should be equipped to make a living, no matter what happened, had been realized in spite of everything. In later life, Margaret was to become a journalist and marry Frank Cobb, the noted editor of the *World*. Hattie, who was one of the early apostles of the religion New Thought, not only wrote books about music but pioneered in the use of musical therapy in hospitals. The extensive work done in this field today dates directly back to Hattie's fiercely determined early efforts which finally broke down the prejudices of laymen and medical people alike.

Although Harriet did not live to see her daughters' full fame or happiness, she had no cause to look back on her life with regret. In fifty-four years, she lived three lives: that of a society beauty, that of a famous businesswoman, and that of one of the best known and best loved newspaperwomen of her day. Her great talent and success lay in her originality and her inventive mind in all three of her careers. She scorned pretense of all kinds—a valuable but a dangerous trait, for while it was partially responsible for her success, it also made enemies, sometimes in powerful places. Her beauty, also, gained her jealous enemies as well as devoted admirers. It was a deep satisfaction to the people who loved her that, as she grew older, she seemed to become lovelier; a former secretary of Harriet's wrote Margaret after her mother's death: "Her special beauty came from within." Perhaps she never married again because she had such strength that most men who were attracted by her were dependent on her. Perhaps the strongest man in her life had been James Seymour—who tried to ruin her out of fury because he could not have her. So, in the end, his strength became weakness, too.

Her children were the keystone of her life, always. Her devotion to them may have been partly rebellion against her mother's indifference to her and her sisters and brother. Harriet's greatest personal tragedies were the loss of her baby Gertrude, in the Chicago fire, and the heartbreaking ten-year period when she believed that both other daughters had deserted her. She was over-possessive, but this was part of her enormous strength of character. If she had lived in our time, we would certainly consider Harriet Hubbard Ayer an unusually forceful woman; over fifty years ago, when women were just beginning to think of themselves of having rights, she was extraordinary.

The last years of her life were dedicated to helping people in need. She tried to live, she once wrote, "as though the children of the race were in my care." Despite her frail health, and the demanding hours of her work at the paper, she made regular

trips into the slums to do what she could to help settlement workers and doctors. Her knowledge of languages—French, German
and a smattering of Italian—was useful. But even more helpful
was her warmth and gaiety. She was always an extremely charming and lovable woman, a woman impossible to forget once she
had crossed your path, no matter how casually.

On Saturday, November 18, 1903, she went to the office as
usual and stayed there from nine until five o'clock, writing her
column, correcting copy, reading and dictating answers to her
reader mail, and seeing the many visitors who wanted a glimpse
—or a piece of advice—from Mrs. Ayer. At five o'clock, she went
home to her hotel apartment at 70 West Forty-sixth street where
she lived with Margaret, who was then in *The Red Feather*.
They had dinner together and then Harriet changed into evening clothes to go to the Horse Show. It was a bitter night, and
Harriet was tired. She stayed at the Horse Show about two and
a half hours, constantly on her feet, talking to people, taking
notes. About half past ten, she went home and wrote over fifteen
hundred words of copy about the show. The newspaper messenger whom she called to pick up her material was delayed in ar-
riving. Margaret got home well after midnight and found her
mother still sitting up, too exhausted to remove her shoes from
her swollen feet.

The next day, Sunday, Harriet realized she had caught cold.
She stayed in bed, hoping to be well enough to go into the office
on Monday. But by Monday, she was worse. Margaret called
the doctor, who refused to let Harriet get up. On Tuesday, he
knew it was pneumonia, a serious case. Margaret did not go to
the theatre and she and Hattie stayed up all Wednesday night
with their mother. On Thursday morning, as they waited for the
doctor, Hattie bent over her mother and whispered: "You are
going to get well, my dearest, I feel it."

Harriet smiled up at her. "You are a sweet little faker."

Those were her last words; a few seconds afterwards she died.

She left $3,000—"enough to pay for my funeral and a little
over for you girls," as she had always promised Margaret. There
were a few treasures and keepsakes, little Gertie's baby dress and
the General's letters, in her private strong box. But the most

important heritage she left her daughters, and their children, was the memory of her strength and courage.

Many newspapers in the United States and in Paris and London printed the story of her death. In a few cases, her participation in the sensational trials and her incarceration in the asylum were mentioned, but for the most part, the reporters and editors who had known Harriet as a fellow-worker praised her professional skill and eulogized her as a "friend of the needy, mourned by hundreds who either knew of her charities or were benefited."

The *New York World* said: "Mrs. Ayer was the most prominent newspaperwoman in America. The achievements of her lifetime constituted a history of courage that misfortune, no matter how severe or frequent, could never affect. It is seldom that one woman has so thoroughly commanded the respect and admiration of the reading public, as well as the love and friendship of all who came within the wide range of her personal influence.

"For her to hear of a case of need was to relieve it. It mattered not whether its object were a friend or a total stranger. She often said that her religion in life might be summed up in two words—'lift up.' "

Funeral services were held at Trinity Church. Traffic was blocked by the crowds who could not get in the church. Margaret remembers:

"Promptly at noon, the beautiful old bell of Trinity tolled. The great Trinity organ began the processional. Many famous people were there, people whom my mother had met through her newspaper work and who had become her friends, and I suppose some others had come out of curiosity. But also in the church were scores of the poor and humble people whom she had been able to help a little and who, in return, never forgot either her kindness or her beauty.

"I saw Mary, the apple woman, who always *gave* my mother an apple each day, in return for some kindness my mother never told about. There were the White Wings who cleaned the streets, in uniform; I heard afterwards that when they found out who was being buried, they asked the police for permission to come in and say a prayer for her. And there were many others, shabbily dressed, obviously poor people who wept openly.

"The pallbearers were all members of the staff of the *World*. Afterwards Don Seitz, the business manager, went back to the office. He was a very clever man, with dark, shrewd eyes, whom my mother had admired very much. He found two reporters from other papers waiting for him. They had seen the flag on the World Building at half-mast. Don Seitz told them it was for my mother.

"They looked astounded. 'You did that for a woman?'

"Mr. Seitz's dark eyes flashed, I was told. Perhaps he was thinking of the long working day my mother had put in on her last Saturday on the job, for he answered: 'She was the best man on the staff.'"